# A Claim of Right for Scotland

To the Memories of

HUGH MacDIARMID

and

SYDNEY GOODSIR SMITH

# A Claim of Right for Scotland

EDITED BY

Owen Dudley Edwards

**Polygon**
*determinations*〉

© 1989 Polygon
22 George Square, Edinburgh

Typeset using the Telos Text Composition System
from Digital Publications Ltd., Edinburgh
and printed in Great Britain by
Redwood Burn Limited, Trowbridge

ISBN   0 7486 6022 4
          0 7486 6023 2 pbk

# Contents

## A CLAIM OF RIGHT FOR SCOTLAND: *COMMENTARY*

# Series Preface

CAIRNS CRAIG

Scotland's history is often presented as punctuated by disasters which overwhelm the nation, break its continuity and produce a fragmented culture. Many felt that 1979, and the failure of the Devolution Referendum, represented such a disaster: that the energetic culture of the 1960s and 1970s would wither into the silence of a political waste land in which Scotland would be no more than a barely distinguishable province of the United Kingdom.

Instead, the 1980s proved to be one of the most productive and creative decades in Scotland this century—as though the energy that had failed to be harnessed by the politicians flowed into other channels. In literature, in thought, in history, creative and scholarly work went hand in hand to redraw the map of Scotland's past and realign the perspectives of its future.

In place of the few standard conceptions of Scotland's identity that had often been in the past the tokens of thought about the country's culture, a new and vigorous debate was opened up about the nature of Scottish experience, about the real social and economic structures of the nation, and about the ways in which the Scottish situation related to that of other similar cultures throughout the world.

It is from our determination to maintain a continuous forum for such debate that *Determinations* takes its title. The series will provide a context for sustained dialogue about culture and politics in Scotland, and about those international issues which directly affect Scottish experience.

Too often, in Scotland, a particular way of seeing our culture, of representing ourselves, has come to dominate our perceptions because it has gone unchallenged—worse, unexamined. The vitality of the culture should be measured by the intensity of debate which it generates rather than the security of ideas on which it rests. And should be measured by the extent to which creative, philosophical, theological, critical and political ideas confront each other.

If the determinations which shape our experience are to come from within rather than from without, they have to be explored and evaluated and acted upon. Each volume in this series will seek to be a contribution to that *self*-determination; and each volume, we trust, will require a response, contributing in turn to the on-going dynamic that is Scotland's culture.

# Introduction

On 1 March 1979 a majority of Scottish voters taking part in a referendum on the setting up of a representative assembly for Scotland, cast their ballots in its favour: 32.9% voted 'Yes', 30.8% voted 'No', in a 63.9% poll. The referendum has been in widespread use throughout many countries for many years, but the British politicians, as opposed to the Scottish electorate, showed themselves as a body unable to grasp what it entailed: the only previous use of it (in 1975) had been to confirm, that British voters now agreed that the then government had been right to enter the European Economic Community over two years before (the other countries debating entry in the early 1970s had had their referenda on the issue at the time of entry). Before the Scottish referendum of 1979 (held the same day as Welsh referendum for an Assembly of consultative, not — as proposed for Scotland — limited executive, powers), Westminster had attached a provision that 40% of the Scottish electorate — including persons who for death or other reasons were no longer at the addresses given in the electoral registers — must vote in favour before the Government would proceed with the establishment of an Assembly. The referendum therefore obtained its majority of approval, but failed to satisfy restrictions attached by politicians hostile to the referendum system and accepted by politicians ignorant of it.

No further Governmental attempt having been made to seek Scottish opinion on an Assembly — indeed, on the tenth anniversary of the referendum the Government of Mrs Margaret Thatcher held celebrations in both London and Edinburgh rejoicing in the continued denial of implementation of the wishes of the majority of Scottish voters, who consistently voted against them in elections — a Scottish-based campaign for a Scottish Assembly set up a Constitutional Steering Committee under the Chairmanship of Sir Robert Grieve. Its membership was as follows: William Anderson,

Scottish Secretary of the National Federation of Self-Employed and Small Businesses; Ian Barr, then Chairman of the Scottish Postal Board; the Reverend Maxwell Craig, at that time Chairman of the Church and National Committee of the Church of Scotland; Sandra Farquhar, a worker with the Scottish Women's Aid in Stirling; Nigel Grant, Professor of Education in the University of Glasgow; Joy Hendry, editor of the magazine *Chapman* and free-lance dramatic and literary critic; Jock Hendry, a Trade Union leader and formerly Deputy General Secretary of the Scottish Trades Union Congress; Pat Kelly, Assistant Secretary of the Scottish National Union of Civil and Public Servants; Isobel Lindsay, Lecturer in Sociology at Strathclyde University; D. Neil MacCormick, Professor of Jurisprudence and Public Law at Edinburgh University; Dr. C.M. Una Maclean, Lecturer in Community Medicine at Edinburgh University and widow of Scottish political scientist Professor John P. Mackintosh, MP; Paul H. Scott, a retired Diplomat and leading member of the Saltire Society, Scottish PEN and other Scottish cultural organisations; Judy Steel, Cultural Festival Organiser at Ettrickbridge, Selkirkshire (whose husband was at that time leader of the Liberal Party in Britain); and Canon Kenyon Wright, a Methodist clergyman, General Secretary of the Scottish Council of Churches. Councillor Derek Barrie, Convener of the North-East Fife District Council, and Dr Joseph Devine, Roman Catholic Bishop of Motherwell, were also founder-members of the Committee, but both resigned at an early stage through pressure of other commitments. The Secretary, Jim Ross, was a retired Civil Servant, who had been Under-Secretary in charge of Devolution at the Scottish Office from 1975 to 1979. Sir Robert had been Chairman of the Highlands and Islands Development Board at what is widely acknowledged to have been its most successful and seminal phase. It is of importance that he is generally held in affection as well as respect.

On 6 July 1988 Sir Robert sent the completed Report of his Committee to Mr Alan Armstrong, Convener of the Campaign for a Scottish Assembly (hereinafter CSA): it was entitled *A Claim of Right for Scotland* and was duly published in that month in the form which follows in the present volume. It elicited widespread interest, some of which was publicly admitted, some not. As it stated, Scotland's distinctiveness had been formally preserved down the centuries through the existence of specific institutions including a separate Law from England and Wales, and a separate established Church (Presbyterian, as opposed to the Protestant episcopalian church established in England and Wales and subsequently disestablished in Wales). The issuance of *A Claim of Right for Scotland* was in itself a peculiarly Scottish action born of this institutional consciousness. Apart from its citation of earlier Claims issued in 1689 and 1842, it took its place in a tradition going back to the Declaration of Arbroath of 1320 when Scottish nobility and clergy formally instructed Pope John XXII that they would resist any attempt at abridgment of their independence from England even if approved by a King of Scotland including their present one, Robert I, victor of Bannockburn over the forces of Edward II of England six years earlier. *A Claim of Right for Scotland* did not call for Scottish independence: at least three of its signatories (Ms Lindsay, Professor MacCormick and Mr Scott) are members of the Scottish National Party which does, and other signatories in or out of that party may have agreed with them, but several certainly did not. What all signatories did clearly agree on was a greater degree of Scottish self-dependence. Scotland had become united with England by consent through the Union of Parliaments in 1707; a Union of Crowns had existed since 1603, but the presence of many heirs to Queen Anne in 1707, some of them possibly seeming more attractive to the Scots than the Electress of Sophia of Hanover designated by Englishmen, meant that security required a pan-British parliament. Scots had economic disadvantages occasioned by the hostility of English commerce which a Union was expected to allay. But the Union was assumed by Scots then and since to have guaranteed certain forms of Scottish identity, of which the Law and the Church were the most evident. *A Claim of Right for Scotland* did not take its stand on the need to dissolve the Union, but on the question of whether its assumptions were being satisfactorily fulfilled. It found they were not, and proposed steps to deal with this. Its issuance and its reception in some quarters was a symbol of the survival of a form of Scottish identity, although much (arguably, most) of its thought was conditioned by the needs of the Scottish future more than the pieties of the Scottish past.

*A Claim of Right for Scotland* has important Welsh. Irish and English implications as an example, but it emerges because Scotland, unlike Ireland or Wales, is not present in the United Kingdom by the right of conquest, an ancient formula in political theory however dubious in ethics. The United Kingdom has been challenged in the past by both Protestant and Catholic movements in Ireland embodying parliamentary and extra-parliamentary agitation; it has been more subtly challenged by cultural evangelism in Wales. Individual thinkers in both countries have produced arguments and manifestoes from time to time. But it is difficult to see national or ethnic self-expression in either country asserting itself through the origination of an instrument such as this, although now that Scotland has done so the example may prove infectious. The legalistic, and at times somewhat theological, tones in which the instrument is cast suggest the primacy of institutional consciousness around which a nucleus of national self-consciousness spins itself.

The importance of *A Claim of Right for Scotland* was reflected in the interest it engendered, and the growing sense of a popular demand for some constitutional change in Scotland's present situation was reflected in the by-election at Glasgow Govan, on 10 November, when the existing Labour majority of 19,500 was swept aside to return the candidate of the Scottish National Party (hereinafter SNP), Mr. Jim Sillars, who had campaigned for Scotland's 'independence in Europe'. The vote was less of an upset in terms of known Scottish enthusiasm for independence, which had been fluctuating around the 35% mark for some years, but which had not been thus translated into a vote for the party pledged to independence in the general elections of 1983 and 1987. This is not to say that *A Claim of Right for Scotland*, or its impact on public opinion, had necessarily played a large part in the change in voter behaviour. It is more likely that the makers of *A Claim of Right for Scotland* had diagnosed currents in Scottish public opinion which expressed themselves in a new form. The grievance against the incumbent Labour party stemmed less from any repudiation of the local tradition of support for its social principles as from an apparent conviction that a Labour-supporting Scotland would no longer be well served by a party unable to obtain governing power while striving to do so by courting supposed preferences of the English electorate with which Scots might find themselves unsympathetic. Defence was not an issue in the by-election, but it is clear since then that the Labour Party in Scotland remains pledged to unilateral disarmament where London-based leaders of the Labour Party meditate on a Defence policy more in keeping with some of the assumptions of the present Tory government. Voter support for 'independence in Europe' was at the very least an expression of confidence in a party which prides itself on not being swayed by English priorities.

By this time feeling was growing that some more permanent form than that of a pamphlet was required for *A Claim of Right for Scotland*, and a number of persons raised the question of its republication with commentaries by a selection of politicians and others who had sympathy for ideas of greater, and in some cases absolute, Scottish self-dependence. Polygon Books was approached on the matter. The firm had significant credentials as imprint for such a publication. Four years before taking its present name in 1979, Polygon, under the general imprint of Edinburgh University Student Publications Board, its parent body, had published *The Red Paper on Scotland* under the editorship of the then Rector of Edinburgh University, a history postgraduate student, who today is Dr Gordon Brown, MP. It was a massive exploration of many themes in Scottish politics, economics and society, and constituted the first substantial theoretical contribution to the public debate on Scotland after the SNP victories of 1974. Polygon has since produced many other contributions to the Scottish debate from a variety of hands, both in book form and in its journal *New Edinburgh Review* (now renamed *Edinburgh Review*). In Summer 1988 Polygon was taken over by Edinburgh University Press, whose Secretary, J.M. Spencer, made it clear that the firm would maintain its vigorous, wide-ranging and thought-provoking role in Scottish culture and politics, and it is fair to say of him that he has maintained the spirit of exciting and sometimes iconoclastic enterprise which characterised such Founding Fathers of the firm as Dr Brown, Mr Bill Campbell (now of Mainstream Publishing), Mr John Forsyth and Mr Jonathan Wills. Mr Spencer discussed the proposal with a number of persons including contributors to this volume, and signatories of the *Claim* (among the latter Paul H. Scott, C.M.G. was particularly helpful). He asked me to undertake the editorship and we designed the book together. We would now find it impossible to say from which of us many of its ideas came, but the responsibility for any editorial decision deemed to be political must rest with me. I have never discovered what Mr Spencer's politics are.

Our first thanks are due to the Campaign for a Scottish Assembly for permitting the republication of *A Claim of Right for Scotland*. Particular personal thanks must be given to Mr Alan Armstrong, its Convener, for his courtesy and aid. Mr Alan Lawson of the CSA, also editor of *Radical Scotland*, has been of outstanding assistance to us, both in furthering the reproduction of the *Claim* and in providing invaluable information for the editor, much of it peppered with a deliciously abrasive wit. Professor MacCormick's essay in part reworks material from a lecture published by the SNP of February 1988, and we thank Mr Angus MacGillivray of SNP Publications for permission to use it here; internal evidence makes it clear, however, that the work is primarily from 1989. Dr Gordon Brown would have liked to have accepted an invitation to contribute, and for a time hoped to do so, but his duties during the illness of Mr John Smith, MP (now happily over) obliged him to decline: his present position in British Labour leadership, and his personal influence in Scottish Labour leadership, make him a man to be watched closely, and upon his actions (not now inhibited by any commitment in these pages) much may turn, although it is one of our findings that Labour MPs in Scotland are now according, almost imperceptibly, a greater value to their own individual perceptions than has hitherto been the case, and as Dr Brown and others proceed to eminence in Westminster Opposition they must be increasingly concerned not to lose touch with Scotland. In the last analysis my chief regret about Dr Brown's absence from these pages is our loss of his felicitous style, his charm of address and his place as our great forerunner. We will in the future discover in what manner he who wound our clock so well, will hear it strike. Meanwhile, I thank my old friend for the good advice and stimulating argument he, as my former editor on the *Red Paper*, gave me for this venture.

Convalescence from illness also lost us another essay, in this case from Mr Alick Buchanan-Smith, MP. Mr Buchanan-Smith, as a Tory whose principles on devolution led him to resign the Shadow Secretaryship for Scotland of its party, and recently to decline office within its Government, deserves the respect and gratitude of his people. It would have been an honour to have included him, quite apart from the special perspectives and knowledge he would bring to his paper. Any criticisms of his party which appear in these pages do not apply to him.

We also suffered some other refusals to contribute, some after significant intervals. It is tempting to list them, but not constructive.

The one exception is Mr Neal Ascherson, also prevented by pressure of work from contributing, but in a sense he is present. He and I are fond of the character of Thomas Yownie in John Buchan's *Huntingtower*, who at the crisis is of outstanding effectiveness as a powerful voice off-stage. Mr Ascherson's voice is heard in several of these essays, sometimes by direct citation, sometimes by its influence. I have drawn specifically in the Epilogue upon his remarks to a one-day Conference 'What Scotland Wants: Ten Years On', organized by the Unit for the Study of Government in Scotland at Edinburgh University on 25 February 1989, and all of my Ascherson quotations come from my notes of his speech. But it is impossible for me to convey the psychological strength which his elegant mingling of passion and wit, and his saurian schoolboy grin, give to his hearers and readers. 'You'll no fickle Thomas Yownie.'

Of the actual contributors my gratitude is due to all, and additional services to the effectiveness of my own work were performed by Mr Griffiths, Professor MacCormick, Mr Maxwell, Mr McLean, Mr Nairn, Mr Osmond and Professor Crick. But Dr Tom Gallagher, happily for me on leave in Edinburgh, has pride of place. He laboured into long nights as second reader of text and proof, and Mr Spencer and I entrusted the final decision on certain knotty points to his judgment where we found ourselves in minor disagreement (each of us being excessively deferential to the other's opinions). In particular, it is thanks to them both that my Epilogue has been saved from many excesses. I should add that I have left almost all contributions unchanged save for trifling (and probably pedantic) corrections on purely factual matters in a few cases. Dr Cairns Craig, general editor of Polygon's 'Determinations' series in which this volume takes its place, has worked himself to the bone on it. His industry and his idealism are as infectious are they are invaluable.

I am deeply indebted to Ms Marion Sinclair of Polygon for her encouragement and assistance; and Mr John Davidson has worked wonders in rapid design and production. I also want to express my thanks to my wife, Bonnie Dudley Edwards, my mother-in-law, Elizabeth Balbirnie Lee, and my children, Leila, Sara and Michael, and our friend Mr Mark Kennedy, for constructive and forceful comments which have concentrated the mind wonderfully. I apologise to them for any nuisances this book has presented, and equally to the wives and families of Mr Spencer and Dr Craig. I am also most grateful to the research staffs of certain of the contributors, to Mr. Richard McAllister and to Mr C.D. Raab.

The dedication is my own action. I know both of the recipients would have strongly disagreed with much that is here, perhaps amongst it much that is in my own writing. But they taught me and their fellow-Scots so much, and were so kind to me personally, that however imperfect it may be I place this tribute to before them, coupled with my love and gratitude to Hazel Goodsir Smith, and to Valda, Michael and Deirdre Grieve.

*University of Edinburgh*

Owen Dudley Edwards
March 1989

# A Claim of Right for Scotland

*Report of the Constitutional Steering Committee*
*Presented to the Campaign for a Scottish Assembly*
*Edinburgh July 1988*

# PROLOGUE

Twice previously Scots have acted against misgovernment by issuing a Claim of Right; in 1689 and in 1842. Circumstances now may be thought less stark and dramatic than on these previous occasions. But they are none the less serious.

Now, as then, vital questions arise about the constitution and powers of the state. Then it was clearly understood that constitution and powers were the issue. Now there is a danger that this will not be fully recognised; that symptoms, such as the Poll Tax, the Health Service, Education and the Economy, are mistaken for causes, which lie in the way in which Scotland is governed.

It is for a larger body than ourselves to set out in full the constitutional rights Scotland expects within the United Kingdom. That would be the true equivalent of the Claims made in 1689 and 1842. But we hold ourselves fully justified in registering a general Claim of Right on behalf of Scotland, namely that Scotland has the right to insist on articulating its own demands and grievances, rather than have them articulated for it by a Government utterly unrepresentative of Scots.

[signed on behalf of the Committee]

Robert Grieve                                           (Chairman)
Jim Ross                                                (Secretary)

# PART I

# The Need for Change in Scottish Government

'The Scottish Members of Parliament should therefore
lose no time—not an instant—in uniting together in their
national character of the Representatives of Scotland

[Sir Walter Scott; The Letters of
Malachi Malagrowther, (Edinburgh 1826)]

# Introduction

**1.1** We were appointed because, in the opinion of Campaign for a Scottish Assembly, Parliamentary government under the present British constitution had failed Scotland and more than Parliamentary action was needed to redeem the failure. We share that view and in this report set out what we consider must be done if the health of Scottish government is to be restored.

**1.2** Our direct concern is with Scotland only, but the failure to provide good government for Scotland is a product not merely of faulty British policy in relation to Scotland, but of fundamental flaws in the British constitution. We have identified these and pointed out their relevance to the problems of Scotland. They do not, however, afflict Scotland only. So far from giving Scotland an advantage over others, rectifying these defects would improve the government of the whole of the United Kingdom, more particularly those parts of it outside the London metropolitan belt.

**1.3.** In this report we frequently use the word "English" where the word "British" is conventionally used. We believe this clarifies many issues which the customary language of British government obscures. Although the government of the United Kingdom rests nominally with a "British" Parliament, it is impossible to trace in the history or procedures of that Parliament any constitutional influence other than an English one. Scots are apt to bridle when "Britain" is referred to as "England". But there is a fundamental truth in this nomenclature which Scots ought to recognise - and from which they ought to draw appropriate conclusions.

**1.4** We do not wish to create ill-will between Scots and English. But our report must be based on a clear understanding of the motor forces of the "British" State, the allocation of power within it, and the effects of these forces and that power on Scotland. That understanding can best begin with some essentials of Scottish history.

# 2 The Past: essential facts of Scottish History

**2.1** Much ink is wasted on the question whether the Scots are a nation. Of course they are. They were both a nation and a state until 1707. The state was wound up by a Treaty which clearly recognised the nation and its right to distinctive government in a fundamental range of home affairs. The fact that institutional forms, however empty, reflecting these distinctions have been preserved to the present day demonstrates that no-one in British government has dared to suggest openly that the nation no longer exists or that the case for distinctiveness has now disappeared.

**2.2** Scottish nationhood does not rest on constitutional history alone. It is supported by a culture reaching back over centuries and bearing European comparison in depth and quality, nourished from a relatively early stage by an education system once remarkable by European standards. Since the Union, the strength of that culture has fluctuated but there is no ground for any claim that, overall or even at any particular time, it has benefited from the Union. On the contrary the Union has always been, and remains, a threat to the survival of a distinctive culture in Scotland.

**2.3** The international zenith reached by that culture in the late eighteenth century is sometimes facilely attributed to the Union, but that leaves for explanation the subsequent decline of the culture as the Union became more established. No doubt some benefit was derived from the relatively settled state of Scotland at the time. More, probably, stemmed from the minimal interference of London in Scottish affairs in those days. But the roots of that philosophical, literary and scientific flowering lay in the social soil of Scotland itself and its long-established cross-fertilisation with mainland Europe.

**2.4** That cross-fertilisation diminished as the pull of London increased and the effects of the removal of important stimuli to Scottish confidence and self respect were felt. In mid-nineteenth century Scottish culture eroded and became inward-looking in consequence. It has struggled with mixed success to revive as Scots realised what they were in danger of losing. The twentieth century, up to and including the present day, has been a period of extraordinary fertility in all fields of the Scottish arts; literature, visual and dramatic arts, music, traditional crafts, philosophic and historical studies. In particular the indigenous languages of Scotland, Gaelic and Scots, are being revived in education, the arts and social life. We think it no accident that this trend has accompanied an increasingly vigorous demand for a Scottish say in Scotland's government.

**2.5** The nation was not conquered but it did not freely agree to the Union of the Parliaments in 1707. We need not go into the details of the negotiations about the Union. What is beyond dispute is that the main impetus for Union came from the English and it was brought about for English reasons of state. Likewise, the form of Union was not what the Scots would have chosen but what the English were prepared to concede. However, the considerable guarantees which Scots won in the Treaty of Union reflected the fact that, until the Treaty was implemented, they had a Parliament of their own to speak for them.

**2.6** The matters on which the Treaty guaranteed the Scots their own institutions and policies represented the bulk of civil life and government at the time; the Church, the Law and Education. However, there was never any mechanism for enforcing respect for the terms of the Treaty of Union. Many of its major provisions have been violated, and its spirit has never affected the huge areas of government which have evolved since. The say of Scotland in its own government has diminished, is diminishing and ought to be increased.

**2.7** The forms of Scottish autonomy which, until recently, had multiplied for almost a century are misleading. The Scottish Office can be distinguished from a Whitehall Department only in the sense that it is not physically located in Whitehall (and much of its most important work is done in Whitehall). The Secretary of State may be either Scotland's man in the Cabinet or the Cabinet's man in Scotland, but in the last resort he is invariably the latter. Today, he can be little else, since he must impose on Scotland policies against which an overwhelming majority of Scots have voted.

**2.8** The apparent strengthening of Scottish institutions of government since 1885; the creation of a Secretary of State, the enlargement of the functions of the Scottish Office, the extension of Scottish Parliamentary Committees; has been accompanied by an increasing centralisation and standardisation of British government practice which has more than offset any decentralisation of administrative units.

## 3 *The Present, and the Future being forced upon us*

**3.1** Scotland has a team of Ministers and an administration who are supposed to exist in order to provide Scotland with distinctive government according to Scottish wishes in those fields of British government which affect Scotland only. They cannot possibly do so.

**3.2** The creation of these offices and procedures was a sop to Scottish discontent, not a response to Scottish needs. The team of Ministers is chosen from whichever political party has won a British general election. That election must be fought on British, not Scottish, issues. The Scots cannot concentrate on Scottish issues when casting their votes, but must simultaneously reflect their opinions on such matters as foreign policy, defence, the EEC, and Northern Ireland. So far as the Scots vote for United Kingdom parties, these parties will themselves regard Scottish issues as subsidiary to the winning of British votes. At present, the Scots cannot vote for other than a UK party without implying a vote for independence. And the political arithmetic of the United Kingdom means that the Scots are constantly exposed to the risk of having matters of concern only to them prescribed by a government against which they have voted not narrowly but overwhelmingly. Yet Scottish Ministers and the Scottish administration must implement these policies, even where their implementation affects only Scotland.

**3.3** Scottish Ministers and the Scottish Office are not the only parts of the special machinery of current Scottish government. But the other parts are no more effective.

**3.4** There is a Scottish Grand Committee for general debate of Scottish issues in Parliament; there are Scottish Standing Committees for detailed consideration of Scottish legislation; and there used to be a Select Committee on Scottish Affairs to scrutinise the working of Government policy in Scotland.

**3.5** The Scottish Grand Committee rarely votes. Its debates have no effect except so far as the Government chooses to pay attention to them and its agenda is subject to Government manipulation. The Scottish Standing Committees operate only when the Government chooses to handle Scottish legislation separately. If it prefers to combine Scottish legislation with English, it can usually find an excuse for doing so. And if need be, Scottish Standing Committees can be filled out with English members. The Select Committee on Scottish Affairs must have a Government majority, no matter how slight a minority the Government may be in Scotland.

**3.6** Even this unsuitable and inadequate "government" of Scotland is no longer working. There is a constitutional flaw in the present machinery of Scottish government: it can work only within a limited range of election results. Providing a Scottish Ministerial team, Scottish Whips and Government representation on Standing and Select Committees, requires a certain minimum number of Government party MPs from Scottish constituencies. There is no guarantee of such a number being elected.

**3.7** At present the governing party is below the minimum and there is no certainty that this situation will be short-lived. As a result, we have no Select Committee on Scottish Affairs, so Government policy in Scotland is not subject to the scrutiny thought necessary elsewhere. And the use of the other elements of Scottish Parliamentary procedures is being minimised.

**3.8** We are not aware of any other instance, at least in what is regarded as the democratic world, of a territory which has a distinctive corpus of law and an acknowledged right to distinctive policies but yet has no body expressly elected to safeguard and supervise these. The existing machinery of Scottish government is an attempt either to create an illusion or to achieve the impossible.

**3.9** In that attempt it was bound to fail eventually and the failure can no longer be hidden. The choice of adhering to present Scottish government is not available. Either we advance to an Assembly, or we retreat to the point at which Scottish institutions are an empty shell and Scottish government is, in practice, indistinguishable from that of any English region. The latter process has already begun.

**3.10** So far as Scottish Ministers and the Scottish Office have a real, as distinct from an illusory, purpose it is merely to solicit for Scotland a larger share of what the British Government of the day thinks Scotland ought to want. Even when this soliciting succeeds, it regularly fails to produce what Scotland wants and there can be little confidence that it produces what Scotland needs. It is also invidious within the United Kingdom. It arouses the jealousy of English regions and it concentrates Scottish attention on lobbying in London rather than initiating in Scotland. It creates the very dependency culture of which the present Government professes to disapprove.

**3.11** Because of the constitutional flaws long latent in Scottish government, also because it is now imagined elsewhere that Scotland has an unfair advantage, Scottish government as developed over the last century is being rapidly eroded. It cannot be preserved. It must be rejuvenated or it will fade away.

# 4 The English Constitution — an Illusion of Democracy.

**4.1** The English constitution provides for only one source of power; the Crown-in-Parliament. That one source is now mainly embodied in the Prime Minister, who has appropriated almost all the royal prerogatives. She/he appoints Ministers who, with rare exceptions, can be dismissed at will, and has further formidable powers of patronage. Because of Party discipline and the personal ambition of members the consequence is that, so far from Parliament controlling the Executive (which is the constitutional theory) it is the Prime Minister as head of the Executive who controls Parliament.

**4.2** Historically, the power of Parliament evolved as a means of curbing the arbitrary power of Monarchs. We have now reached the point where the Prime Minister has in practice a degree of arbitrary power few, if any, English and no Scottish Monarchs have rivalled. Yet he or she still hides behind the fiction of royal sanction and the pretence of deference to Parliament to give legitimacy to a concentration of power without parallel in western society. The American constitution was framed largely with a view to making such a development impossible. Even the centralised and Executive-biassed French constitution distributes power, demonstrated by the recent balance between the President and Prime Minister there.

**4.3** Every feature of the English constitution, every right the citizen has, can be changed by a simple majority of this subordinated Parliament. That applies even to the requirement to hold Parliamentary elections every five years - or at all. It applies to the very existence of Parliament, with no more than minor delaying qualifications.

**4.4** As a product of these constitutional facts, Parliamentary procedures are subject to heavy pressure to conform with Government convenience and rest on the tacit assumption that the primary purpose of Parliament is to facilitate Government business. The power of dissolving Parliament has largely passed to the Prime Minister who, with rare exceptions, can manipulate it both to benefit and to control her/his party. In fact, if not in theory, the Prime Minister is Head of State, Chief Executive and Chief Legislator, and while in office is not circumscribed by any clear or binding constitutional limitations. Against all this there is in the United Kingdom not a single alternative source of secure constitutional power at any level.

**4.5** This unique concentration of power is reinforced by a voting system which has always been commended as yielding strong government. In the English case, a system which already gives government excessive power adds to that power through the voting system. Specifically, a large majority of the electorate may have voted against the Prime Minister wielding the enormous powers described above, supported by a crushing Parliamentary majority.

**4.6** The effects on Scotland now can be statistically measured. In the last election, political parties expressing the intention of creating a Scottish Assembly won 57% of the United Kingdom votes cast and 76% of the Scottish votes cast. In spite of which there is currently a Prime Minister dedicated to preventing the creation of a Scottish Assembly and equipped, within the terms of the English constitution, with overwhelming powers to frustrate opposition to her aims.

**4.7** It is sometimes said that Scotland cannot complain when it is governed by a Party which is in a minority in Scotland, since the same can happen to England. In marginal cases, where voters in England are almost equally divided between Parties, there may be something in this point. But there is no possibility of England ever being governed by a Party which had won only a seventh of the seats and a quarter of the votes there.

**4.8** It would be wrong to isolate any one of the above features. Any one of them might be tolerable without the others. Taken together they represent an indulgence to Party dogma and a hazard to human rights, in particular to the rights of minorities. Within the United Kingdom the Scots are a minority which cannot ever feel secure under a constitution which, in effect, renders the Treaty of Union a contradiction in terms, because it makes no provision for the safeguarding of any rights or guarantees and does not even require a majority of the electorate to override such rights and guarantees as may once have been offered.

**4.9** Some may argue that all the above is irrelevant because the Scots had a referendum on the Assembly issue in 1979 and failed to vote for it. That is a misrepresentation on three counts. First, by the criteria of British general elections, which are regarded by British Governments as justifying policy and constitutional changes of every kind and magnitude, the Scots did vote for an Assembly in 1979 but were refused it. Secondly, during the referendum campaign, The Conservative Party promised that, in the event of a "No" vote, it would propose a constitutional conference to consider the improvement of the government of Scotland. The implications of the negative votes, let alone the abstentions, are therefore suspect. Thirdly, no referendum is forever. All current evidence suggests that the demand for an Assembly is now much stronger.

# 5 Fundamentals of an Assembly

5.1 However convinced Scots may be of the defects of their present system of government, some may be daunted by the apparent complexities and uncertainties of change. It is not our function to draw up a scheme for a Scottish Assembly. But it is part of our terms of reference to convince doubters not only that present Scottish government is bad but that an Assembly would make it better. A number of doubts about the practic-ability or desirability of an Assembly have been expressed. We deal with the main ones below.

## 5.2 An Assembly and Independence

5.2.1 It is sometimes argued against an Assembly that it will inevitably lead to "separatism", by which those concerned presumably mean Scottish independence. As those who profess to think this usually also profess the opinion that, if the Scots want independence they ought to have it, we must conclude that they believe that an Assembly will somehow lead the Scots into independence without wanting it.

5.2.2 The planning of a Scottish Assembly within the framework of United Kingdom government is a complex task, made considerably easier, however, by the fact that a great deal of it has already been done. The negotiation of Scottish independence would be a vastly more complex task. It would take a considerable time, it could not be kept secret and its details would be the subject of active public debate. The Scots could not be faced with independence either suddenly or in ignorance of its implications. Hence, the argument that an Assembly will inevitably lead to independence can imply only one of two things.

5.2.3 On the one hand, it may imply a belief that independence offers the best long-term prospects for Scots and that an Assembly will help them to perceive this. That is a legitimate and honest belief but there is no guarantee that it will prove well founded. It is at least equally possible that refusal of an Assembly will convince the

Scots that only independence offers them any prospect of acceptable government, whereas achievement of an Assembly will satisfy them.

**5.2.4** Alternatively, the argument implies an insult to the Scots by suggesting that, once an Assembly is in place, they will lose all power of political judgement and will be manipulated by a particular faction in despite of their own interests. The Scots will indeed have lost their political judgement if they succumb to such an argument. They are entitled to point out that they already suffer from an English constitution which allows manipulation by a particular political faction
and that the quest for an Assembly shows a determination to put an end to such manipulation and a resolve to decide for
themselves.

### 5.3 The West Lothian Question

**5.3.1** This is the name given to an anomaly that would result from an Assembly scheme such as that in the Scotland Act 1978. Scotland would continue to send MPs to Parliament, which would continue in its present form. The Scottish MPs would be able to vote on, say, health matters affecting England, but English MPs would no longer be able to vote on health matters affecting Scotland. It has been argued that this renders a Scottish Assembly impracticable unless there is a federal arrangement for the whole of the United Kingdom, or Scotland becomes independent.

**5.3.2** This is equivalent to saying that Scottish government cannot be further improved unless the English agree to restructure their government or the United Kingdom breaks up. In default of an Assembly, Scottish government is now at a dead end or worse. The efforts of those who encouraged Scots to vote "No" in 1979, on the grounds that better ways of improving Scottish government could and would be found, have resulted in the weakening of such Scottish government as then existed.

**5.3.3** The United Kingdom is a political artefact put together at English insistence. If it is to continue, it must work for its living and justify its existence. It is for the English to decide how to govern themselves, but they must allow the continuing improvement of Scottish government. If they dislike the Parliamentary anomaly created by a Scottish Assembly, the remedy is in their own hands - a federal system. But the anomaly would be of practical effect only occasionally and temporarily. The defects of Scottish government are fundamental and continuing.

## 5.4 Overgovernment

**5.4.1** Some describe an Assembly as an additional tier of government and argue that we have enough tiers already. This is a misunderstanding. An Assembly would not add to government, it would transfer from London to Scotland that part of government affecting Scotland only. This could result in duplication only if London government continued to interfere unnecessarily in Scottish government and failed to give the Assembly appropriate freedom to exercise its functions. It is both practicable and essential to draw up an Assembly scheme which avoids this.

**5.4.2** In this context others argue that, if there is to be an Assembly, the present two tier local government system must be replaced by a single tier one. Since the Assembly would not be an extra tier of government, its creation would not necessitate any change in the structure of local government. Some change in that structure may be desirable irrespective of an Assembly. If so, the change should be made in an orderly and democratic way. It would not be orderly to set up an Assembly and restructure local government simultaneously. And if the Scots want their local government restructured, they can be surest of getting it done to their own satisfaction by allocating the job to their own Assembly. The order of procedure is, therefore, to set up an Assembly and to call on that Assembly to consider urgently the case for reorganising local government.

## 5.5 The Cost of Government

**5.5.1** It has been argued that an Assembly would condemn the Scots to taxation permanently higher than that elsewhere in the United Kingdom. Any Assembly scheme which does will have been wrongly conceived.

**5.5.2** The Scotland Act 1978 provided for an Assembly without taxing powers. It is now agreed by all political parties proposing an Assembly that it should have taxing powers. We do not dispute that an Assembly with taxing powers will be stronger, and therefore potentially better, than one without. But even one without would be much better than no Assembly.

**5.5.3** Even if Scotland could not decide the volume of resources available to it, it would be better governed if it could decide the allocation and management of these resources. This need not lead to either irresponsibility or to a dependency culture if the powers and functions of an Assembly are clearly spelt out and there is an open and acceptable process for deciding the volume of resources the Assembly is to have. We make this point not to recommend an Assembly without tax powers, but to stress that their absence is no reason for not having an Assembly.

5.5.4 There is a variety of tax powers which could be devised for an Assembly, giving it the freedom to have higher, lower, or the same level of taxation as the rest of the UK. The difficulties are not inherent. They lie in slavish adherence to the present United Kingdom tax regime, which has been developed to suit a totally centralised government. It might therefore take time to develop the operating system for whatever taxes were put under the Assembly's control.

5.5.5 Even granted that an Assembly need not levy higher taxes unless the Scots vote for policies which require them, there are those who think an Assembly is bound to add to the expense of government, because of the additional elected members, civil servants and related accommodation required.

5.5.6 This extra requirement is marginal. A Scottish administration already exists covering the full range of Assembly functions. The purpose of an Assembly is to give this administration better and more thorough political supervision, and to create policies based on Scottish needs rather than cosmetically adapted from London dictates. Only the elected members and their immediate staff would be additional to present administrative costs.

5.5.7 It was estimated that the administrative costs consequent on implementing the Scotland Act 1978 amounted to one half of one per cent of the budget the Assembly under that Act would have been managing. It is generally accepted now that that Act included many needless provisions for interference by London in Scottish affairs. Some of the extra cost would have been occasioned by the duplication resulting from that interference. The 1978 estimate can therefore be regarded as high. Even at one half of one per cent, it would not be difficult for an Assembly to represent a net economy when the results of more apt policies and more thorough management were taken into account.

## 5.6 An Assembly and the Scottish Economy

5.6.1 Every large state is almost bound to contain within it a series of micro-economies differing appreciably from each other. It is almost impossible to devise a single macro-economic policy suited

to all the micro-economies. This is true of the United Kingdom
and it applies with particular force to Scotland, which regularly
suffers from macro-economic policies designed to suit the economy
of southern eastern England, particularly, though not only, policies
of restraint applied to the United Kingdom when capital and labour
are underused in Scotland.

**5.6.2** In the absence of tariffs, controlled trade and a local
exchange rate, all of which present difficulties, the problems of
declined or underdeveloped micro-economies can be relieved only
by strong regional policies designed to correct both existing defects
in the local economy and the adverse effects of central macro-economic policy.

**5.6.3** The need for such policies is recognised by the European
Economic Community, although a combination of political factors
and the demands of the Community Agricultural Policy have limited
the results to date. Since before the Second World War, British Governments have acknowledged a need for regional policies. Doubts
are beginning to arise as to whether the present British Government
acknowledges that need, yet the need is as great as ever and may
intensify when the Single European Act comes into force.

**5.6.4** It has generally been argued that past regional policies have
ameliorated the problem. Some at least seem to have been cost
effective in doing so. But the problem, summed up in the phrase,
"North - South Divide", not only remains but is widely regarded
as having become worse in recent years. Does this mean that the
wrong regional policies have been chosen, or that the right policies
have been irresolutely applied, or that regional policies can never do
more than suppress symptoms of the disease?

**5.6.5** There is little historical evidence to suggest that market
forces alone can be relied upon to retrieve economies such as
Scotland's now is, and much to suggest that they can't. In any
case, market forces aren't allowed to work freely in the interests of
Scotland, because they are distorted by fiscal and economic policies
tuned to the needs of London. The evidence suggests that past
regional policies have proved inadequate because they have been
inadequately conceived and executed.

**5.6.6** We conclude that, for Scotland within the framework of the
United Kingdom, strong regional economic policies are essential.
The Scots, therefore, have a simple choice. They can allow these
economic policies to be decided by a machinery with a record of

failure to solve the problem, by a London Government to which Scotland is a peripheral issue, in which the only Scottish spokesman can be censored before he speaks and the only Scottish executive must do as London tells him. Or they can have an Assembly which could devise and publicise its own policies, argue for them openly in Scotland and with London, and at least in part implement them.

**5.6.7** There is a clear need to do more than is being done to maintain and develop, for example, a strong Scottish financial sector which can nurture Scottish industry and commerce. This has no necessary connection with subsidies or what is generally described as protectionism. Other countries have demonstrated mechanisms to develop and maintain strong local finance sectors with a commitment to native industry under native control. But these arrangements have not come into being without some kind of political underpinning.

**5.6.8** It has been argued that, because Scotland did very well economically between about 1770 and 1870, when it had less formal political machinery than it has now, the Scots are better off when their voices are lost in the London chorus. Apart from being insulting to Scots, the analogy is false. Between 1770 and 1870 Scotland suffered much less economic intrusion from extraneous capital and London Government than it does now. In the present world, established competitive strength lies elsewhere, and the current lack of it in Scotland cannot be made good without a co-ordinated effort on a number of fronts, which is much more likely with a Scottish political stimulus than without.

**5.6.9** Fear has been professed that an Assembly would damage the Scottish economy because business would move elsewhere. It is difficult to believe the argument sincere. Larger businesses will stay in Scotland if the conditions for a healthy economy prevail. Smaller businesses, with stronger roots in the local economy have a greater incentive to stay.

**5.6.10** The present southward bias of the UK economy, and the failure of regional policies to counteract it, have two results. First, there remains a financial pressure to locate nearer the centre of power. Secondly, there is the danger that publicly quoted businesses come under take-over threats from financially stronger companies based in the South. This will result in a further shift of control away from Scotland.

**5.6.11** In the case of smaller businesses that danger is much less, as most are locally based and a shift of control is usually only accompanied by a voluntary shift in domestic location by the owner or partners. However, the problem in Scotland has remained the lower rate of business start-ups compared with the South. This problem has obviously not been lessened by the present form of government in Scotland and there is no reason to believe that a Scottish Assembly would exacerbate it. On the contrary, there is good reason to believe that it would improve the situation help matters.

**5.6.12** Furthermore a shift of a centre of power to Scotland could give a valuable fillip to the provision of venture capital funding for indigenous Scottish enterprise. In general, business congregates where it can find politicians to lend it an ear and fight its cause. Scottish Assembly Members would know that their prospects of re-election depended at least in part on what they were judged to have done for the Scottish economy. If the close propinquity of politicians frightened off business the City of London would have decamped long ago.

# 6 The Lessons of Experience

**6.1** There is an inherent contradiction between the acknowledgement that Scotland should retain its own legal system and much of its own law, and that it should have its own policies over extensive areas of civil affairs, and the absence of any elective body to nurture and manage that system and these policies.

**6.2** The executive elements of the present machinery of Scottish government put the interests of current London government first, the interests of Scotland a long way behind. The two do not necessarily coincide. The non-executive elements of the present Scottish machinery are more illusion than reality, far more noisy than effective. The machinery is also constitutionally unsound in that it can work only if the governing party in the United Kingdom has a certain minimum of support in Scotland.

**6.3** That there are special problems about the economic and social fabric of Scotland is not disputed. That there is a need for regional policies to deal with these problems has been accepted by all British governments, except perhaps the present one, for many years. Yet the policies devised and applied by British government unaided by an effectively representative Scottish input have been only marginally successful.

**6.4** On both theoretical and practical grounds, therefore, the case for a Scottish Assembly seems conclusive. The question to which we now have to address ourselves is how to bring about its creation in face of intransigent Government opposition.

**6.5** Many Scots would invoke the doctrine of self determination. Although the application of that doctrine is not always clear, it seems beyond question that acceptance within the United Kingdom of a separate Scottish legal system, and at least a theoretical right to a significant area of distinctive policy, carries with it acknowledgement of the right to some degree of self-determination. The present English constitution, or at least its manner of operation, denies that and thereby calls into question the Scots' obligation to abide by that constitution.

**6.6** The convention of loyal opposition and obedience to the government of the day, cardinal to English practice, is a valuable barrier against violence, disorder and, ultimately, rule by force. It should not be lightly abandoned. But it can command continuing respect only if it is not subject to prolonged exploitation.

**6.7** However relatively superior the English constitution may have been a hundred and fifty years ago, it is by modern standards fundamentally flawed. It is now acceptable only so far as Governments in general and Prime Ministers in particular exercise restraint, show sensitivity and do not drive the constitution to its limits. It is unrealistic to expect such qualities in every case and they have been markedly absent recently.

**6.8** The prescribed way of getting an Assembly is to vote for a political party undertaking to provide it. But the figures quoted earlier in this report show that, in the United Kingdom, this does not necessarily work even when Scots vote for it overwhelmingly and the majority of the United Kingdom electorate accepts it.

**6.9** The reasonable expectations of Scots will be fulfilled only within a changed system. However, the system is unlikely to be changed by any action the system itself authorises. The flaws in the present constitution offer incentives to its abuse and an interest in maintaining its abuses. Any party which has power has a temptation to cling to the unreasonable powers available. Even a party which merely has a hope of power may be tempted to support retention of powers it hopes to wield.

**6.10** The Scots are thus offered no constitutional opportunity of self determination in relation to any part of their own machinery of government, no matter how little it may impinge on the government of other parts of the United Kingdom. They must create their own constitutional machinery.

## 7 Freedom, Choice and Representation

**7.1** We make our report against the background of a drive to diminish democracy - to reduce the range and influence of representative institutions. Elective bodies outwith Whitehall are being shorn of their powers or done away with. Areas long regarded as being within the domain of public affairs are being taken outwith that domain. It is in that context that the Government resists the creation of a new elective body, a Scottish Assembly.

**7.2** The Government claims to act in the name of freedom and choice. There are two kinds of choice; choice from what is offered, and choice of what is to be offered. Only the latter is effective choice. The crucial question is, "Who edits the choices that are to be offered?" The ordinary citizen's power to edit the choices that are to be offered can be exercised better through elective institutions than in any other way. These institutions are also the only means by which those exercising power can be made accountable to those affected by its exercise. The United Kingdom has never suffered from an excess of accountability, and it is now experiencing a progressive diminution of accountability.

**7.3** There are many ways of structuring the institutions through which power is made accountable. There is often room for debate about the delineation of the geographical units on which accountability is to be based. In local government, boundaries may be based at least partly on circumstances and connections which change over time. Hence there is room for periodic change in the structure of local government.

**7.4** The boundaries of Scotland, on the other hand, have been fixed for centuries and within Scotland there are laws and policies which apply nowhere else. If there is a geographical unit anywhere in the United Kingdom which ought to have its own elective machinery of accountability, it is Scotland.

**7.5** There is a profound hypocrisy in saying that the Scots should stand on their own feet while simultaneously denying them management of their own political affairs, and that denial is a clear deprivation of choice for Scots. Scots can stand on their own feet only by refusing to accept the constitution which denies them the power to do so.

# PART II

## The Road to Change in Scottish Government

# 8 The Way to Resurgence

**8.1** We have described a situation in which the spirit underlying the Treaty of Union has been eroded almost to the point of extinction; in which the letter of approved Scottish Parliamentary procedures is no longer being honoured; in which the wishes of a massive majority of the Scottish electorate are being disregarded, and in which there is only remote hope of a response to Scottish wishes through Parliamentary action. In such a situation one would expect to see signs of a breakdown of respect for law. They are beginning to appear.

**8.2** It is not part of the Committee's remit to pronounce on the legislation for what is generally known as the poll tax. But the existence of, and the reaction to, that legislation illustrate our point. Whatever the arguments for and against the legislation, its unpopularity is beyond dispute. Equally beyond dispute is the fact that it is attracting greater resistance and creating a more serious risk of disobedience to the law than any other issue in living memory. Now that the legislation is being enacted for England and Wales, its defects are being highlighted by the Government's own backbenchers, though nothing was heard from them when it was forced through for Scotland against the opposition of six sevenths of the Scottish MPs. Probably no legislation at once so fundamental and so lacking in popular support would have been initiated other than in a territory within which the Government was unrepresentative of and out of touch with the electorate.

**8.3** We fully understand the pressure for refusal to comply with the requirements of the poll tax legislation. In all the circumstances the Government cannot reasonably expect anything else. But we do not believe that random rejection of the law on particular issues is the answer to the problem facing Scotland.

**8.4** Misconceived and undemocratic legislation for Scotland is not the product of occasional aberration by a particular British Government. It is a consequence of the flaws in the machinery of government which we have already pointed out. Resistance to one mischief will not prevent other mischiefs and may well fail because it does not address the real weaknesses of the Government's case.

**8.5** Scots must create for themselves a focus of resistance and political negotiation, which rejects comprehensively the authority of existing government on matters peculiar to Scotland, which describes and demands the appropriate cure of present ills, namely a new form of Scottish government, and which encourages civil disobedience of any kind only so far as this forms part of an orderly programme to achieve it. The appropriate form of that focus of resistance is a Constitutional Convention.

## 9 *What is a Constitutional Convention?*

**9.1** A Constitutional Convention is a representative body convened to fill the democratic gap when the government of an existing state has partly or wholly failed, or when a government needs to be created for a new, or re-created for an old, country. It may perform several tasks, but one invariable task is to draw up a new constitution.

**9.2** A definition applicable to Scotland was given in a Consultative Paper issued in 1985 by Campaign for a Scottish Assembly. This stated that a Scottish Constitutional Convention would:—

(a) articulate and represent the Scottish demand for an Assembly;

(b) draft the provisions of an Assembly scheme, setting out the powers of the Assembly, its sources of finance and its relationship with British Government;

(c) negotiate with British Government the timetable and implementation of that scheme;

(d) arrange any necessary test of Scottish support for the scheme, eg., by referendum.

**9.3** The Constitutional Convention idea is not a new one. It has been discussed in various quarters in Scotland for several years. Internationally, it has a history covering two hundred years and several countries, beginning with the bodies which controlled the American War of Independence and subsequently drafted the United States Constitution.

**9.4** The definition is more important than the title. Various titles have been given to such bodies including; Convention, Constituent Assembly, National Assembly, Parliamentary Council. However,

"Constitutional Convention" has the merit of describing more accurately than any other title the purpose for which the body is convened - to draw up a constitution and, so far as appropriate, to take steps to implement it.

**9.5** Constitutional Conventions may be, but are not necessarily, challenges to Government. Governments have recognised the political sense of Constitutional Conventions in particular circumstances. In Germany, after the Second World War, the Allied Powers promoted the setting up of a Convention (though the Germans used a different name) as a means of creating a new German constitution.

**9.6** Past British Governments have recognised that, where existing government machinery clearly failed to command respect in some part of the United Kingdom, the creation of a Convention might represent a sensible step towards a solution of the problem. The Government set up an Irish Convention in 1917, and a Northern Ireland Convention in 1975.

**9.7** The first of these failed in its objective because it was too little and too late. The results of the second were aborted because of difficulties peculiar to Northern Ireland. But these failures do not affect the inherent good sense of the expedient as a solution to the very problem which exists in Scotland, namely that existing government has failed and that there is no political body which can speak for Scotland and deal with Government to negotiate a resolution of the Scottish problem.

**9.8** The absence of a body which can speak for all Scots on constitutional matters presents a difficulty whichever Party is in power at Westminster. An Assembly achieved by the normal legislative route might carry the authority of one Party only. While even a flawed Assembly would be an advance, an Assembly carrying the authority of a Constitutional Convention would have greater authority. A Constitutional Convention has merits, therefore, regardless of the prospects for future elections.

# 10 How can a Constitutional Convention be set up?

**10.1** The precedents give only limited help in deciding how to set up a Scottish Constitutional Convention. There is no standard pattern. The creation of Constitutional Conventions has usually required some improvised response based on local circumstances, and exploiting local traditions and such native political mechanisms as were functioning at the time.

**10.2**  The originating mechanics of Conventions have ranged along a spectrum from, at one extreme, formal de jure legitimacy with direct elections and a remit prescribed by Government to, at the other extreme, semi-clandestine gatherings, mainly appointed or delegated and with only a de facto claim to be representative. The 1975 Northern Ireland Convention is an example of the first. The German Vorparlament of 1848 and the French Assemblee Consultative, which began work in Algeria in 1944 and was later transferred to France and enlarged after the recovery of Paris, are examples of the second.

**10.3** Two other possible aspects of Constitutional Conventions are worth noting. They need not spring up full grown in the first instance; and groups or bodies initially formed for another purpose may turn themselves into Constitutional Conventions. The French case mentioned is an example of gradual growth. Examples of transformation can be found in France, where the Estates General of 1789 turned themselves into a National Assembly with the remit of drafting a constitution, and Ireland at the end of the First World War, where MPs elected in British elections withdrew from Westminster and set themselves up as a Dail in Ireland.

**10.4** The essential is that a Convention, whether its origins are de jure or de facto, whether it is created complete as a single act or grows gradually, must achieve acceptance by those on whose behalf it presumes to speak and act. The more difficult the circumstances in which the Convention is created - in other words the less help it gets from established government - the more difficult it will be to make it wholly representative. By strict criteria, most Constitutional Conventions to date have been representative only to a limited degree. However, a wise and mature community should be tolerant about the criteria of representativeness when the body representing it has been convened in circumstances of difficulty and obstruction.

**10.5** Ideally a Convention should be specifically elected for its purpose. But few past Constitutional Conventions would have come into existence had this been a requirement. There are a variety of other means of choosing the members of a Convention, carrying quite sufficient representative status for the purpose.

# 11 The Creation of a Convention by Government

**11.1.1** The creation by Government of a directly elected Scottish Constitutional Convention, with the task of preparing an Assembly scheme for consideration and adoption by Government, is the most obvious and suitable way of resolving the Scottish problem. The legislation creating the Convention could provide for a Scottish referendum either as a pre-condition of holding the elections to the Convention, or as a pre-condition of putting the Convention's handiwork to Parliament.

**11.1.2** It is not too late for the present Government to recognise the necessity for constitutional change in Scotland, its potential benefits for British government generally, and the consequent merits of setting up a Scottish Constitutional Convention. However, in light of both its past actions and its current professions, we have no ground for supposing that it will do so. We therefore go on to consider how a Convention might be set up in face of Government hostility.

## 11.2 Size, Composition and Mechanics of a Convention

**11.2.1** We see no need for fixed assumptions about the appropriate size of a Constitutional Convention. By varying the methods of working, a wide range of sizes can be accommodated. The essentials are that the Constitutional Convention should be efficient in its work and in touch with Scottish opinion while devising its proposals.

**11.2.2** For certain tasks; drawing up an Assembly scheme, negotiating with Government, and week to week co-ordination of a programme of protest, a compact group is obviously appropriate. But that group would need the support of a larger, widely representative body. There is room for debate as to whether the Convention itself should be the larger body, appointing committees for specific tasks, or whether the Convention should be relatively small but in regular contact with a larger group. In the latter case, that larger group might have either consultative or ultimate policy control functions.

**11.2.3** It will be important to settle the size, detailed composition and at least some of the mechanics of the Convention before it is set up. But in the first instance it is far more important to decide on the criteria which will maximise the prospects of the Convention being established, and ensure its being accepted as representative. Our thoughts on the mechanics of a Convention will emerge from Part III of our Report. We do not think it necessary to take our thoughts on size and composition beyond the analysis of criteria which follows.

### 11.3 A Directly Elected Convention

**11.3.1** Orderly and democratic elections involve the provision of offices, polling stations and the availability of numbers of experienced staff with appropriate equipment. All this costs money. In this country, the equipment, the expertise and the powers to conduct elections lie with local government, subject to central government control.

**11.3.2** Whether local government would be prepared to conduct elections for a Scottish Constitutional Convention in face of central government opposition can be tested only in the event. Whether they would be able to incur the consequent expense, or would be free of legal challenge if they did so, are equally matters we cannot examine realistically now. But it does seem that it would be significantly more difficult to convene a Convention by this method than to convene it by the methods we consider below.

**11.3.3** That difficulty would be increased by the need to decide on the voting system to be adopted. We have already pointed out that the current British voting system has been discredited in practice by its recent results. A widespread reluctance to adopt it for elections to the Convention is likely. On the other hand, unanimity about changing it, or about the precise system to replace it, might not be reached easily. An attempt at an elected Convention is likely to put the creation of the Convention in some doubt.

**11.3.4** Elections for a Convention would not be the only possible opportunity of a vote on the issue of a Scottish Assembly. At some later stage there could be a referendum. A referendum on a specific proposal for an Assembly would be more precisely focussed and more easily understood than a vote for a Constitutional Convention. With a Convention in existence to organise the referendum, the prospect of efficient and comprehensive voting arrangements would be greater. The complexities of the voting system would be less. And if there is to be a need for special efforts to raise money to finance voting, that effort could better be devoted to financing a referendum than to financing elections to a Constitutional Convention.

**11.3.5** We do not suggest that the possibility of an elected Convention should be dismissed out of hand. We appreciate that our report can be no more than a basis for discussion between interested groups and authorities who might take action on it. Only when these groups and authorities come together can the practicability of an elected Convention be tested. But it would be a mistake to pursue the ideal of direct elections if this were to put the creation of a Convention at risk, or even significantly delay it.

## 11.4 An Elected Member based Convention

**11.4.1** If there is to be no elected Convention, there are two alternative strategies for the construction of a Convention; it could be based on existing elected representatives, either MPs alone or MPs together with local councillors; or it could approximately follow the precedent set by the Scottish Economic Summit convened in July 1986. It may be possible to mix some elements of each of these strategies.

**11.4.2** The attitudes and actions of Members of Parliament for Scottish constituencies will be a cardinal factor in the prospects for, and composition of, a Convention. Unless the MPs are actively involved, their relationship with the Convention is bound to be delicate as, otherwise, a Constitutional Convention must come to seem a rival source of representative authority.

**11.4.3** In light of their role in representing Scotland, the primary responsibility for taking the lead in forming a Scottish Constitutional Convention must rest with the Scottish MPs. Taking the lead in forming a Convention, and actively supporting it, does not necessarily imply that the Scottish MPs form all, or even part, of the Convention's membership. That would be a decision for the MPs to take. However, they must face the fact that, if they decline to form part of the membership, their influence on the Convention's decisions and actions will be diminished accordingly. If the majority of pro-Assembly MPs and the Convention are later found disagreeing with each other, the repute and authority of both will suffer.

**11.4.4** It may be argued that it would be counterproductive for the the MPs to abandon Westminster. Bearing in mind our criticisms of the existing constitution, we think this argument can be exaggerated. Considerable doubt has already been thrown on the extent to which the Scottish Opposition MPs can influence matters in the present Parliament. However, we accept that there would be services for their constituents which the Scottish MPs would want to continue to provide, and that not all MPs have exactly the same role at Westminster. In any case, membership of the Convention would not require their presence in Scotland on every day of every week. It should be possible to combine the essentials of work at Westminster with active membership of the Convention. Membership of the latter would enable the MPs to make a substantially greater impact within Scotland than they can when constantly at Westminster.

**11.4.5** If it is felt that, even with these qualifications, regular attendance of MPs at the Convention would be difficult, a system of alternates could be devised, whereby each MP who was a member of the Convention could name a substitute, who would attend in the MP's absence and keep in regular touch with her/him about Convention business. However, though we do not press it, the idea of MPs totally deserting Westminster should be borne in mind. It would have a symbolic value both because of the greater emphasis on the rejection of Westminster, and because Westminster would be plainly seen to be governing Scotland with no, or marginal, Scottish participation.

**11.4.6** Provided an overwhelming majority of Scottish MPs took part, directly or indirectly, and provided they took effective steps to consult and involve others, a Convention consisting only of MPs or their named substitutes could be adequate. But it would be more authoritative if supplemented. It should be supplemented on two counts, possibly three; to provide for the representation of local government, to make greater room for political groups who strongly support an Assembly but who are under-represented in the present Parliament, and perhaps from non-political interests who support an Assembly.

**11.4.7** Local councillors, though not nominally elected on national issues, have a more representative status than delegates can have, no matter how chosen. No less important, local authorities have resources and executive power. How far they would be willing and able to use them on behalf of the Convention we cannot predict, but everything possible should be done to bring these resources and powers into play. Finally, local government has been a principal victim of the defects of the English constitution which we have described above. Local government councillors should, however, be appointed to the Convention as representatives of local government generally, not as representatives of their own local authority.

**11.4.8** It is not part of our remit to propose reforms of the present voting system. But we have pointed out some of its distorted results. While the present Party composition of the Scottish MPs is a not unfair reflection of the total demand for constitutional change in Scotland, it is not an accurate reflection of the distribution of that demand between Parties. We do not suggest that the Convention should reflect precisely the votes cast on any particular occasion, if only because it might be difficult to agree which occasion should be chosen. But we do suggest that the Convention should be supplemented by members nominated by or on behalf of Parties so as to redress some of the Party imbalance resulting from the 1987 election.

**11.4.9** There are attractions in having Convention members outwith the political Parties. They could add to the popularity of the Convention and to mass involvement in its doings. But, given that the Convention will be a decision taking body and the Parties will naturally want to be assured that nominally non-Party members do not in practice give the Convention a Party balance out of accord with electoral voting, the scope for such members in the Convention itself, as distinct from the consultative body proposed in para. 16.3 below, seems limited.

**11.4.10** On the basis of their own professions, recently and emphatically renewed, we must assume that the Conservative Party will oppose a Convention. While their absence will not prevent the remaining Parties representing the overwhelming majority of the Scottish electorate, we believe the possibility of the Conservative participation in a Convention should be held open, although the scale of their representation must be viewed in light of the extent to which the Party as a whole pronounces in support of a Convention.

**11.4.11** We have set out in Annex A three illustrations of the way in which the criteria suggested above might be interpreted. These illustrations are a guide rather than specific recommendations. In the event the approach must be flexible, taking account of the circumstances of the time and the precise quarters from which the strongest support comes.

### 11.5  A Delegate Convention

**11.5.1** The Scottish Economic Summit Conference of July 1986, which established the Standing Commission on the Scottish Economy, offers a framework which could be adapted for the creation of a Scottish Constitutional Convention. The Economic Summit was the consequence of a joint initiative by Strathclyde Regional Council and the Scottish Trade Unions Congress. It comprises individuals from local authorities, trade unions, the Scottish Council (Development and Industry), Chambers of Commerce, CBI (Scotland), the churches and all Scottish political parties.

**11.5.2** An analogous body, addressed to constitutional change, could be convened. This body might either itself be the Scottish Constitutional Convention, appointing committees as appropriate, or could appoint a Constitutional Convention, with a request to report back to a Summit Conference periodically.

**11.5.3** However, there is a great difference between calling a conference to express generalised anxiety and to arrange the preparation of reports for the Government's consideration and, on the other hand, convening a body setting itself up to replace the Government as the channel of Scottish aspirations and to lead action designed to force constitutional change. The Economic Summit Conference is the latest and most developed example of an expedient with a useful history in Scotland. No doubt that expedient is capable of further development. But it needs considerable further development to render it capable of the very great and immediate leap required to serve as an effective Constitutional Convention?

**11.5.4** A body of this type could have little authority to act as a Constitutional Convention unless it comprised not merely individuals from a wide range of organisations, but delegates carrying with them the full authority and wholehearted support of these organisations. A substantial degree of local authority support would be important. Even then, the authority of the Convention would depend heavily on the range of other organisations represented and there would be room for debate about the support they commanded.

**11.5.5** We consider that the view we expressed in 11.4.2 above, about the role of MPs, is crucial to the setting up of any kind of Constitutional Convention, other than a directly elected one set up by Government. It is possible that MPs, taking the lead as we propose, might promote a Convention of a predominantly delegate structure but the difference in origin would be crucial. If the MPs collectively, and with them the Parties they represent, do not give clear support to a Convention, it will operate under serious difficulties.

**11.5.6** If the Scots want and need a Constitutional Convention and the MPs and their Parties will not take the lead in giving them one, not only has the English constitution broken down, so has the Scottish party system. If that proves to be so, the Scots have no alternative but to pursue the concept of a delegate Convention, with or without some local authority support, and develop it as far and as fast as they can. But their first recourse is to require their elected representatives to represent them.

## 11.6 Level of Support Required

**11.6.1** Below a certain level of support, no Constitutional Convention of any of the three categories we have described would command any authority. However, we think it would be a mistake to suppose that, until some predetermined level of support has been indicated, no steps to set up a Convention should be taken. We reiterate that it has been known for Constitutional Conventions to grow rather than to spring to life full-grown. The Scots, whose closely law-abiding nature has been the subject of both admiring and regretful comment, may swallow hard and hesitate before launching a Constitutional Convention in despite of Government, whatever the provocation. But that is a reason to give encouragement to those who face the necessity first and act accordingly.

**11.6.2** Acting accordingly, we suggest, means setting up the Convention as soon as a significant level of support has been indicated, even if that initial level is not sufficient to carry through the Convention's task. The Convention itself can then act as a means of building its strength to the point at which it can discharge its full task.

# PART III

## A Constitutional Convention at Work

## 12 The Tasks of the Convention

**12.1** The Convention, when set up, will have three specific tasks:-

(i) to draw up a scheme for a Scottish Assembly;
(ii) to mobilise Scottish opinion behind that scheme;
(iii) to deal with the Government in securing approval of the scheme, or an acceptable modification of it.

The Convention will decide for itself how to carry out its tasks, but we need some analysis of them in order to complete our picture of a Constitutional Convention in the Scottish context, and in particular our assessment of its composition and mechanics, also as a guide to Campaign for a Scottish Assembly in the follow up of our Report.

**12.2** The Convention must be distinguished from an Interim Assembly. The latter would seek to act in part as a legislative and executive body by debating the policy issues of concern to Scotland at the time and building up such massive support for its views on these issues that the Government felt obliged to comply with them. If there were serious delays in achieving an Assembly scheme by legislation, the Constitutional Convention might be pressed to act also as an Interim Assembly and it might be appropriate for it to do so. But its primary objective should be to achieve an Assembly by legislation and it should not allow other activities to interfere with that objective.

## 13 Drawing up the Assembly Scheme (*)

**13.1** There is no "right" scheme for an Assembly. Machinery of government is an ever-changing process. Whatever Assembly scheme is initially adopted will change over time and there is room for negotiation about the provisions of that initial scheme. Scots should be prepared to give their Convention members latitude accordingly.

[*Throughout this report we have used the term Assembly, first introduced in this connection during the drafting of the Scotland Act 1978. All previous proposals for Scottish self-government have preferred the historical term, Parliament, used in Scotland for many centuries. We believe that there are good arguments for returning to the traditional usage of Parliament rather than Assembly, but this is a matter which should be considered by the Constitutional Convention.]

**13.2** But the drafting will not begin from scratch. There have already been two elaborate exercises in drafting Scottish Assembly Bills; that leading to the Scotland Act 1978, and that leading to the Bill presented by the Labour Party in November 1987 but aborted by the Government. A substantial scheme of a different character from the two Labour Bills has now been presented by a group of Scottish Conservatives. In addition, a Convention can draw on a considerable body of literature from academic sources analysing the possibilities and their prospective consequences, as well as the Report of the Royal Commission on the Constitution, policy documents by the Democrats and SNP, and consultative documents by the Labour Party and Campaign for a Scottish Assembly.

**13.3** It will make sense for the Convention to start from where others have left off and to compare the two Labour schemes, both of which follow the same principles though one is a considerable development of the other, with the recent Conservative scheme, looking at both against the background of the literature. But it should bear in mind both that views as to the powers the Assembly needs have changed over the years, and that the Assembly ought not to be hidebound by traditional Parliamentary practice.

**13.4** If the suggestions made in the previous paragraph are followed, the task of preparing the Assembly scheme need not take long.

## 14 Mobilising Scottish Opinion

**14.1** Whatever the composition of the Convention itself, the practices followed and the standards achieved in informing Scottish opinion and invoking its support will have to surpass those shown in the ordinary course of British Parliamentary government. A challenge to the authority of Government, expressed through new channels, needs greater commitment than traditional Parliamentary initiatives.

**14.2** The aim must be to involve at every level and in every part of Scotland all organisations with any interest in public affairs. This implies a vital distinction between the pattern of working of the Convention and the pattern of working of, for example, the House of Commons. The latter spends most of its time in London, debating. It spends only a small part of its time, and even less of its effort, involving the electorate in its doings. The Convention should do the reverse.

**14.3** This is not necessarily a criticism of Parliamentary methods, which are a separate issue. The Convention differs from the House of Commons in that it is a representative body brought together for a single purpose and it is concerned only with action designed to achieve that purpose as quickly as possible. It must adapt its methods accordingly.

## 15 Dealing with the Government.

**15.1** The Convention will require to correspond with, make representations to, and in due course negotiate with the Government.

**15.2** There will probably be much more to this third task than superficially appears. We cannot assume that the Government will accept the need to treat with a Constitutional Convention as soon as it is set up. Powerful indications of Scottish support for the Convention and resistance to the Government may be needed before the latter acknowledges the facts of Scottish opinion and the need to take account of them. Deciding on, planning and supervising these indications would be part of the Convention's responsibilities.

**15.3** We cannot predict what this might involve. One seemingly obvious prospect is the organisation of a referendum, both to satisfy the Convention itself that its proposals commanded support and to convince the Government that they did. However, it is a debatable point whether the Convention should itself endeavour to conduct a referendum, or should strive to force the Government into conducting a referendum on lines agreed between Government and Convention. That will be a matter of judgement for the Convention. But a wide range of other action is possible, either to force a referendum or to force the Government to recognise the results of one. Whatever forms this action takes, it will achieve its object only if the Convention has effectively mobilised opinion on its side.

## 16 The Needs of the Convention

**16.1** In light of the above review of the forms of action the Convention must be prepared to undertake, we can now assess what it will need to do its job and what implications this has for its detailed composition and organisation.

**16.2** Drafting an Assembly Bill for consideration by the Convention should be the first task put in hand. If the suggestions in paras 13.2 and 13.3 are accepted, this could be done with the part-time services of a secretary and a circle of specialist advisers whose work might well be voluntary, all working under the supervision of a drafting management committee drawn from the Convention.

**16.3** Since it must both take decisions and either take action or supervise it, the Convention must from time to time vote on issues. The Convention itself must, therefore, reflect reasonably closely the recent voting patterns of the Scottish electorate, otherwise its decisions will be open to serious question. But the need for massive public support, which we described in paras 14.1-3, suggests that the Convention could usefully be reinforced by a consultative body.

**16.4** Because this body would not be executive, it need not be rigidly structured and political balance within it need not be a primary consideration. It would not normally vote, but it would give the Convention a regular means of sounding public opinion on a broad basis, and a channel of communication through which the Convention's decisions and proposals could be disseminated widely, quickly and effectively.

**16.5** This consultative body could include representatives of all the substantial national organisations declaring themselves in support of a Convention. It could also include individuals drawn from organisations, or social, cultural, economic and religious groupings, which did not collectively declare themselves in support, but an appreciable number of whose members supported the Convention. The body could most conveniently be called forth by the Convention and it would make sense for the Convention to devise a regular pattern of consultation with it. In default of the early creation of a Convention, the consultative body might arise by spontaneous action as a means of putting pressure on those who ought to form the Convention to do so.

**16.6** The work of the Convention designed to persuade the Government that it must accede to the demand for an Assembly will be the most important part of its task, whether or not that part of its work includes the organisation of a referendum. The preparation, and the approval, of an Assembly scheme should involve less effort in light of the work already done. Also, it is more important for the Scots to get an Assembly, and to get it soon, than to ensure from the outset the ultimate refinement of the Assembly's powers. Negotiating with the Government, when it faces the need to negotiate, will no doubt be a delicate task involving weighty decisions. But the basis for taking these decisions will be the effectiveness of the work done on demonstrating the strength of Scottish demand.

**16.7** In terms of its week-to-week operations, the committees it will need, etc., any body with 50 or more members is likely to be enough for the Convention itself, excluding the supplementary consultative body. But in the interests of its representative authority we think its membership should be at least equal to the number of Parliamentary constituencies in Scotland.

**16.8** At the other end of the spectrum, we can see no objection to a body twice that size, but no great advantage in it either, except so far as the Convention was thereby made more representative. It would be an advantage if there could be a representative from every Scottish constituency, whether that representative were a Member of Parliament, an alternate, or a local councillor. The examples of Convention composition given in Annex A broadly accord with these criteria.

**16.9** The consultative body should probably be larger than even the higher figure suggested for the Convention. Local councillors on the Convention itself would be there not to represent their local authority, but to represent local government generally, though they could also speak for the general area from which they came. The consultative body could usefully include a representative of each local authority, in addition to representatives of all those national organisations; social, economic, cultural and religious wishing to take part.

**16.10** The needs would be different if, regrettably, a delegate Convention as described in section 11.5 above had to be attempted. Once it was fairly launched, the model of a relatively compact executive body and a larger consultative body would probably remain valid. But a Convention of this sort would have to devote greater effort in the first instance to establishing its credibility and demonstrating its support. This might well take the form of a struggle with, within, or between political parties. That very process would probably have an effect on the structures eventually adopted and we see no point in trying to predict that effect.

**16.11** The Convention would need staff and accommodation, but there seems scope for providing much of both from existing resources. We have stressed that the Convention must not be confused with Parliament and should not imitate it. The Convention will have more of the attributes of a campaign than of a legislature. There need not necessarily be a permanent meeting place. Indeed, moving meetings about could be turned to advantage.

**16.12** There will have to be a permanent office for the promulgation of instructions, the conduct of communications and the maintenance of records. It will be convenient if this is nearby the most frequently used meeting place, better still if it can be physically within it. If our proposals are adopted, most or all members of the Convention will have established arrangements for carrying out political or administrative work in Scotland and will not need personal offices associated with the Convention. A number will already have research and perhaps other assistance.

**16.13** We see grounds for hope that enough organisations, local authority or other, possessing office and meeting space, would provide what the Convention needed of both at modest or no cost. We would also hope that the individuals forming the membership of both the Convention and the consultative body, or their organisations, would meet most travelling and incidental expenses.

**16.14** There appears to be scope for voluntary work in aid of the Convention in that much of the assistance it will require need not be rendered by full-time staff. For example, preparation of the Assembly scheme on the lines we have described in paras 13.1-3 would need the part-time services of a secretary and a number of specialist advisers. The secretary probably would have to be part of a full time staff, but the advisers could almost certainly combine their advisory functions with existing employment, possibly with some co-operation from their employers. Communications and publications are likely to be an appreciable part of the Convention's activities and may be another field in which voluntary workers can be useful.

**16.15** Some full-time staff, to provide both high grade and routine secretarial services, would be needed. There might be some scope for obtaining these by secondment and at a cost to their existing employers.

**16.16** In effect, we are suggesting an operation of fund-raising in kind. It is impossible to predict how much this will cover. A great deal depends on what sympathetic organisations, notably local authorities, are empowered and willing to do to assist the Convention. But we do not imagine this will be enough. Additional cash is likely to be needed to discharge the Convention's functions, though it is impossible at this stage to say how much. It should therefore be assumed that a cash fund-raising operation will have to be mounted.

**16.17** It should be mounted at the earliest possible stage. There would be little point in mounting it until at least some promising consultations about setting up a Convention had taken place. But it should not await the formal establishment of the Convention. A fund should be set up on the basis of returning all moneys if no Convention is created and devoting moneys eventually unspent by a Convention to a Scottish public purpose. A Committee, preferably comprising mostly prospective members of the Convention and the associated consultative body, should be established for this purpose.

> "It should seem, therefore, to be the happiness of man to make his social dispositions the ruling spring of his occupations; to state himself as the member of a community, for whose general good his heart may glow with an ardent zeal . . . we need not enlarge our communities to enjoy these advantages. We frequently obtain them in the most remarkable degree, where nations remain independent, and are of a small extent."
>
> [Adam Ferguson; An Essay on the History of Civil Society, Edinburgh 1767]

# EPILOGUE

Scotland faces a crisis of identity and survival. It is now being governed without consent and subject to the declared intention of having imposed upon it a radical change of outlook and behaviour pattern which it shows no sign of wanting. All questions as to whether consent should be a part of government are brushed aside. The comments of Adam Smith are put to uses which would have astonished him, Scottish history is selectively distorted and the Scots are told that their votes are lying; that they secretly love what they constantly vote against.

Scotland is not alone in suffering from the absence of consent in government. The problem afflicts the United Kingdom as a whole. We have a government which openly boasts its contempt for consensus and a constitution which allows it to demonstrate that contempt in practice. But Scotland is unique both in its title to complain and in its awareness of what is being done to it.

None of this has anything to do with the merits or demerits of particular policies at particular times, or with the degree of conviction with which people believe in these policies. Many a conviction politician contemptuous of democracy has done some marginal good in passing. Mussolini allegedly made the Italian trains run on time. The crucial questions are power and consent; making power accountable and setting limits to what can be done without general consent.

These questions will not be adequately answered in the United Kingdom until the concentration of power that masquerades as "the Crown-in-Parliament" has been broken up. Government can be carried on with consent only through a system of checks and balances capable of restraining those who lack a sense of restraint. Stripping away the power of politicians outside Whitehall (and incidentally increasing the powers of Ministers inside Whitehall) restores power not to the people but to the powerful. The choice we are promised in consequence will in practice be the choice the powerful choose to offer us. Through effectively answerable representative institutions we can edit the choices for ourselves.

Whether Government interferes unnecessarily or fails to interfere where it should, political institutions answerable alike to consumers and producers, rich and poor, provide the means of correcting it. If these institutions are removed, restricted or censored, Governments do not get accurate messages - or can ignore any messages they do not like. If past conduct of politics has given cause for complaint, the answer is to open up and improve politics to give more accurate messages sooner, not to close politics down so that the few remaining politicians can invent the messages for themselves.

It is a sign of both the fraudulence and the fragility of the English constitution that representative bodies and their activities, the life-blood of government by consent, can be systematically closed down by a minority Westminster Government without there being any constitutional means of even giving them pause for thought. It is the ultimate condemnation of that constitution that so many people, in Scotland and beyond, have recently been searching in the House of Lords for the last remnants of British democracy.

Scotland, if it is to remain Scotland, can no longer live with such a constitution and has nothing to hope for from it. Scots have shown it more tolerance than it deserves. They must now show enterprise by starting the reform of their own government. They have the opportunity, in the process, to start the reform of the English constitution; to serve as the grit in the oyster which produces the pearl.

It is a mistake to suppose, as some who realise the defects of our present form of government do, that the route to reform must lie through simultaneous reorganisation of the government of all parts of the United Kingdom. That will lead merely to many further years of talk and an uncertain prospect of action. Tidiness of system is a minor consideration. The United Kingdom has been an anomaly from its inception and is a glaring anomaly now. It is unrealistic to argue that the improvement of government must be prevented if it cannot be fitted within some pre-conceived symmetry. New anomalies that force people to think are far more likely to be constructive than impossible ambitions to eliminate anomaly.

Even if Scots had greater hopes than they have of voting into office a Party more sympathetic to the needs of Scotland, it would be against the long-term interests of Scotland to offer credibility to the existing constitution. There is no need for Scots to feel selfish in undermining it. They can confidently challenge others to defend it.

We are under no illusions about the seriousness of what we recommend. Contesting the authority of established government is not a light matter. We would not recommend it if we did not feel that British government has so decayed that there is little hope of its being reformed within the framework of its traditional procedures. Setting up a Scottish Constitutional Convention and subsequently establishing a Scottish Assembly cannot by themselves achieve the essential reforms of British government, but they are essential if any remnant of distinctive Scottish government is to be saved, and they could create the ground-swell necessary to set the British reform process on its way.

# A Claim of Right
# for Scotland

COMMENTARY

# 1

## Retrospect and Prospect

NIGEL GRIFFITHS

When the Conservative vote in Scotland reached a thirty year nadir in 1987 the pressure for constitutional change was bound to increase. Traditional Tory strongholds like Edinburgh had elected Labour councils and more Labour MPs than ever. Local authorities had fallen to Labour, the SDP/Liberal Alliance (now the SLD) and the SNP. 'Routed' is not too strong a word to describe the state of Scottish Conservatism post 1987. But those expecting a moderation of Conservative Government policies were quickly disappointed, as public services came under the auctioneer's hammer and the poll tax was imposed. Parliamentary scrutiny of Scottish matters was severely curtailed. With only 10 MPs left in Scotland the Tories were unable to staff the Select Committee on Scottish Affairs. Their English colleagues, while willing to sit on short-lived Bill Committees and vote legislation through, simply refused to take part in any Scottish committee which inquired into the Government's management of Scottish affairs.

For the first time since 1936, the largest department of Government, the Scottish Office, had no-one outside Government examining its activities and calling it to account. With a majority of 100 in the House of Commons, sufficient to defeat even its own rebels, the House of Lords became the Parliamentary block to a few of the worst excesses of Thatcherite rule. Outside Parliament the political parties had to contend with criticism that they were impotent and this jibe was most keenly felt by Labour.

Labour has long been sensitive about its commitment to devolution for Scotland which was first declared in the 1880s, but quietly dropped from the manifesto by 1945.

After 1987, all non-Tory parties recognised the frustration of people in Scotland at the prospect of 4 or 5 years of unfettered Tory rule. A majority supported some form of devolution and within months of the General Election, the Campaign for a Scottish Assembly invited 16 prominent Scots to draft a claim of right for Scotland to articulate that frustration and recommend a solution. A year later, the *Claim of Right* focused on the frustration and proposed a partial solution. A Constitutional Convention, representing the various political parties and powerful interest groups was to be established with a remit to provide a blueprint for a Scottish Assembly and campaign to ensure public support and to secure Government approval. An Interim Assembly would be established if the Government refused to agree to a Scottish Assembly.

*The Claim of Right*, with its Constitutional Convention did not receive unanimous support from the Labour Party when published in June 1988. Some Labour MPs reflected this concern and thought that the chances of getting all the non-Tory parties round the table was slim. Some were rightly worried that even if the Convention succeed in producing an agreed programme, Labour would then be blamed for the failure of the Tories to pay any heed to it. They feared that the Interim Assembly members would be likened to Mensheviks deliberating on great matters while the Bolsheviks held the reins of power. Labour would be ridiculed as powerless — the very label it had been trying to shrug off since June 10 1987 saw 50 Scottish Labour MPs elected. Shadow Scots Secretary Donald Dewar, a quick witted, if cautious man voiced these fears.

Within the Labour Party, objections were overcome by a combination of optimists who were emotionally and ideologically committed to devolution, and pragmatists who, although short on analysis preferred to do something rather than nothing.

The Govan by-election result in November 1988 certainly galvanised the latter. At the same time, it gave focus to those people within the Labour Party whose patience with Labour as a credible force for change had been exhausted. They viewed the Govan campaign, reiterating as it did a Labour commitment to opposition within the law (especially on the poll tax), as the last straw. Party members like Alex Wood, the articulate former leader of Edinburgh District council left Labour to set up a breakaway party to campaign for an independent socialist Scotland. Like Jim Sillars, he was a former hammer of nationalism, but unlike Sillars, he was not a supporter of devolution in the 1970s.

Within the Labour Party ten years of Tory rule had removed all but the vestiges of opposition to Scottish devolution among the English and Welsh.

The effect of Government policies and the perception in parts of England and in Wales that they have no effective way of ameliorating the effects of these policies have converted politicians in the north of England as well as elsewhere to the desirability of a local assembly with legislative powers.

Two obstacles blocked the progress of devolution in the 1970s. One was the West Lothian question — which postulated a reduction in the number of Scottish MPs at Westminster as the price for more power being delegated to the Scottish Assembly, and the consequential disputes over the barring of Scottish MPs from discussing English, Welsh and Northern Irish business. The second was the powers of the Assembly which were perceived to be limited. This latter objection gave Lord Home cause for recommending a 'no' vote on the grounds that any Assembly should have tax-raising powers. It is somewhat ironic that the Tories now use the same reasoning to oppose the Assembly. All pro-devolution parties now invest the Assembly with fiscal powers.

The definitive answer to the West Lothian question was not available to us in 1977, 1978 and 1979. There was no significant demand for other assemblies outside Scotland then. However both Wales and the North East of England now want assemblies of their own — perhaps as a reaction to 10 years of centralised Conservative rule which has not been popular in the local areas. In 1989 the national Labour Party drafted proposals of a federal nature to embrace all regions. As well as deliberating on local matters, it was suggested that these assemblies could collectively perform the function of the House of Lords as a second chamber. This has the merit of replacing an unelected upper house with an elected one, and an unrepresentative one with one whose members are accountable.

The Convention's participants gathered against a background of economic as well as political polarisation. The 'North/South Divide' has become a byword for the regional differences in income, health care, unemployment, housing standards and other 'life-opportunities'.

In ten years Scotland saw the largest reduction in manufacturing employment in the UK. 209,000 jobs in factories disappeared. Scotland's industrial production declined, and took a decade to regain its previous levels. 9,000 jobs in construction vanished, as did 21,000 in agriculture. Investment in housing and schools slumped. Most Scots rejected the political party which brought this about.

When the steering committee of the Convention met in January 1989, the hopes of many Scots were pinned on a united front against the Conservatives and their hardline unionist stance. But the SNP felt that their power in Scotland was not being reflected in balance of representation. The Tories' opponents in Scotland united in genuine sorrow at the attitude of the SNP towards the Convention. Their fears that it would be swamped by Labour representatives and Labour policies were perfectly legitimate.

However in this imperfect world we have to make the best of things as they are, and it was up to the Nationalists to keep Labour in check by demonstrating to the people that Labour is using its powers in the convention in a domineering and intolerant way. Labour was equally keen to avoid such criticism, wanting to give appearance and substance to listening to the voice of minorities and incorporating their views in both the structure and the final deliberations of the Convention. There was no point in Labour sitting at the table if it was going to reach conclusions irrespective of the views expressed by other parties. I could deploy the same arguments and logic against Tory critics of the Convention. They too needed practice being an effective opposition. Instead Tory voices which supported a separate assembly for Scots have fallen silent. Ian Lawson joined the SNP and Malcolm Rifkind joined the Cabinet. Intelligent Tories realised the danger of hoping that nationalism would destroy socialism and leave the path clear for them.

As for the Nationalists, their demand for a referendum at the end of the Convention's deliberations shows that they have not learned the sad lessons of recent history. Getting a straight 'yes' or 'no' answer on devolution in March 1979 proved impossible, as those of us who were involved in that debacle know only too well. It brought down a Labour Government and gave erstwhile Tory supporters of devolution the excuse to say the referendum result demonstrated no overwhelming desire for devolution among Scottish people. The prospect of a referendum ten years later with 3 or 4 options on the ballot paper should worry every proponent of Scottish autonomy. The Secretary of State would ridicule a result which showed (for illustration) 20% wanting separation, 50% who want devolution, 20% supporting independence in Europe and so on. Instead of the Yes and the No campaigns of the 1970s, there would be 4 or 5 campaigns and the anti-status-quo campaigns could end up dividing their energies between promoting their cause, and denouncing not just a 'Tory-No' campaign, but the other devolutionists. And what legitimacy would the ballot have if it was organised without any Government support? Tory central office would tell its supporters to boycott the vote, it would then say whatever the turnout, that all the no-votes were anti-devolution/independence votes — we've all been through this before.

The participation of the SNP in the Convention is vital because they articulate the concerns of many people, and they offer solutions which have some support but which are not espoused by the other parties.

*The Claim of Right* sets out the framework for a campaign to achieve an Assembly. The 1977 Act detailed the powers which have been expanded since. But beyond the desire to bring legislative power closer to home, the Convention members must also discuss the transfer of power from the centre. Nye Bevan said that we must ourselves take power in order to give it back to the people. That is the key rationale for devolution — not simply that the Scots can better administer and manage their affairs than can Westminster, but that an Assembly would be more responsive to the individual and collective aspirations of Scottish people. Nor do I believe for one moment that it can be left at that — a body whose members merely reflect or represent the views of the people is far too limited. People want a greater say in the decisions which affect their lives and the Assembly cannot be content only to carry out Westminster's functions closer to home.

The Thatcherites have been stripping local authorities of powers on the pretext of protecting ratepayers. Councillors have become the scapegoats for the Government's own mismanagement of rating revaluation and for their dishonest attempts to label as 'spendthrift' those councils who have done no more than try to compensate for the loss of grants which previous governments thought essential to run schools, clean streets and stock libraries. Lothian Region's Labour controlled council was actually destabilised by rate capping during 1981. In 1982 the Scottish Secretary achieved his objective when Labour was voted out of office. The fact that the Tory/Alliance administration couldn't attain the Government's spending guidelines in any of their 4 years of office says more about the unreasonable nature of the guidelines than anything else. By 1986 the people of Lothian had had enough of high rates and deplorable services and Labour was returned with a record majority. Throughout Scotland the Tories were trounced.

This should have served to warn the Government that people may not like paying high sums for local services but they certainly do not want their services dismantled.

Labour itself has questions it must answer. To what extent does local Government reflect the views and desires of people? A sub-committee of the Convention should examine the structure of local government in Scotland. I am a strong supporter of one-tier councils, not least because the public are confused enough about where responsibility lies without being shunted from town hall pillar to post. The more people are confused about the differing responsibilities of the Regional and District councils, the more they feel the 'system' is rigged to deprive them of their rights and the less they feel inclined to support their local councillors. A Scottish Assembly is an ideal opportunity to let one tier of local government absorb the other. On the basis that small is more accessible, I favour District councils within the existing structure, or in a new scheme, councils which are closer to the size of current District authorities than the regional ones. To benefit from the pooling of resources and to avoid creating more departmental chiefs which would occur if 59 Directors of Education were appointed instead of the present 12, it may be possible for District councils to form geographical federations which are resourced by the same administrators.

But we cannot be content with a decision-making apparatus which limits participation in decision making to a vote every 4 years. Those councils which have been setting up residents and tenants committees, which are consulting local people on a regular basis and which are giving the control of decision-making to people at a local level must be encouraged. New legislation should enshrine new rights so that people have a stake in their own communities.

The Constitutional Convention sets the Scots a test. Can we work together for the good of our country and communities? Is there enough of a common political philosophy among non-Tory parties in Scotland to achieve an elected body, different from Westminster and more responsive to local needs and aspirations? The answer must be 'yes'.

# 2

## The Claim

GEORGE FOULKES

*A Claim of Right for Scotland* should be dedicated to the late John P. Mackintosh, who did more for the cause of Scottish Home Rule than anyone else since the war.

If it had not been for his untimely death in 1978 there would now be a Scottish Assembly. The 'yes' campaign in the 1979 Referendum did not have a powerful articulate and committed leader within the Labour Movement to ensure support surged over the unfair and artificial barrier of 40% of the electorate. John Mackintosh, author of the basic text on devolution, powerful orator and adroit television performer would have provided such leadership.

Just over a decade earlier we devolutionists, including, to be fair, Donald Dewar, were a lonely and beleaguered bunch within the Labour Party.

Although Home Rule had been a central part of Keir Hardie's Labour manifesto and had been pursued strongly by most of the Labour Leadership since the foundation of the Scottish Home Rule Association by Ramsay MacDonald in 1886, by the early 1960s it had reached a nadir within the Labour Party.

While it can be argued that the 1945–51 Labour Government had greater priorities rebuilding war damaged Britain, creating the NHS and bringing the major sectors of the economy into public ownership, it remains a source of great disappointment to many of us that the 1964–70 Government ignored the Home rule pledges of its forefathers.

It was this failure which resulted in the SNP upsurge, starting with Winnie Ewing's victory in Hamilton in 1967 and followed by substantial advances in the local Government elections of 1968 and 1969.

The obstinacy of the Scottish Labour Party in opposition to Devolution was led by the late Willie Ross with strong support from his

Ayrshire allies Jim Sillars and John Pollock. It was Pollock who, as Chairman of the Labour Party, rounded violently on all of us who pursued the cause, which explains our current mild cynicisms at the undue zeal of the converts.

But it was John Mackintosh who filled us all with hope and optimism even in the darkest hours and provided the determination necessary to keep arguing the case.

After the debacle of the Referendum and the subsequent Tory victory in 1979 the same determination was necessary to keep the devolution cause alive in spite of the negativism of most of the media as well as some of the Labour panjandrums.

Within the Labour Party the Labour Campaign for a Scottish Assembly kept the devolution flag flying. While the Campaign for a Scottish Assembly mobilised all party and non-party opinion, the task of the LCSA was to get the Labour Party successfully recommitted to an Assembly with even more powers than previously.

In doing this we discovered a rare talent — Jim Ross — a quiet retired civil servant who had worked on the 1978 Scotland Bill and knew the issues inside out. The skilled argument and draughtmanship he employed for us has been even more skilfully applied in his authorship of the *Claim of Right*.

It is also fitting that one of the Members of the Constitutional Steering Committee which produced the document was John Mackintosh's widow, Una Maclean, herself a long term supporter of the Home Rule cause.

So, where are we now? In 1968 Professor Gordon Donaldson wrote in *Government and Nationalism in Scotland*, published by the Edinburgh University Press:

> It is especially important to review this period because it shows that the nationalist agitation which has become familiar in recent years is far from being a novelty. Very little has been said in the last decade which had not been said many times before.

— and there is some validity for saying that this is just as true today. But there are important new factors which must be taken account of.

The SNP would have us believe that the crucial new factor is Britain's membership of the European Community and especially the effect of the Single European Act which is intended to create a single European Market by 1992.

Their hope is that the negative effect on the public of the rupture of separation of Scotland from the rest of the UK will be offset by the cushion of continuing joint Membership of a European Community where the real focus of central power is Brussels and where Scotland and England are equal partners.

This is fallacious on at least four grounds. First the effect of the Single market is grossly overstated, the integration will be limited and London will remain the centre of decision for most of the areas which affect our lives.

It also ignores the historical links of family and heritage, economy and education, art and sport, language and culture and a thousand and one others which have bound Scotland to the rest of the UK for over 280 years. These are sometimes difficult to describe but are so widely understood as to be almost tangible and the European Community is seen for the loose association it is by comparison.

But the narrow nationalists of Scotland also ignore the knock-on effect a Scottish claim for separate membership would have elsewhere in Europe where, for example, Italy became a united kingdom far more recently than ourselves.

However their greatest deception is the way they pretend Scotland could somehow 'continue' as a separate member of the European Community without difficulty. The obvious reality is that first we would have to go through the trauma of separating our economy, infrastructure and all major aspects of our life from the rest of the UK and then apply anew for separate membership of the Community, without certainty of acceptance. Already from divisions within the SNP, it is not altogether clear that, having achieved independence, all nationalists would then wish to submerge their sovereignty again within the European Community, at least not without a referendum.

And of course all of this presupposes that there would be agreement on what would constitute a mandate for separation in the first place. Would an SNP majority of Scottish seats at Westminster suffice or would a subsequent referendum be necessary? What would then happen if the referendum rejected separation?

A second new factor is the knowledge that we have had an Assembly almost in our grasp only to have it unfairly snatched from us.

The Assembly building was ready, and is still available, but even more significant was the way in which almost all sectors of Scottish life had become psychologically prepared for an Assembly. The media had planned new offices and new jobs, voluntary bodies had prepared a new lobbying strategy and the Arts were looking forward to a new Scottish renaissance. It was therefore understandable that it took some time for many to recover from the state of clinical shock induced by the loss.

Perhaps the most significant new factor, however, is the rise and rise of Thatcherism. We no longer have the consensus politics of 'Butskellism' which took account of the needs of minorities, representation from the regions or the anxieties of the opposition.

Thatcherism does not just mean the worship of the creed of greed, privatisation of almost all public assets, emasculation of the unions and the all too familiar policies of her Government. It has meant the development of an elected Dictatorship, based on 43% support at the last Election. The British Constitution has never provided the in-built checks and balances of the USA and Canada, Germany or most developed Western democracies. It has always been possible for almost absolute power to be wielded by a Prime Minister, but before now, wisdom and moderation have prevailed.

Now we see a Prime Minister, unassailable within her party, presiding over a supine Cabinet, controlling a large majority in the Commons with fear and patronage, brandishing power unmatched by Presidents or Prime Ministers elsewhere in the Western World.

The inbuilt anachronistic Conservative majority within the Second Chamber can be mobilised to meet even the mildest challenge; the media are almost wholly subservient through indolence or pliant ownership; we have no Supreme Court with the power to challenge, although I would not be too optimistic about their desire to do so even if they had; and we lack the dynamic tension inherent in a federation.

Local authorities which dared to question, let alone challenge, have been either abolished or emasculated along with the unions, and voluntary bodies are increasingly powerless to mobilise effectively.

This new Thatcher factor is recognised in *A Claim of Right* where Section Four rightly describes our present constitution as 'an illusion of Democracy'.

The latest resurgence of Nationalism is clearly mainly a response to the imposition of Thatcherism on Scotland, which rejected it at the polls, and the constitutional impotence of the largest and most active ever Scottish Group of Labour MPs to prevent it.

But successive polls and elections have shown that Scotland does not want separation, even with the illusory protection of possible membership of the European Community. Again and again we see the development of majorities for, demands for and logic for Home Rule within the framework of the United Kingdom.

However the one hurdle remaining is the really difficult one — how to persuade an unwilling Tory Government to concede an Assembly. All other parties are now committed and a Labour Government or a coalition would give it priority but a Tory Government, particularly a Thatcher Government, is not just unreceptive but hostile. This is where the CSA and the *Claim* provide the way forward.

As a founder member of the CSA I have always supported its aims and now with this elegant and persuasively argued Report it gives us the blueprint we need, ideal for present circumstances by a fortunate coincidence of time and chance.

The *Claim* gives us the mechanism but wisely it neither offers a guarantee of success nor prejudges the exact form of constitutional change.

Success will depend on genuine and sustained commitment by all the opposition parties in Scotland, a willingness to compromise and a determination to succeed.

In order to be successful the Constitutional Convention will need substantial resources because it must work efficiently and in a sustained way otherwise the Government will find it all too easy to brush aside.

The necessary level of resources can only come from the local authorities and trades unions, with small amounts from others as a token of commitment. So the support of both the STUC and COSLA for any plan is vital to success.

The legitimacy of the Convention will derive from the participation of Scottish Members of Parliament and they must form the core and the majority of the Convention or of its decision making Executive, whatever model is decided. It is only the majority of Scottish MPs who have any authority to challenge the legislative and executive legitimacy of the Secretary of State and any assembly of the great and the good, however broadly representative, could be dismissed by Malcolm Rifkind as worthy but of no constitutional account.

The need for compromise and consensus to challenge the Tory 'mandate' must be accepted by all parties involved. This will involve difficult internal party conflicts and an even more difficult self-control not to exploit such differences in other parties. It would be naive and over-optimistic to believe this can be fully achieved but it must be sought after, particularly by the leaders of each party involved.

Of the three tasks for the Constitutional Convention — drawing up a scheme, mobilising public opinion and securing Government approval for the scheme — the last is undoubtedly the most difficult.

The difficulty of it will be reduced in proportion to the success of the other two and in turn it will be easier to mobilise public opinion if the agreed scheme is as sound and widely acceptable as possible.

The *Claim* is right to say that the Convention should start drawing up its scheme from where others left off because much work has been done on this, not least by the last Labour Government.

The main deficiency of the Scotland Act was perceived as the 'West Lothian Question' named as such because it was most persistently put by Tam Dalyell, then M.P. for West Lothian. He asked why he, as a Scots MP in Westminster after Devolution, would be able to vote on Education in Blackburn, Lancashire but not in Blackburn, West Lothian. He pursued the alliterative examples *ad nauseam*.

Although, this Question is not as anomalous as much of the present system of Government, we who are arguing change need to show that it will be better and so we must acknowledge and try to deal with this anomaly.

Equally, the plea in the Epilogue to the *Claim* that reform in Scotland should not await simultaneous change throughout the United Kingdom, because Scotland is constitutionally and electorally ahead of all other parts of the UK, is equally, if not more, important.

The difficulty of reconciling the claims and needs of the diverse nations and regions within the UK and the need to aim for reform which is relatively more stable and balanced than the present system is the recurring problem of our constitutional reform.

Professor H.J. Paton in his own *The Claim of Scotland* first published in 1968 argues throughout his classic book that the ideal solution is a complete federal system such as the USA where each state has equality in the Senate as well as full representation in Congress. If this is impossible he argues support for the devolution case but warns 'If this too is resolutely ruled out what is left open except to seek for independence?' Thereby he offers us both hope and a warning.

A federal solution would certainly be the most stable, would provide the answer to the West Lothian Question and may even offer some hope for the Northern Irish problem.

The difficulties remain of the relative size of England compared with Scotland and Wales and the lack of any demand within England for a separate Assembly as distinct from the Westminster Parliament which they, by definition, must dominate.

The way to reconcile this, which I have advocated for some time, and is now gaining wider acceptance, is phased federalism, incorporating within it reform of the Second Chamber.

First we should set a long term objective of a Federal UK Parliament dealing with major economic matters, taxation, social security, defence, foreign affairs, overseas trade and general oversight of the good government of the United Kingdom, and state or provincial parliaments for Scotland, Wales, England and Northern Ireland responsible for education, health, housing, social services, and all matters which the Scotland Act devolved to the Scottish Assembly.

Within the Federal Parliament the first chamber would be elected from constituencies of roughly equal size throughout the whole United Kingdom and the second chamber would have a form of representation which took account of the national or regional assemblies.

Such a solution not only deals with the legitimate demands for devolution but also offers an opportunity to reform the totally anachronistic House of Lords which is an affront to democracy and, if it existed in any third world country, would be condemned by British MPs as feudal and undemocratic.

This ideal solution would, however, be difficult, if not impossible to achieve at one time and so should be phased over a number of years.

The long term objective of complete federalism would answer the West Lothian Question in that any such anomaly caused by devolution would be temporary but the phasing ensures that we in Scotland do not have to wait for our Assembly until the whole jigsaw is completed.

The Scottish Assembly would be set up first, closely followed by Wales and, meanwhile, discussions could take place on whether England would better have one National Assembly or a number of regional assemblies and whether legislative as well as executive powers would be appropriate. At the same time consideration could be given as to how Northern Ireland could best fit into this developing pattern.

This scheme should be acceptable to the Democrats, as heirs to the Federal tradition of the Liberals, it is becoming the orthodoxy within the Labour Party as a result of the excellent work of Roy Hattersley and Alastair Darling and, although it does not satisfy the fundamental aim of nationalists, there should be no conflict with the pragmatic majority within the SNP if they put the good government of Scotland first.

Donald Dewar had already seen this general trend when he wrote in July 1987 in a Fabian Tract: 'An Assembly for Scotland may be a special case based on a powerful sense of identity, a cultural tradition buttressed by distinct religious and legal systems, but it can still be more comfortably set in a United Kingdom which recognises the need for more general reform.'

A Scottish Assembly can lead the reform, and show the way to the rest of Britain. There is a socialist case, a national case, an efficiency argument and an historical claim but above all the case, the cause, the argument is for democracy.

*A Claim of Right*, now three hundred years after its original namesake, should be used as the springboard for eliminating the democratic deficit we now have, for restoring confidence, enthusiasm and hope to the people of Scotland and making it a country we are proud to hand over to the next generation.

# 3

## Sovereignty of the People

DENNIS CANAVAN

In the immediate aftermath of the 1987 General Election, there was much exciting talk of a constitutional crisis in Scotland.

The election result, both in Scotland and in the UK, was not exactly unexpected. The Conservatives, for the third consecutive time, won an overall majority in the House of Commons. In Scotland, however, they were rejected by 76% of voters and Scots Tory MPs were reduced to a discredited rump of 10.

Scotland's 62 opposition MPs all came from parties committed to some form of Scottish Parliament. Even some Conservative supporters were concerned about how difficult it would be for a nation to be governed by a party which had been so resoundingly rejected at the ballot box.

Despite all this, no serious constitutional crisis has yet emerged. Firstly, because of the lack of a coherent strategy on the part of Scottish Opposition MPs to force the issue of constitutional change; and secondly, because of the Government's ability to manipulate the over-centralised British Constitution in order to retain the *status quo*.

It probably would not have mattered very much to the present Prime Minister if the Conservatives had lost every single Scottish constituency, as long as she had her over-all majority in the House of Commons. To her, the Scots are just part of her United Kingdom. She would probably have appointed some remnant of the Scottish aristocracy as Secretary of State for Scotland — or even abolished the Scottish Office completely and imposed direct rule from Whitehall.

That scenario must be faced by those whose recipe for Scottish constitutional change is to make Scotland a Tory-free zone through an electoral pact at the next General Election. There is no guarantee that the recipe would work and the problem requires a more immediate solution.

Such a solution will not be easy. The following extract from *A Claim of Right for Scotland* tells us what we are up against:

The reasonable expectations of Scots will be fulfilled only within a changed system. However, the system is unlikely to be changed by any action the system, itself, authorises. The flaws in the present constitution offer incentives to its abuse and an interest in maintaining its abuses. Any party which has power has a temptation to cling to the unreasonable powers available.

We have seen many examples of such abuses in recent times. Faced with the difficulties of their depleted Scottish team in the House of Commons, the Government flouted Parliamentary tradition by using their English majority to facilitate the appointment of English MPs to Scottish Standing Committees. They then passed a motion to breach the Commons Standing Orders requirement to set up a Scottish Select Committee. This repeated bending of the rules or changing the goal-posts not only offends the people of Scotland. It also makes a joke of any meaningful division of powers between the Executive and the Legislature, in the British Constitution.

The effect has been to make the Scottish Office less accountable to Parliament and to make it easier for the Government to foist upon the people of Scotland legislation which has been rejected at the ballot box. As a result, there has been incalculable damage done to the National Health Service, to Scottish Housing, to the Scottish Education System and many other services and these damaging policies have been imposed contrary to the wishes of the majority of the Scottish people.

To add insult to injury, there has been an unprecedented abuse of the power of patronage to produce a job creation scheme for failed Scottish Tory MPs. It is Glasnost in reverse, Sir Alex Fletcher received a seat on the board of the Scottish Development Agency as compensation for losing his seat in Parliament. The Solicitor General, Peter Fraser, also suffered humiliating defeat at the polls but was afterwards promoted to the post of Lord Advocate, with a seat in the house of Lords. Other examples include the appointment of rejected MPs Michael Ancram to the board of Scottish Homes, Anna McCurley to the Horse-race Betting Levy Board and John Corrie to the chair of the Scottish Transport Users' Consultative Committee. Scotland is being treated worse than a colony and a neutral observer could be forgiven for wondering if the Scottish General Election result had ever happened.

In Parliament, it is even worse than if nothing had happened. Scottish Question Time is now regularly invaded by English Conservative MPs seeking to turn the whole event into a farce and the result is that Scottish Opposition MPs find it even more difficult to raise matters on behalf of their constituents.

Shortly after the General Election, the Scottish Group of Labour MPs published a Scottish Assembly Bill, the product of nationwide consultations on their Green Paper. It was 1988 before the Official Opposition at last forced an all-day debate on the Scottish constitutional question but predictably Westminster again refused to respond to the wishes of the people of Scotland as expressed through the majority of their elected representatives.

How can we counteract this continuing intransingence? There is a great deal of talk about the need for a sustained campaign but, until the publication of *A Claim of Right for Scotland*, little in the way of concrete proposals had emerged. Yet the British and Scottish General Election results were predictable and predicted and it is an indictment of Scottish Opposition parties that pre-election calls for a contingency plan fell on deaf ears.

What are the prospects for delivering constitutional change in this Parliament? The defeatists say that there is no chance and that we are wasting our time even trying. The people of Scotland will not thank us if we simply tell them that they must wait until the next General Election in the hope of changing the British Government. There is a great deal of understandable frustration in Scotland and no sign yet of a significant sea-change in political attitudes in the South-East of England.

It is deeply insulting to the people of Scotland to tell them that, because of the Treaty of Union, they will just have to hang on until 1992 or 1997 or 2002 or whenever, until political change takes place in another country. If the Treaty of Union means that the people of Scotland are constantly denied their democratic demands as expressed in the ballot box, then it is a Treaty of Treachery which is not worth preserving *A Claim of Right for Scotland* correctly states that the Scottish nation did not freely agree to the Union and, because of the absence of any mechanism for enforcing the Treaty of Union, many of its major provisions have been violated to Scotland's disadvantage.

Of course, defenders of the Union, especially those with a vested interest, will assert that the people must wait until the next UK General Election before they can achieve political or constitutional change. But to many Scots that is pie in the sky. They want firmer action and they want it now.

The only action plan on the table at the moment is the proposal of the Scottish Constitutional Steering Committee for the setting up of a Scottish Constitutional Convention. Ideally, perhaps, the

Convention should be directly elected but this would delay the start
of its work and surely there is general acceptance that the elected
Parliamentary representatives of the people of Scotland should have
some input to discussions on the future governance of Scotland.

All Scottish MPs, regardless of party, should therefore be invited
to take part. The Tories would almost certainly all refuse but, in
order to give the Convention legitimacy, they should be formally
invited nevertheless. There is a strong case for 'topping up' the
representation from some of the smaller parties and an even stronger
case for broadening out the membership to include representatives
from local government, trade unions, churches, industrial and other
interests. With such a comprehensive membership, the Convention
would be better equipped to speak with authority on behalf of the
people of Scotland as a whole and would command widespread
respect.

It is to the credit of members of the all-party Campaign for a
Scottish Assembly that they have persistently pursued the idea of a
Scottish Constitutional Convention, even in the face of adversity. In
the immediate aftermath of the 1987 General Election, the Labour
Party leadership showed no enthusiasm for the idea but, even before
the Govan by-election, there were signs of movement under pressure, mainly from members of Scottish Labour Action.

The Labour Party has now agreed to participate in the Convention
along with the other opposition parties in Scotland. They are all committed to some form of Scottish Parliament and Labour should not
use its dominant position to exclude serious consideration of all the
options put forward. After all, at the last General Election, Labour
won only 42% of the Scottish vote, even though it has 49 of the 72
seats. The Labour Party cannot therefore claim to speak on behalf
of a majority of the people of Scotland and, besides, Labour's policy
on home rule needs up-dating and all thinking politicians should be
open-minded enough to listen to new ideas.

A fresh examination of the Scottish constitutional question should
begin with acceptance of the sovereignty of the people of Scotland
as oppressed to the absolute sovereignty of the Westminster Parliament. The people of Scotland, like the people of any nation in
the world, are entitled to as much self-determination as they want.
There may be little if any evidence that Scots want to exercise that
right by setting up a completely separate Scottish state but there is an
abundance of evidence that the vast majority of them want a Scottish
Parliament with legislative and economic powers.

It will not be easy finding cross-party agreement on the exact
nature and powers of a Scottish Parliament. No party or individual

should be expected to surrender on a matter of deeply-held principle but it would be wrong for any party to go into the Convention with a pre-conceived blueprint and expect other parties to accept it in its entirety.

Surely many lessons have been learned since the repeal of the Scotland Act ten years ago. Under the 1978 Act, the Scottish Assembly would have had no revenue-raising powers and the devolved Scottish Government would therefore have been completely dependent on a block grant from Whitehall. Indeed, a valid general criticism of the 1978 Act was that the Scottish Assembly would have been too tied to Westminster and that there was no real diminution of the ultimate sovereignty of Westminster.

The initiators of the 1978 legislation seemed to start with the question: 'How much could and should be devolved, without threatening the unity of the United Kingdom?' If, however, there is general acceptance of the sovereignty of the people of Scotland, then a better starting point might be the question: 'To what degree do we want to share that sovereignty with any other nation or group of nations, whether in the United Kingdom or the European Community or both?' If that question is adequately addressed, then a much more radical measure than the 1978 Act could emerge from the debate.

On the matter of economic powers, for example, the Scottish Treasury could be responsible for raising all revenue within Scotland, including income tax, VAT, oil revenues and company taxes. A block payment could then be made to the Westminster Government for any shared services such as defence and overseas representation. That such a scheme has been suggested even by a group of Conservative Party members is perhaps indicative of the potentially broad support it might have.

The agenda of the Convention will be confined to the constitutional future of Scotland but that will inevitably have repercussions elsewhere in the UK. There are growing demands from Wales and some of the English regions for some form of devolution or decentralisation. There are certain attractions, therefore, about introducing some form of federal structure for the whole of the UK. It is neat and logical and it answers the vexed West Lothian question. But it would require re-writing the British Constitution or rather putting it all down in writing for the first time. This would be a gargantuan task and no clear consensus has yet emerged from the English regions as to what exactly they want in terms of devolved powers.

The debate in England must not be allowed to block or hold up the clear demand of the people of Scotland for a Scottish parliament. The

Scottish case must be prioritised because it is unique. It is not about a region but a nation, indeed the only nation in the world with its own Department of State, its own legal system and laws but no legislature to enact those laws. The setting up of a Scottish Parliament will probably eventually lead to fundamental and welcome constitutional change throughout the whole of the UK but that is in the longer term. Scotland's case deserves an answer now.

Similarly, the setting up of a Scottish Parliament will almost certainly lead to fundamental change in Scottish local government. There is considerable and justifiable concern about the steady erosion of what little local democracy is left in Scotland because of increasing intervention by central government into what was traditionally the sphere of local government. The setting up of a Scottish Parliament will present an opportunity to restore the powers of local authorities but hopefully the Constitutional Convention will not allow itself to be side-tracked into a long-ranging debate on the future structure of local government.

There are obvious advantages in a one-tier system with a single door approach for the client and better co-ordination between services such as social work and housing, which at present are split between two different tiers. A one-tier system would also help to counteract the argument that a Scottish Assembly would lead to yet another layer of government, thereby making the Scots the most over-governed nation in the world. But the Constitutional Steering Committee has it absolutely correct when it states that the order of procedure is to set up an Assembly and to call on that Assembly to consider urgently the case for re-organising local government.

One of the most contentious issues to be considered by the Convention is likely to be the method of electing the Scottish Parliament. Virtually every party has a vested interest in one system or another and it is therefore very difficult to have an objective debate on electoral reform.

The weaknesses of the first past the post system are obvious when we consider that, at the last General Election, the Conservative Party won 58% of the UK Parliamentary seats with only 42% of the vote. In Scotland, the Labour Party won a similar share of the vote but captured 69% of the seats. On the other hand, some forms of proportional representation weaken the local constituency link between the elected representative and the electors, while strengthening the central control of the party in the selection of candidates. No system of democracy is perfect in every respect.

Recently there have been signs of politicians reconsidering their positions on electoral reform and some interesting cross-party alignments could emerge. Members of the Convention should not be expected simply to toe the party line, especially on this issue, and it will be interesting to see what transpires on a free vote. Whatever happens, it would be tragic if the work of the Convention was sabotaged by any party making acceptance of its preferred electoral system a pre-condition for supporting the establishment of a Scottish Parliament.

With goodwill on all sides, there should be enough common ground for a consensus to emerge in favour of a scheme for Scottish constitutional change. What is more problematic is how to deliver it. The aim should be to get into a negotiating situation with the Government.

A delegation of leading members of the Convention could demand a meeting with the Prime Minister but, if they succeeded in getting past the door of 10 Downing Street, it is inconceivable that they would be welcomed with open arms. The present Prime Minister has made it clear that she does not believe in the need for Scottish constitutional change. Furthermore, she firmly rejects the claim that she has no mandate to govern Scotland just because she did not win a majority of Scottish seats. She repeatedly points out that four out of the past five Labour Governments did not win a majority of English seats but nobody claimed that they had no right to govern England.

This argument must be answered. Under those four Labour Governments, there was never any demand from the people of England for any measure of 'English home rule' and no political party or group of parties could claim a mandate for any degree of English self-determination. By contrast, at the last Election, political parties committed to a Scottish Assembly or Parliament won 57% of the UK votes and 76% of the Scottish votes.

In these circumstances, it is clearly absurd for the Prime Minister or anyone else to claim that there is insufficient demand for a Scottish Parliament. If, despite the Convention's conclusion, Government ministers persist in this absurd claim, then Scottish political leaders should call their bluff and demand a referendum. If the Government refuse to hold an official referendum, then it should not be beyond the wit of the Constitutional Convention to organise one, with the co-operation of Scottish local authorities.

Continuing Government intransigence should be countered by an escalating campaign of widespread resistance, designed to maximise pressure on the Government to accede to the legitimate demands of the people of Scotland. The Scottish Constitutional Convention could develop into an unofficial Scottish Parliament, meeting regularly to discuss not only the constitutional question and the strategy for delivering constitutional change but also other important issues facing the people of Scotland such as unemployment, the National Health Service, Scottish Education and the Poll Tax.

Critics would try to dismiss such a forum as a mere talking shop but what is the Scottish Grand Committee at present? It cannot even determine the dates and venues of its meetings, it cannot set its own agenda, it does not debate substantive motions, it rarely votes and merely reports back to the House of Commons. Even an unofficial Scottish Parliament would have more autonomy than that!

Complete withdrawal from Westminster might be an option worth considering at some stage but there is undoubtedly some advantage in all Scottish Opposition MPs trying to sharpen up their collective attack on the Government in the House of Commons. A determined group of 62 could make life very difficult if not impossible for the Government, especially with its Scottish legislative programme. To achieve this, they should not simply abide by the hallowed traditions and conventions of Westminster. All co-operation between the Government and the Scottish Opposition should be broken off, until the Scottish question is adequately answered.

The campaign must not be confined to Parliament. The aim must be not only to make Parliament unworkable but to make Scotland ungovernable until the Government agrees to negotiate. The people of Scotland as a whole must therefore be mobilised and involved in that campaign.

It is interesting that *A Claim of Right for Scotland* does not rule out the possibility of civil disobedience as long as it forms part of an orderly programme to achieve a new form of Scottish Government. Until recently, the people of Scotland showed little if any support for civil disobedience but the advent of the Poll Tax may yet change all that. Many people who were previously cool on the idea of a Scottish Parliament now realise that it could and would have stopped such a blatant injustice as the Poll Tax being foisted on the people of Scotland. A widespread campaign of non-payment of the Poll Tax could therefore be a useful weapon in the campaign for a Scottish Parliament.

The Constitutional Steering Committee sets out three tasks for the Scottish Constitutional Convention: firstly to draw up a scheme for a Scottish Assembly; secondly to mobilise Scottish opinion behind that scheme; and thirdly to deal with the Government in securing approval of the scheme or an acceptable modification of it.

Undoubtedly, the third of these tasks is the most difficult because it involves persuading the British Government to change the British Constitution when that Government clearly has a vested interest in retaining the status quo. The British Constitution, for the most part unwritten, has a time-tested way of resisting change. No-one can forecast with absolute certainty what would be the outcome of any course of action designed to change it. Only one thing is certain. If Scotland's political leaders do nothing, then they will get nothing.

The British Constitution has been exposed as incapable of delivering to the people of Scotland what they have voted for. Scottish MPs must therefore ask themselves the basic question: 'Is our first loyalty to the British state or to the people we were elected to represent?'.

# 4

# The Democratic Deficit

DAVID MARTIN

'Stimulating and enlightening' was how Sir Robert Grieve described his work on the Report entitled *A Claim Of Right For Scotland* in a letter to Alan Armstrong, Convener of the Campaign for a Scottish Assembly. Stimulating and enlightening was my experience of reading the document.

I found much of the reasoning tough, pragmatic and realistic; leading inevitably to a conclusion I agree with: that a Constitutional Convention ought to be set up in order to facilitate the establishment of a Scottish Assembly. However I should mention at this stage that I did not agree with all the premises. I will get these out of the way first before I go on to discuss the area of substantive agreement. Firstly, my inclination would differ slightly with the authors' desire to locate the claim of right in Scotland the nation state rather than with the Scottish people. For me nation-statism is an historic concept whereas democracy is an eternal political principle based on equality and leading to socialism.

Secondly, I would not agree that Scotland's constitutional problems can be dealt with in isolation: either from the UK, or the European Community (EC). This does not mean an Assembly could not be set up in Scotland until problems at these other levels had been dealt with. But I do believe that the world's economic and geopolitical systems are so integrated now that such problems would have to be identified and their reform, in some way, anticipated in order for us to achieve the best form of government possible for the Scottish people at the time. If not any improvement could be short lived.

Now, for the area of substantive agreement. Where the *Claim of Right* is at its strongest is in its analysis of what it calls the 'The English Constitution - an Illusion of Democracy'. It is convincingly argued that 'The English constitution provides for only one source of power; the Crown-in-Parliament. That one source is now mainly embodied in the Prime Minister, who has appropriated almost all the royal prerogatives'. The consequence of this under the present regime is that: '....far from Parliament controlling the Executive (which is the constitutional theory) it is the Prime Minister as head of the Executive who controls Parliament'. We are living in what has been called an elective dictatorship.

The authors adequately convey the reality that, in the process of writing about an important historical phenomenon, they are actors as well as observers and commentators. They are writing their Report '...against the background of a drive to diminish democracy'. The United Kingdom they claim '...has never suffered from an excess of accountability, and it is now experiencing a progressive diminution of accountability'. With the abolition of the GLC and the Metropolitan Counties, the assault on the rights of trade unionists, the imposition of the poll tax and the use of advertising agencies rather than Information Offices to communicate with the electorate, who would disagree with their assertion about the erosion of democracy?

All of these centralising anti-democratic trends are, of course, greatly accentuated in Scotland where there was an overwhelming rejection of Thatcherite policies at the last General Election. We are suffering what the *Claim Of Right* calls a 'democratic gap'. The solution, they suggest, is to convene a Constitutional Convention which could temporarily fill that gap by formulating a constitution and structure for a Scottish Assembly which would restore democracy to the people of Scotland.

On first reading the *Claim Of Right* I had the feeling that its authors had been down a similar road to the one which I took within the European Parliament — albeit they had travelled somewhat further. When I was elected leader of the British Labour Group in the European Parliament in June 1987 I resolved to use that year to argue vigorously for a change in Labour Party attitude to the European Community (EC) even although I knew I would probably lose the leadership for my efforts.

I reasoned that it was time to take a pragmatic approach towards the EC. The world had moved on since 1975; there was no way we were going to withdraw, at least for the next four years of Thatcher rule and probably not at all. It was imperative in my view that we must cease the sterile 'in out argument' and unite round a policy of winning economic and social improvements for our people from the EC whilst, at the time, arguing for democratic reform that would make such a process more fruitful. I put my ideas on this subject into a Fabian pamphlet entitled *Bringing Common Sense To The Common*

*Market — a left agenda for Europe*, the most controversial section of which was the last one entitled 'Towards A Democratic Community'.

The main motive for writing that chapter stemmed from the observation that the European Community operates in an undemocratic and inefficient manner. It was a criticism of bureaucratic power, patronage and unnecessary secrecy. The increasing secrecy and centralising of power in the UK, identified in *A Claim Of Right For Scotland*, has always existed in the EC. I believe these two trends are not only getting worse but they are related. In the EC 236 million voters are asked to vote every five years for a democratic fig leaf on an undemocratic system. Proposals which take a greater cogniscance of the needs of the regions and unrepresented nations must be framed to reform this system.

Democracy should be both our starting point for analysis and our objective in making proposals.

The European Community is in fact dominated by a sclerotic decision-making process. Its principal decision-making body, the Council of Ministers, is the only legislative (i.e. law-making) body which meets in private. Laws are made as a result of horse-trading between different issues. In practice, agricultural decisions are swapped for budget decisions, VAT rates can be swapped for deals on harmonisation of insurance laws without the citizens of the EC knowing exactly what went on.

It is this permanent confusion, the contrast between the bold ideas regularly reaffirmed by heads of government and the sordid reality of semi-permanent blockage, which explains and justifies public disillusionment on an EC level similar to that in Scotland with the Thatcher Government. Scotland, the UK and the EC now all, in fact, need massive doses of democracy.

Just as it is argued in the *Claim Of Right* with reference to Scottish legislation, the situation in the House of Commons has become untenable as regards EC legislation. From time to time general debates are held in which details cannot be explored or, on other occasions, extremely detailed points are debated in committee or late at night without the general approach of the government coming under scrutiny. The ineffectiveness of House of Commons debates are re-inforced by the press coverage given to meetings of the European Council of Ministers. The average citizen could be forgiven for thinking that these are called twice a year simply to allow Mrs Thatcher to wave the Union Jack under the noses of other Community heads of states. This combination of low level press information and lack of House of Commons scrutiny have allowed such major pieces of legislation as the Single European

Act (SEA) to go ahead in this country with almost no public discussion.

The general problem of the relationship between the executive and the legislature in the UK as outlined in *A Claim Of Right For Scotland*, has been exacerbated by our membership of the EC and the adoption of the SEA, particularly in the foreign policy field where it has increased the power of the government to bypass the House of Commons or, at best, to treat it as no more than a rubber stamp. The question is now much deeper than the petty discussion about how effective the opposition front bench has been, or whether the Committee for Scrutiny of EC legislation should have more power.

A report prepared by the Institutional Committee of the European Parliament speaks openly of the 'democratic deficit'. It observes that EC structures are developing at the 'expense of the member states' parliaments'. The development of the European Internal Market in the years to 1992 will enhance this tendency. The Parliament report speaks bluntly of a 'violation of the elementary principles of democracy', pointing out that in spite of having an elected European Parliament 'the involvement of the people in the exercise of power. . .is very limited as far as Community legislation is concerned'. In short, there is a continuing transfer of power from the national to the Community level without the concomitant strengthening of democracy at that level.

This process is continuing. The left must therefore decide how best to influence and participate in changing that process. Pretending that it is not taking place or arguing that we must deal with Scotland's situation first may be a convenient strategy for those who fear a frank and open discussion about what is going on. It would be better to take a strengthening of democracy at all levels as our primary objective and then to see how best that can be achieved. To do this at a European level an analysis of the differing roles of the various Community institutions will be needed in order to come to grips with the serious and continuing conflicts which characterise decision making in Brussels.

The Commission consists of 17 politicians appointed under patronage of governments not only to run the bureaucracy but to make proposals for legislation. The council consists of twelve ministers each representing their national governments, parties and parliaments; the ministers are the only people who can actually decide upon legislation; Council meetings are prepared by lengthy meetings of civil servants whose mastery of the details of national positions and role in the implementation of EC legislation gives them enormous uncontrolled power. The parliament consists of 518 elected politicians who can discuss all aspects of the life of the Community but even when they are united can only exercise influence on Community legislation. The most powerful institution, the Court of Justice, against whose decision there is no appeal, is also appointed by governments and has enormous power.

The specific problem at the heart of the Scottish and European debate is not shrinking sovereignty as outlined in Mrs Thatcher's Bruges speech but the democratic deficit, or gap as outlined in *A Claim Of Right For Scotland*. The way forward for Scotland and the EC is to freeze all further transference of power and make the areas of legislation that have been ceded to the European level the legitimate preserve of the European Parliament which would be accountable to the people who elect it; similarly with a Scottish Assembly and Scottish affairs.

Democracy is not about nations, or supranations, having a say: it is about people having a say. From a democratic point of view Scotland joining the EC as a neutered nation-state — given the restrictions of the SEA — as advocated by the Scottish National Party, would be a step back for democracy as it would, in a sense, legitimise the undemocratic nature of the EC. Furthermore, if we were to seek membership of the EC because we think Thatcher and the undemocratic nature of her government cannot be defeated in the UK then it is more likely that the EC, post 1992, would be Thatcherite.

A more tantalising glimpse of the future direction the people of Scotland and Europe should be travelling in is the one put forward by the growing number of people, and I count myself amongst them, calling for national and regional agencies with devolved economic powers — an enlarged democratic Europe of the regions. This path of devolved economic and democratic structures at national and regional level connecting into a more democratic European Community, could indeed be the way forward for the people of Scotland and would suit exactly a Scottish Assembly. Such a move could resolve the objections countries within the EC such as Spain, Italy, Germany, Belgium and other states would have to an independent Scotland seeking membership. It would also sidestep the question of England's veto.

Before going through the traumatic upheaval of creating an independent Scotland that might be ill-equipped for Europe and the world of the 1990s and beyond, it would be much more productive to look at the possibilities offered by a democratic Europe of the regions. I am sure a Scottish Constitutional Convention could take on such a task. It would make much more political sense for the people of comparable nations and regions to combine in a truly democratic European parliament to argue for resources for their respective areas. Such a move would be radical and democratic. The reality is that the future of radical policies in a Thatcherite world means restoring democracy — that is the bottom line.

Thatcher has intuitively grasped the link between democracy and socialism. Her stated aim of rolling back the frontiers of socialism is being achieved by destroying local government, consolidating the power of the UK parliament in her office and refusing to allow any growth of democracy within the EC.

The authors of *A Claim Of Right For Scotland* have clearly identified and articulated the fear about the centralising nature of Westminster and Jacques Delors, the President of the European Commission, has stated that 80% of the social and economic decisions affecting our lives will be taken by an undemocratic bureaucracy in Brussels within the next ten years. Here are two worrying anti-democratic trends taking power from the people.

If we look at the developing geopolitical world trends we will observe the increasing domination of the USA and Japan. Viewed from one side it could be that the whole rationale behind 1992 and the completion of the European Internal Market is the construction of what is known as 'Fortress Europe'; a trading bloc of 320 million consumers and big enough to take on the Japanese and Americans. The development of such a superstate (because that is what it would be) without a sufficient democratic structure would be likely to result in extreme right wing government. If we examine an historical parallel of a customs union and free trade area developing into a nation state, or superstate, with inadequate democratic structures, we have the example of the *Zollverein*. Under Prussian auspices the *Zollverein* developed into the German state with consequent trade and then military world war.

A worrying trend in Scotland is that the Scottish National Party (SNP) wants to counter the centralising nature of Westminster by locking itself into the corrupt anti-democratic set up in the EC; it wants to jump out of the London frying pan into the Brussels fire. Jim Ross, the author of *A Claim Of Right For Scotland*, stated in an article after the Govan by-election, in *The Scotsman* (Monday November 14, 1988), that although he did not know whether November 10 would prove good or bad for the chances of a Convention he was sure that: '...an independent Scotland in or out of Europe is, for the foreseeable future, a mirage'. Perhaps that statement explains some of the SNP's subsequent antics towards collaboration in the Constitutional Convention. Whether or not this was the case I am sure Jim Ross is quite right; the *Claim Of Right* and the Constitutional Convention must be about increased democracy and not independence.

I believe that the future of the people of Scotland is inextricably bound up with the future of the EC; that the question of sovereignty and the crisis of democracy in Scotland and the UK is mirrored by a similar question and crisis within the Community and that the answer to the questions and the solution of the crises will ultimately involve interlocking changes at all levels. It is not shrinking sovereignty but the democratic deficit, at all levels, which poses the greatest threat.

In some senses the nation states of the EC have become, at the same time, both too large and too small to realistically and democratically deal with the re-structuring taking place in the geopolitical arena at global level. For democracy to be saved and extended it is necessary to have constitutional changes which bring political and social organisation into line with economic reality. In shaping and implementing these constitutional changes it is crucial to remember that democracy is about people having power at all levels and therefore to make sure that when we make changes at the local level they will be compatible with increased democratic power at the global level. In terms of the programme immediately before us that means interlocking the changes in Scotland with those in the EC. This task could clearly fall within the remit of a Scottish Constitutional Convention. If it does, and if the cause of democracy is furthered, then the people of Scotland and the European Community will clearly owe an enormous debt of gratitude to the authors of *A Claim Of Right For Scotland* and to the Campaign for a Scottish Assembly.

# 5

## The Highland Question

CHARLES KENNEDY

Scotland and its *Claim of Right*. My first thought is anecdotal. It is pre-Govan 1988 and I am sitting on board a British Airways 757 shuttle from London to Edinburgh. From my window seat, it being a fine, cloudless morning, I enjoy the panoramic view surrounding our nation's capital. The Forth road and rail bridges, Arthur's Seat, and the Castle itself. We land safely and the standard metallic air hostess voice intones the usual greetings and litany of BA propaganda as we taxi into the terminal. She concludes: 'So, welcome to Edinburgh, where the local time is. . .'

Some passengers chuckle at the gaffe, others experience a surge of outraged nationalistic sentiment. Being a committed political centrist, I recall vaguely my own reaction falling somewhere between the two. We are not yet on a different time zone from our southerly neighbours; indeed the Eurocrats persist in trying to defy both logic and geography by placing the Butt of Lewis on the same hour of the day as the heel of Italy. But we are, and I trust will always remain, on a different wavelength from the folk south of Hadrian's Wall.

Yet, for all the trappings and accoutrements of that quite different attitude and environment which do abound in Edinburgh — from the Scottish Regalia to the General Assembly of the Church of Scotland Hall, from the Scottish Office to the National Gallery — it still evokes, for me, a strange eeriness where the ethic of nationhood in concerned. It can only be the contradiction which arises from possessing the artefacts and yet lacking the actuality of real national political control.

A contrast with two other European capital cities makes the point : Warsaw and Dublin. The former, for obvious reasons of downright subjugation, is a capital whose flavour is sucked dry and left desolate by the will of Moscow being imposed through locally propped-up puppets. It is a capital of the lost cause called Communism. Dublin, by contrast, conveys a genuine sense of vigour and vitality — which is surely derived from the fact that, within its city boundaries, resides the reality of governmental decision-making. Edinburgh should be that way too; almost became so in the late seventies; and the converted Old Royal High School stands today in historical tribute to the inadequate Devolution Act and the unjust 40% rule of that period. But, as national consciousness again seems to be reawakening, and as the Scottish system stands poised — perhaps — to reassert itself, the question must now be asked: does the empty Assembly chamber represent the ultimate symbol of Scottish apathy or, instead, does it signal a sense of national anticipation yet to be fulfilled?

It will be frustration breeding apathy again if the politicians do not manage a better showing at constructive cooperation this time round than was the case a decade ago. Notwithstanding legitimate ideological differences between (and indeed within) parties there remains sufficient common ground and collective national interest to make the Scottish Constitutional Convention work — and thus bring the big prize of a Scottish Parliament that much closer.

That truth is one which must act as a focus for all the participants. At the time of writing the SNP's position remains unclear: it is surely to be hoped that they recognise the overwhelming national opinion in favour of some degree and some form of constitutional change for the better. That must be the motivating force behind the entire exercise.

In so saying, however, none of us can be blind to the obstacles and pitfalls ahead. Take one old chestnut, for example — the vexed West Lothian Question. Although *The Claim of Right* document reads as commendably lucid and invigorating prose it nevertheless fails to resolve that central dilemma, save for the casual comment that 'It is for the English to decide how to govern themselves, but they must allow for the continuing improvement of Scottish government.' Is it? Must they?

Now I consider myself to be a nationalistic Scot in politics — but that is not the same thing as being, politically, a Scottish Nationalist. The party political nationalist would encounter no difficulty over the above sentiment, nor should someone of that particular persuasion be expected to. Such a conviction, after all, is part of their political *raison d'être*.

The same cannot be said for those of us involved in projecting our political preferences across an electoral stage which encompasses England, Wales and ( hopefully in time) Northern Ireland — as well as Scotland. By definition we will seek support within two nations, a principality and a province respectively — but that support manifests itself unavoidably in the division lobbies of only one House of Commons. It is there that the UK unitary state governmental legitimacy is represented by the Mace in position.

Therefore the longer-term, post-Scottish Parliament structure and role of that Commons' chamber will have to be resolved in this respect. It is a tricky question which suggests no straightforward answer — and it is one component of the constitutional trawl facing the Convention which, necessarily, will demand Westminster input. It seems that the Curse of Tam is with us yet.

Recognising this 'anomaly' the *Claim of Right* document goes on to pronounce — both with some reason and some lack of it — that it 'would be of a practical effect only occasionally and temporarily. The defects of Scottish government are fundamental and continuing.' I'll buy the second proposition but just try selling the first to a Westminster institution which, in terms of its capacity for internal improvements to working procedures, displays all the imaginative dynamism of a Stalinist Five Year Plan.

Political problems have created the constitutional opportunity; that opportunity creates obvious problems of its own, of which the West Lothian Question is but one. In the remainder of this short contribution I shall dwell upon, in the main, one other significant regional problem within Scotland, which any consideration of the case for a Scottish Parliament carries with it. And for reasons of unashamed regional bias I shall term it 'The Highland Question' — although readily acknowledging that it applies in equal if not greater measure to the Western & Northern Isles, the Borders, Grampian, and other parts of rural Scotland as well.

Mackenzie King, Canada's long-serving and whimsical Prime Minister, used to refer to his country as possessing too much geography and not enough history. The Highlands lay claim to more than their fair share of both. That reality obliges me to express a few truths from home itself.

'For 200 years' announced Willie Ross, 'the Highlander, has been the man on Scotland's conscience.' I doubt if the same could be said less than twenty-five years later. Ross was speaking against the backdrop of historical injustice and inhumanity endured by those whose fate was to have been born into the distinctive life-patterns and settings of the crofting counties. 'No part of Scotland has been given a shabbier deal by history from the '45 onwards. Too often there has been only one way out of his troubles for the person born in the Highlands — emigration.' He sought some redress for their long-term deprivations through introducing (with that speech) the

Highland Development Bill which set-up the Highlands & Islands Development Board.

A generation later things have changed in at least one dramatic sense. It is not that the Scots have lost their sense of national empathy or fairness — far from it, as reaction to last year's Lockerbie tragedy showed. Instead it is simply that the agenda has been influenced, sadly, by modern day social harshness visiting itself upon other large tracts of our land.

The historic legacy of the Clearances as recognised by the 1886 Crofting Act, coupled to the persisting regional drawbacks and disadvantages experienced by the Highlands in the twentieth century, gave rise to the consensual sixties emphasis upon the encouragement and location of large-scale industry at key points within the area. The HIDB was seen as both a social and economic tool to complement such development although, given its creation under a Labour government, was also mistakingly suspected — by the Tories at the time — of being a political instrument as well.

Industrial encouragement was linked to social engineering — with the combined lure of an engaging environment alongside apparently secure employment prospects acting as a magnet for many workers and their families. The talk was of repopulation, with some even envisaging a 'linear city,' stretching along the coastline of the Moray Firth.

Today these social advances, if that is what they were, are in abject retreat. The Corpach pulp mill has gone, the Invergordon aluminium smelter closed, Dounreay fast-breeds into a highly uncertain future. And, in the concurrent but separately encouraged on-shore oil-related sector, the huge fabrication yards have met with mixed fates. Kishorn lies in receivership while Ardersier and Nigg scramble for orders in an ever-cyclical industry, made worse by the oil price fluctuations of more recent years, the changing technological nature of the industry and the related periodic contractions of available large-scale work.

Yet for Corpach there is Bathgate; for an Invergordon a Linwood; for Dounreay, Gartcosh; with the longer-term oil-related activity mirroring the social and economic anxieties associated with Ravenscraig. So it is not that the Scots have become harsher — had they, then Thatcherism might begin to sound its sour note with more resonance in our society — it is just that the economic realities across Scotland have become harsher. The Scottish conscience is now spread wider, and so thinner, than before.

This inescapably sad fact is likely to accentuate a genuine anxiety for those domiciled in outlying Scotland; that a legislature in

Edinburgh would run the risk of being insufficiently attuned and thus responsive to their particular problems and priorities. Indeed, the fear can be expressed in even more barbed political fashion : what is the point, such a Scot may enquire, in swopping an apparently remote Tory dominated Westminster system for socialist control dominated through the Labour Party of the Central Belt?

This is not party point-scoring. Rather it is a statement of the obvious. And recently history bears it out — as a glance at the regional breakdown of the Devolution Referendum results demonstrates. Borders, Grampian, Dumfries & Galloway and Tayside all voted 'no'. In Orkney and Shetland the anti vote was emphatic, over 70% in both cases. Highland Region recorded only the narrowest of 'yes' margins (51% to 49%). Hardly a ringing endorsement, even allowing for the failings of the scheme on offer at the time. (Remember also that the Act did not grant the proposed Assembly any tax-raising powers — which in these regions under the political and financial climate prevailing then could have been a source of still greater anxiety, and so opposition.)

Ironically, the poll tax proposals give current confirmation of this outlook. There is deep resentment elsewhere across Scotland at the imposition of what has become known as the 'Strathclyde surcharge' — an additional contribution which has been deemed necessary to provide an effective safety-net for the country's most populous region. Clearly, a certain lack of communal identity continues to figure prominently within Scotland. As such, if it is to provide reassurance and carry national conviction, any legislative tier at Edinburgh must be structured in such a way so as to meet the attitudes and aspirations of those outwith the Central Belt itself.

The obvious way to overcome this significant stumbling block is, of course, through proportional representation. Increasingly throughout the UK, most definitely across Scotland, this long overdue electoral reform is being understood not only as a question of party political fairness but also as one of regional balance. UK democracy is debased by the near no-go zones of the Tory south and the Labour north; in Scotland, as the Kilbrandon Commission noted, only PR would guarantee that any legislature could not be dominated by a single party 'elected' on a minority national vote. Correspondingly, a proportionately based chamber would also ensure greater leverage and direct political input for the less populous regions. It would lessen the fear — and the risk — of geographic disenfranchisement becoming a permanent institutional feature.

Given today's political reality, where Scotland faces a Government deeply hostile to constitutional change, the PR prerequisite assumes still further importance. Acknowledging the unfavourable political backdrop, the *Claim of Right* document stresses the preparatory work which will have to be undertaken by the Convention, before going on to argue: 'Also, it is more important for the Scots to get an Assembly, and to get it soon, than to ensure from the outset the ultimate refinement of the Assembly's powers. Negotiating with the Government, when it faces the need to negotiate, will no doubt be a delicate task involving weighty decisions. But the basis for taking these decisions will be the effectiveness of the work done on demonstrating the strength of Scottish demand'.

There is a strong dose of chicken and egg here. If 'demonstrating the strength of Scottish demand' is the name of the game — and so it should be — then that demand, by logical definition, must be as near all-Scottish as is attainable. Yet to make it so, to enable the package to command sufficient respect and support throughout outlying Scotland, inevitably entails the Convention demonstrating sensitivity to the anxieties aroused over Central Belt domination. The *Claim* is therefore correct in according less priority in the earlier stages of the Convention to that 'ultimate refinement of the Assembly's powers' — but the electoral basis through which the Assembly members would attain their legislative offices and so shape that 'ultimate refinement' later on is of the highest priority. If the voting system on which the Assembly was founded was seen to be insensitive to regional disparities, then what chance that the eventual structure which emerged would be any better? Chicken and egg could run the risk of becoming pig in a poke.

This important question of principle can be resolved satisfactorily. Both the Democrats and the SNP are formally committed to PR; there are growing trends in its favour within the Labour movement; as earlier noted it already carries the imprimatur, and specifically in this context, of one Royal Commission. Assuming then that it is resolved, what kind of broader governmental structure is likely to commend itself to the Scotland outside the central conurbation?

Appropriately, the answer is to be found amongst our furthest-flung communities: the trio of single-tier all purpose Councils instituted for the Western Isles, the Orkneys and the Shetland Isles. They provide the ready-made blueprint for the reformed local government system which should follow on from the establishment of a Scottish Parliament. (Although, in each of their cases, there are strong arguments in favour of devolving further powers, with the Orkneys and the Shetland Isles specifically being accorded greater autonomy.)

Additionally, such reform also kills the leaden talk of an extra tier of government, ever more bureaucracy and the like, which is

so frequently trotted out by the apologists for the status quo. There
are two important considerations here. First, as the *Claim* document
points out, a legislature per se does not constitute additional government, merely a 'transfer from London to Scotland [of] that part of
government affecting Scotland only'. Second, a consequential reform
of local government into all purpose, single tiers across Scotland
would enhance regional community identity. A simpler, smaller and
more locally identifiable level of decision-making would ensue. This
is preferable to the current dual system — not least with its over-large
and geographically remote regional tier — and as such would be a
consistent and popular reform.

A Scottish Parliament, elected under proportional representation, coupled to a reformed single-tier system of local government
throughout Scotland, would give us more efficient and effective
decision-making. Efficient because policy options could be properly
explored and weighed by Scots in Scotland. Effective because those
options would be decided far closer to the people and the communities upon which their implications would impact.

If, as runs through the entire *Claim of Right* text, we begin with
the assumption that the UK unitary state is failing us, then there is
no reason why we should opt for a smaller model of the same mess
in Scotland. Instead we should recognise our national diversities and
seek to evolve a governmental structure which works in sympathy
with them. At the end of the day that is a better way to harness the
talents, unite the spirits and give authentic legislative voice to the
country that is ours.

# 6

## Claim of Wrong

MICHAEL FRY

The terms Conservative and devolutionary are nowadays a contradiction, but they ought not to be. A concern for the vigour of local life and institutions has been one of the most enduring features of Conservatism, here and in other countries. It has reflected two instincts. The first was a liking for the individual and for the particular, even for the eccentric, against the abstract, utilitarian, moralising ideas of progressive liberals. More recently, it has expressed distaste for the centralising and levelling effects of socialism.

It was for these reasons that at various times in the past the Scottish Conservative party has been more nationalist than its opponents. That was true in the time of Sir Walter Scott, who abhorred the anglicising Whigs. It was true in the time of Sir Winston Churchill, who in an intriguing application of the mandate argument, said he would never consent to socialism being imposed on Scotland by a vote of the House of Commons (in those days, of course, the Scots Unionists used to win more votes than Labour). As late as December 1976, when Alick Buchanan-Smith resigned as shadow Secretary of State, it was quite all right for Tories to proffer devolutionary schemes of their own.

Why, then, is the very idea so indignantly rejected now? The Government since 1979 has been a radical one, and such Governments are often centralising, because they cannot get far if they spend too long listening to local or other vested interests. We must also take into account the personal preferences of Mrs Margaret Thatcher, with her British jingoism and the association in her mind between devolution and the other desperate, failed expedients of that low, dishonest decade, the 1970s.

Though her view is in retrospect not entirely unjustified, it still leaves her party in Scotland in an uncomfortable position. Scottish nationalism may at times be ignobly mean and petty, but it certainly is not always so. And the language of patriotism, of nationhood, of inherited loyalty to historic communities is language that Conservatives like to hear, — that comes naturally to them. Everywhere else in the world it is part of the Conservative stock in trade. Here it is forbidden. On the contrary, Scottish Conservatives have got themselves into an extraordinary position where national sentiment actually works against us, something that would be inconceivable for any other Conservative party in any other land. Alone among the Conservative parties of the world, the Scottish one tells its country that nationhood counts for nothing. Can we still then define ourselves as a Conservative party? Is not an unpatriotic Conservative party a meaningless abstraction?

Disraeli was right in saying the first question that must be put to any Conservative party is what it wished to conserve. In our case, the only coherent answer is that we wish to conserve the Union. But I am not sure this really answers our difficulty, because the Union has meant different things at different times. For instance, we cannot reasonably claim to be defending the Union of 1707, with its semi-independence for Scotland under fully autonomous institutions. The original Treaty has been so often amended that few of its articles are in practice applicable today. Nor indeed can we claim to be defending the Union of 1945 to 1979, with its bureaucracies and quangos, its patronage and subsidy, making of Scotland the biggest pressure group in Britain — in all, the very antithesis of Thatcherism. Which Union then? Or is every incoming Government entitled to define the Union in any way it likes? Its measures may well be defensible, but hardly on grounds of their Conservatism.

It should not be thought that these sentiments flow from any disloyalty to the Conservative party. On the contrary, I accept all the basic tenets of Thatcherism. I am sure they have done infinitely more good than harm, and saved a country which was going to the dogs ten years ago, as well as creating for most people a prolonged prosperity such as no other Government this century has been able to achieve.

Still, nobody gets things 100 per cent right, and principles may at times conflict with one another. Doubtless, in 1979, immediate priority had to be given to setting the economy to rights. And perhaps a degree of ruthless centralisation was necessary for that purpose. We should recall the dictum of one of the greatest Conservative thinkers, Edmund Burke, that 'Circumstances (which with some gentlemen pass for nothing) give in reality to every political principle its distinguishing colour, and discriminating effect. The circumstances are what render every civil and political scheme beneficial or noxious to mankind.' What was justifiable, even desirable, in the 1980s will not appear in the same light in the 1990s. There are already signs of popular reaction against centralism. The Tories, the only party really interested in power, are bound to respond — or else in the end yield to someone who does. The more likely course is that they will stay in office, with Mrs Thatcher stepping down sometime in the next decade to an altogether cuddlier figure. If the party has still not solved its Scottish problem, he or she, unshackled by past commitments, may well decide on a new approach. It is against that contingency that devolutionists ought to be planning.

In this context, the *Claim of Right* is obviously a premature document. There is no chance of anything at all happening while Mrs Thatcher is in power with a secure majority behind her in the House of Commons. The same argument applies to a Constitutional Convention. It would, moreover, be open to the charge that its mandate was even weaker than hers. Such self-elected bodies have met before, in the 1940s and in the 1970s, and have never done any demonstrable good. This is because they lack the legitimacy conferred, whether we like it or not, by the normal political process. If 80 per cent of the Scottish electorate voted in 1987 for parties in favour of constitutional reform, 80 per cent of them also voted for parties believing that such reform has to come, if at all, through Westminster, and not by extra-parliamentary means.

The instinct is a sound one. The British system is far from perfect but it has given us two or three centuries of general liberty and prosperity, more than most other countries have had. Our citizens are on the whole wary of speculative schemes of reform. Those who seek such reforms should be ready not to evade the objections, or break off debate about them through the well-tried constitutional channels, but to accept the objections as genuine and, if they can, to meet them with arguments of their own. If they succeed in this, there is no reason why they should not in the end prevail. Our system, after all, exists for giving expression to the will of the people, insofar as it is consistent with good sense and practical expediency. The process may take a long time. In fact, most of our major constitutional reforms have come only after several decades of thoroughly mulling over the issues at stake. I dare say this is frustrating for the reformers. But it strikes me as preferable to running off flightily after every novel proposition, let alone to shooting one another.

My first advice to devolutionists is therefore to prepare themselves for a long haul. My second is to set out from an assumption that the Government's resistance arises not from obtuse malice but from a legitimate point of view which we have to face, not duck. On both counts the *Claim of Right*, despite a tone confident to the point of being dogmatic, is a lamentable piece of work.

One problem is that Scottish political thinking seems to have stopped dead on March 1, 1979. Compared with the fertile, not to say frenetic, atmosphere of a decade ago, the 1980s have been sterile indeed. Though I supported the Scotland Act with my pen and with my vote, I can in retrospect acknowledge that it was in many ways a bad piece of legislation and understand why it failed to excite enough enthusiasm to get through. If we want a new measure, it has to be a better one. Otherwise, any significant devolutionary sentiment is likely to be killed off, probably for good.

The *Claim of Right* offers no hope here. It treats as trivial what were in fact weighty objections to the Scotland Act: the West Lothian Question, the danger of excessive government, Scotland's over-representation at Westminster, the method of election, to name but the most important. Two of these are not mentioned at all in the document, and two are in effect treated as of lesser consideration than the fact that Mrs Thatcher is such an awful woman.

Not being much of a constitutional lawyer myself, I shall confine my remarks to another fundamental matter, of how a Scottish Assembly would be financed. Here I can claim some expertise, at least to the extent of having formulated the new proposals included in the pamphlet, *Unlocking the Future*, brought out last year by the Conservative Constitutional Reform Forum (CCRF).

These were, in my view, the only notable steps forward from the years of aridity in Scottish political thinking to which I have referred. They criticised the failed settlement of 1979 on the grounds of its having rested on two contradictory propositions: first, that there should be more freedom for Scotland (leaving aside the many varying interpretations that might be put upon those words);secondly, that the English should give us much more money.

That Scottish freedom and English money are as incompatible now as they were in 1707 ought to be clear — quite apart from practical question of whether the English, indoctrinated by ten years of Thatcherism, are ready to hand out more money to anybody. If they could be persuaded to hand it over to Scotland, you may be quite sure that they would demand an exact account of how it was spent and put a stop to anything they did not like. More English money is a prescription for less, not more, Scottish freedom. If money is the essence of good relations between the two nations, we surely do better by having as our go-between with Whitehall a Secretary of State, especially one who speaks with an acceptable accent and rides a horse, than some glottal-stopping jumped-up Strathclyde councillor, call himself Prime Minister of Scotland though he might.

That is why the CCRF turned previous ideas about financing on their heads. We proposed that a Scottish Assembly should raise all its own taxes, levy what rates it liked, receive in addition some agreed share of the Petroleum Revenue Tax. It would then pay over to London a just contribution for the services which would continue to be provided in common (defence, foreign affairs, social security, etc.) by the United Kingdom Government. Scotland could forget her mendicant whine and throw away her begging bowl. This excellent scheme was, of course, thrown out at the Tory party conference by 600 votes to 12. Like that great Scottish Conservative, A.J. Balfour, I should rather trust my valet than the Tory party conference.

Recently, however, the Labour party has shown some interest in adopting the CCRF scheme. I wonder if it will also accept one basic premise for the scheme's working at all — which is that Scotland, so far from being a poverty-stricken economic wasteland ravaged by ten years of Mrs Thatcher's rule and groaning under her oppressions, is, as a matter of fact, an averagely rich part of an averagely rich industrial country. To be sure, it has problems (which nation has no problems?). But they are not such as can normally justify the huge transfers of resources which Scottish socialists traditionally see as the answer to everything, particularly not when several English regions are now poorer than we are. In short, money does not grow on trees, and the rest of the world does not owe us a living. Scotland, in or out of the Union, is perfectly capable of standing on her own feet if she wants to.

If she wants to . . .aye, there's the rub. Assuming that the *Claim of Right* is reasonably representative of devolutionary sentiment, one must deduce that she does not want to. For in a rambling and inconsequential discussion of the economy, the only real conclusion it comes to is that 'within the framework of the United Kingdom, strong regional economic policies are essential.' True, it does for a moment penetrate the skulls of these collectivist dotards that such policies have not in the past worked all that well. 'Does this mean that the wrong regional policies have been chosen, or that the right policies have been irresolutely applied, or that regional policies can never do more than suppress symptoms of the disease?' they muse.

We should leave them musing. For all the reasons recited above, anyone who genuinely believes in devolution and thus necessarily rejects the dependence culture should rejoice that regional policy has come to an end and is unlikely to rise again. He or she should equally rejoice that under the EEC regional policy, invoked in support of its arguments by the *Claim of Right*, the Eurocrats concerned are forever trying to stop Scotland getting any of the money, as the Highlanders have recently discovered to their chagrin. The reason is not that they have anything against us. It is rather that they can see, what is indeed the fact of the matter, that Scotland simply does not deserve lavish subsidies when the Community contains such places as Sicily and Portugal.

The nub of the case presented by the *Claim of Right* is this: 'Business congregates where it can find politicians to lend it an ear and fight its cause.' This is the authentic voice of clapped-out corporatism: business will congregate, note, not where it can most efficiently draw on the resources available to it, nor yet where it can best serve its customers, but where it can win access to patronage and subsidy.

I have already advised devolutionists to take a long view, by which I mean to work now on arguments that will strike home in the 1990s — when one may be sure that those just quoted will look positively prehistoric. If I were to look very hard on the bright side, I suppose I might observe a new spirit abroad in Scotland, a spirit which will in due course cast off the dependence culture, take responsibility for the nation's affairs, not demand that the rest of the world should arrange itself for our comfort and convenience, not relapse into querulous self-pity when the rest of the world declines. But I see none of that new spirit reflected in the document I have been discussing. For Scotland, the *Claim of Right* is part not of the answer, but of the problem.

# 7

## Unrepentant Gradualism

NEIL MACCORMICK

Other contributions to the present volume will have higher claims to dispassionate objectivity about the *Claim of Right* than does this one. This is written by a signatory of the *Claim of Right* who is also a member of the Scottish National Party, but one who at the time of writing finds himself in sharp amd public disagreement with the party leadership's posture of opposition to the convening of a convention on the terms proposed in the *Claim*. Rather than pretend to academic objectivity, I shall therefore here present an amalgam of blatant advocacy and apology for a view not much in fashion among my political friends. I hope the argument will succeed as apologia, rather than be dismissed as a mere apology for an argument. However that may be, the argument is not a new one, not even new in the context of the particular present debate in Scotland. At the Scottish National Party conference in Inverness in September 1988, I had the honour of being invited to present the annual 'Chairman's Lecture', taking as my subject 'Constitutional and Democracy'. The case I put then will be substantially restated here. If I now have the misfortune to disagree with the leadership of the party to which I (perhaps all too loosely) adhere, I shall at all events be stating the very same view as I stated to the party conference well before the outbreak of controversy.

The argument here has two main sections. In the first, I state some elements of a general political creed under the rubric of 'Constitutionalism, Democracy, Gradualism', showing the connections of this with some of the themes of the *Claim of Right*. In the second ('On Present Discontents'), I try to justify a view about the way the SNP should respond to the challenge of a Convention, and concede some points of fault in my own view.

### 1. *Constitutionalism, Democracy, Gradualism.*

'Constitutionalism' and 'Democracy' are in my view concepts or ideals essential to the ever elusive goal of human freedom in political society. To make this bold statement is, however, to assert a relatively uncontroversial, not to say vapid, thesis. The real question is not whether these concepts are involved in the issue of political freedom, but what conceptions of them we should propose as defining a favoured ideal of liberty in community. The ones which I propose are certainly congenial to the long standing style and spirit exhibited by the Scottish national movement in almost all its manifestations, and most particularly to the political approach of the SNP. The SNP has been devoutly and unshakeably constitutionalist and democratic throughout its history, and is so now. Even if there were shortcuts to its cherished goal of a free Scotland, the party has never shown any inclination towards them, and rightly, since attempts to dodge round either would put at profound risk the integrity of the objective sought. The general temper of Scottish politics in modern times provides its own guarantee against any successful adventures down such shortcuts.

The point about integrity is fundamental. For the goal of a 'free Scotland' in the favoured sense must be taken as prescribing the freedom and equality of all citizens regardless of creed, class or ethnic origins, and the free participation of them all as equals in the processes of self-government. In a word, democracy. It must also, however, be understood as requiring what our forebears such as George Buchanan and David Hume used to call a 'free government', that is a government which is not only freely chosen by the people but which conducts the business of government with respect to the freedom under law of each citizen and of all of them in such associations as they pursue. In a word, constitutionalism. If the goal of a free Scotland is understood in this way, pursuit of it entails both practical and logical limits on the means that could be adopted for attaining it; if it is not so understood, it is not a goal fit to be pursued.

Sometimes one almost thinks of democracy and constitutionalism as though they were run together and hyphenated, constitutionalism-and-democracy, just one great big compendious concept. This is unhelpful, since it obscures the need for a balancing of values by presenting the balance as already struck pre-analytically. Constitutionalism and democracy represent two internally complex values, two poles to each of which our political life and thought has to be oriented, albeit in tension between the partly opposing pulls from them.

Democracy as a value stresses the equality of citizens (the equal worth, dignity and civil and political rights of citizens), and the sovereignty of the will of the totality of the citizens acting as equals. Constitutionalism is about the need for all sovereignties, not least popular sovereignty, to be constrained and restricted within political structures and legal or quasi-legal limits. It points to the dangers of every sort of absolute and arbitrary power, and stresses the need to divide into parts the powers of a commonwealth, distributing them among several agencies and estates, each jealous of any overweening pretensions of any other, all supplying 'checks and control' (as Hume would say) upon all the others. As well as limits of form and structure, in the modern world constitutionalism is increasingly and rightly seen as stipulating limits of substance upon governmental power, spelt out through charters or bills of right — or 'Claims of Right' such as those stipulated by the Scots Estates in convention in 1689.

Democracy says the people should be sovereign; constitutionalism denies that any sovereignty should be absolute and free of restraints or limits. Rather than plainly asserting the power of the people, it says that even the people will not exercise power wisely or justly save under acknowledged limits. Constitutionalist governments are carefully respectful of the limits on state power. Constitutionalist citizens make it their pride to pursue just reforms through the forms of legality and constitutional propriety — but they must also have the most watchful jealousy against governmental encroachments of constitutional power practised through any of the branches of government.

The long-standing constitutional policy of the Scottish National Party is in my view one which postulates a well-balanced equilibrium between the two poles of democracy and constitutionalism. It insists on equality of citizenship for all residing here. It proposes to entrench equality of voting power for everyone through a fair system of proportional representation in elections. It guards against abuses of majority power by proposing to give substantial minorities in parliament a power of veto subject to control by referendum or fresh general election. It sets out an elaborate scheme to depoliticise judicial appointments and to make the independence of the Courts as nearly as possible absolute. Faithful to understood traditions and usages, it provides for a Parliamentary Executive under limited monarchy. Lastly, but of fundamental significance, it proposes a restriction on all governmental powers under a justiciable Bill of Rights based on the European Convention, but somewhat strengthened.

It is not necessarily a paradox that the party proposing the most radical constitutional change, through dissolution of the present

incorporating union of Scotland with England and its replacement
with a partnership of equals within the European Community, nevertheless proposes a draft constitution for this independent Scotland
in Europe which would guarantee strong elements of constitutional
continuity from the present. On these proposals, the form of self-
government in Scotland would, as it should, be instantly recognis-
able as government within the traditions of governance tested by
experience in these islands over four centuries and perhaps more.
Such a respect for tradition is, I believe, another practical necessity
of constitutionalism. The structure established by and the limits
prescribed in the constitution have to be meaningful to the people
whose constitution it is. At least, they have to be so if democracy is
to have any chance. For democracy requires that the popular exercise
of power is an intelligent one made by persons who understand the
constitution within which they are working. And that entails in effect
that the wisdom of many generations tested out in constitutional
experience has to be gladly accepted as a limit on the ingenuity and
inventiveness of any particular moment.

The important truth that all constitutions presuppose and depend
on tradition and custom rather than on acts of momentary will is
another of the discoveries of the Scottish Enlightenment, particularly well articulated by David Hume. It used to be regarded, not
unjustly, as a special gift of political conservatism to common political wisdom. This makes it all the stranger that the Conservative
Party under Mrs Thatcher appears to have abandoned it in face of
an overwhelming commitment to a political ideology, that of the
so-called 'enterprise culture'. Mrs Thatcher has even on occasion
brought to Scotland a homily for the fathers and brethren of the
Kirk in assembly, not to speak of her sundry lectures to obsequious
gatherings of her party's faithful. In these interventions she has
risked startling the public intelligence with a reading of the Scottish
Enlightenment which almost parallels in strangeness and audacity
her interpretation of St. Francis as a patron saint of Thatcherism or
the Good Samaritan as an advertisement for the unique humaneness
of unqualified capitalism.

In fact, the present government more than any other in living
memory has perfected the skills of what Lord Hailsham used to call
an elective dictatorship (his lordship's anguish against such mon-
strosities having evidently been mightily soothed by regular application of a woolsack to his nether parts). The elective dictatorship
is a perversion of democracy and a corruption of constitutionalism.
As to democracy, our present electoral system regularly awards a
clear and often an overwhelming majority in Parliament to what is

no more in the country than — again let me use Lord Hailsham's words — merely the 'largest organised minority'. Disproportional representation denies equality and clothes substantial minorities with powers so unrestricted that they would be dangerous if exercised even by *bona fide* popular majorities. This is true, mark you, at the UK level or that of England alone — recall Mrs Thatcher's remarkably low winning percentage of the vote in 1987. In Scotland it simply parodies itself when a party has to crowd all its unalienated members into the Scottish Office just to make up an administration. And there is something a bit too self-serving about the thesis that it is only fair for Scotland to put up with a minority administration from time to time since England gets her share too when the left is ascendant in Scotland and Wales. You only have to reflect on the impossibility for a party holding a seventh of the English seats to form a British government in order to see the very restricted conception of equity here involved.

All very well, you may say, to criticise the undemocratic quality of the elective dictatorship. But have I not to admit that it is the traditional British way, hallowed by the constitutional usages and hence as constitutionalist as you like; tried and tested by practice even if criticisable from the view point of fancy theories about proportional representation? The fact is anyway contrary to the objection. The British system as it has evolved presupposes that those who exercise power accept and observe largely conventional constraints on the way power is to be exercised. This has functioned as a necessary counterweight to the massive and potentially arbitrary power held by a proclaimedly sovereign Parliament in fact controlled by an executive with a secure majority from a well-whipped party most of whose members depend on the government for their own secure continuation in Parliamentary if not also governmental office. A Prime Minister as dedicated to a single ideological line (and as intolerant of alternative opinions) as the present one can further, during a long period in power, establish a scarcely challengeable personal ascendancy over the whole apparatus of state.

This is not just an abstract or theoretical danger.It is the way we live now. Local Government when found inconvenient has been swept away without inquiry or commission or any attempt to find or establish a consensus. Local taxation in a new form has been thrust upon us, and in Scotland this was initially done without thought that such a thing, done without local popular mandate and otherwise than as part of a uniform UK scheme, was contrary probably to the letter and certainly to the spirit of the Articles of Union increasingly recognised in modern scholarship as the true fundamental constitution of the United Kingdom as a constitutional union. That particular and strong constitutional objection was no doubt mitigated by the carrying of the parallel measure for England and Wales. Yet what very many see as the profoundest injustice still faces us in the garb of legislation, but legislation thrust through Parliament on the say-so of a ministry without any of the normal, traditional and wise prior airing of ideas and problems in the light of suggestions, objections and considerations from all quarters. A whole system of taxation has been substituted for an ancient and admittedly unsatisfactory one by a process which might have been reasonable for some kind of civil emergency, not by the kind of reflective, well deliberated and consensus-seeking measure appropriate to changes of this kind. (I am not naively supposing that oppositions do not or should not oppose; but the really alarming thing was the way in which the government simply defied the idea that it ought to seek a real consensus among its own supporters.)

Most serious of all has been the steady attrition on freedom of speech and of information, and the withering attack on public institutions of free inquiry. Who but a person crazed with some extremity of conviction in the omnibeneficiality of markets could conceivably suppose that Mr. Rupert Murdoch, with or without a communications satellite, is apt to be a sounder servant of disinterested public information than the BBC? Who felt as though the Prague late spring were upon us when the Special Branch descended upon the BBC by night in Glasgow to execute a warrant whose invalidity apparently none of them had noticed? Or when the journalist who prepared the story had his house ransacked on a pretext of harm to national security? We are entitled to suppose that the Law Officers would have given no countenance to such invasions of valued public institutions and personal rights in a free country unless they had been advised on apparently serious evidence that there were overwhelming grounds to apprehend a real and serious breach of law with attendant damage to the safety of the state. But such advice, if it was given, was evidently flimsy after all, and perhaps it was politically motivated all along. After a delay of almost a year, the tapes were sent back and no prosecutions brought nor any criticism of the offending tapes as themselves affording evidence of the commission of a crime. The only wrong they in fact disclosed was by Government to the Parliament whose nominal sovereignty grounds the overweening power of the Government. Now that same power is as I write being moved into position to steamroller a new official information Bill through Parliament which will create an executive stranglehold over all such information as ministers decide their electorate must never know.

This all comes on top of an unexpected period of governmental bullying of BBC and IBA broadcasting systems alike, most recently symbolised by the response to Lord Windlesham's report on the ITV 'Death on the Rock' film, followed up with Lord Chalfont's appointment to the IBA itself.

The recently published *Index on Censorship* has driven home all the points of such a critique of this government's small respect for constitutionalism in the sphere of freedom of information and of opinion-formation. Perhaps even more telling, because yet wider-ranging, is the critique of present British constitutional doctrine and practice which makes up a substantial part of the argument in the *Claim of Right* report itself. The erosion of constitutionalism in the UK exposes the distortions of democracy in a cruel light. Liberties long taken for granted are under threat. The old semi-autonomy of Scottish government within the UK compromise is a thing of the past. There is just one say in the state, and that say goes regardless of the measure of popular support, regardless of restraints traditionally observed in constitutional practice. Whatever be thought of the *Claim*'s proposals and prescriptions, its diagnosis of present ills in Scotland and indeed the UK at large deserve attention in their own right.

What is to be done, then? One possibility from the SNP's point of view is certainly to stand clear of any proposals other than that for independence, or for independence in Europe, and to press these forward in every forum and election available, starting with the elections to the European Parliament in June 1989. From this point of view, there would be serious objections of principle to any proposal for any sort of all-party convention or conversations which did not include the possibility of a resolution in favour of such a constitutional settlement. Notoriously, however, the *Claim of Right* proposed an attempt to establish a more restricted and perhaps more tactical than strategic short-term consensus towards constitutional change in and for Scotland. The proposal was that in favour of convening, with or without the endorsement of Westminster, a Scottish Constitutional Convention consising all the Scottish MPs willing to participate, together with appropriate representative others. That Convention was envisaged as settling after careful debate a proposal for the future constitution and governance of Scotland, whether inside the UK or outside it. Given the effects of the present electoral system's principle of disproportional representation, the proposal necessarily had undesirable effects in relation to the relative representation of parties in the Convention, and proposals for additional counterweighing members from under-represented parties fell well short of fair proportionality. Further, the electoral opinion represented was that of a quite long past election (that of 1987), not of the present, nor yet of whatever the European elections will reveal.

These are serious deficiencies. They are, moreover, deficiencies of principle if we judge by reference to the ideal of democracy sketched above. What for me justifies the Convention proposal despite the deficiencies and despite their serious character is that it seems to me to offer the best first opportunity to achieve an agreed first step in the way of Scottish constitutional reform. Either before or after the next general election, a plan agreed by a massive Scottish majority and backed by their representatives elected to Parliament will have been determined. If in these circumstances no reform were forthcoming from Westminster, there would be a serious crisis for democracy, and the conditions for a deeper recourse to popular sovereignty would have been summoned into being. The Westminster reply, if it were made, that Scotland must either secede or remain in an unreformed incorporating union would certainly polarise the issue in a manner eminently fit for recourse to a referendum in Scotland at a point at which it had been made clear beyond doubt and across party lines that no serious middle way was available for consideration within the time scale of the crisis.

For myself, I seriously doubt if it would come to that. Just conceivably Mrs Thatcher might choose to remain as implacably opposed to any devolutionary reforms as she is now. But it is open to question whether she could then still command support in party, parliament or perhaps even palace. I strongly believe in the importance of an initial establishment of a Scottish Parliament upon terms of the broadest consensus available, even if such must necessarily fall short of that which the SNP will at the same time propose in the elections it contests.

This view is fairly open to attack as nothing more than advocacy of 'back to gradualism', back to a policy which many hold to have been discredited by the experience of the Scotland Act and the 1979 referendum. Such an attack I regard as wholly to the point but also wholly wrong. For myself, I am an unrepentant gradualist. Gradualism is an all but inevitable corollary of constitutionalism, but also of a commitment to democracy, for we should seek to go at the speed of the greatest majority in promoting constitutional change. On reflection after ten years, I think that what was discredited in 1979 was an insufficient gradualism, a half-hearted gradualism. I remember Jo Grimond challenging members of the SNP during the debates about devolution to promise that we would work for ten

years within the framework of a Scottish Assembly, before again
raising the issue of full independence as a concrete policy proposal
(as distinct from an ultimate aim). The idea got short shrift then.
Ten years on, we in the SNP can say that we did not sully ourselves
with compromise. We also did not have an assembly of any, however
inadequate, sort all these ten years. It is not certain that we would
have had one had we been more openly accommodating to ideas of
that sort. It is certain that we have had nothing as things have been.
One's deepest doubt has to be that Scotland will go on having no
democratic forum of legislation and government if those who most
wish most in the way of self-government find themselves unable to
strike compromises with those who will go some way, but not the
whole way yet.

## 2. *On Present Discontents*

It is not hard to see why the view I just stated may be challenged.
The trouble is the gap which is left between the principles stated as
premises and the practical conclusion argued for, namely the setting
up of a constitutional convention as proposed in the *Claim of Right*
and subsequently set in motion by the Campaign for a Scottish
Assembly. After all, if the arguments of principle start out by being
grounded in democratic equality, it has to be said that the departure
from proportionality is considerable. Those in the SNP who have
lately argued that the convention ought to be directly elected for the
purpose can rightly appeal both to precedent and to the principle
of the thing, as well as to the SNP's own historical commitment
to the idea of setting up a convention. Further, it can fairly be
said that a constitutional convention in the full sense ought to be
preparing proposals which may ultimately be put to the sovereign
people in a referendum as the most appropriate test of popular
approval. Finally, it has to be acknowledged that so long as what
is proposed is revision or alteration of the constitution of a United
Kingdom of which Scotland is to remain a part, one cannot either
upon democratic or upon constitutionalist grounds, to say nothing
of elementary fairness, assert a right to impose change without the
consent of the whole body politic in some form or another.

These thoughts at the very least require some admission of fault
on the part of at least one member of the team who drafted the
*Claim*. To put the point plainly, while I for my part do believe
we were correct in supposing that the greatest care was called for
in the framing of convention proposals if these were to be capable of
winning the participation of the Labour Party, yet I now have to say

also that I at least ought to have contemplated yet more carefully the question what would be sticking points for other parties, particularly the SNP, particularly in the light of its established approach to issues of democracy and of constitutionalism. Whether Labour could ever have settled for anything less than the terms of the *Claim* is far from clear; that more has been asked of the SNP than its officers and tacticians are willing to give is now clear also.

Let me not seek to disguise or to excuse this fault. Still I shall argue on the other hand that the goal we set is a good one. Somehow, some day, we have to find a way of bringing together all those who desire home rule in Scotland, under circumstances which fundamentally challenge the right of governments to continue to override the popular will here. Nothing but a massively majoritarian endorsement of some concrete proposal for workable change can un-jam the present constitutional log-jam. Certainly, this might give rise to charges of double-thinking, even duplicity, on the part of the SNP if it appears to be pretending to endorse a devolutionary or quasi-federal proposal while it is at the same time known to be favouring independence in Europe.

To that, and to the horror of so many in the party over any blurring of the ultimate end, there is I believe a simple reply. There is surely no reason for the SNP ever to campaign electorally on anything other than the plain theme of its well-known policy as that which will be mandated by a sufficient majority vote for the party's candidates. But there is another question to which it is not defeatist to seek a ready answer. That is the question what the SNP would demand and would support politically in the not unlikely event of a repeat of some variant on the 1987 election result, that is, a massive defeat for the Conservatives in Scotland, an increase in SNP support falling short of a majority even of Westminster seats, far less of votes, and the balance of the votes and seats split between Democrats and Labour with a probable large predominance for Labour. Whether the UK Government formed after such an election were Conservative, Labour or some sort of coalition, we should require clarity as to the interpretation of the Scottish result. A highest common factor of a home rule scheme worked out well ahead of time by the proposed convention would answer that question.

Some will say that the very act of working out such a scheme would so dilute the SNP's commitment and demoralise its workers that it would be counter-productive. I doubt it. Further, when one takes it the other way and speculates on the morale and drawing power of a party which appears to have walked away from the attempt to articulate an all Scotland consensus as to one workable scheme, one is left doubting whether the course of non-participation in the convention is not the course which incurs by far the greater damage. I am sure it is. I admit some measure of fault in the *Claim*'s proposals, given the severe strain they cause for the SNP. But I have to conclude still that, in terms of Scotland's good, the greater fault is in non-participation. I hope it will not prove permanent.

# 8

## Claim of Right or Cap in Hand?

CHRIS MACLEAN

It has been argued by many nationalists and indeed by some hard-line unionists, that independence and devolution are not points on the same scale, but incompatible opposites. This may not be strictly true in terms of political strategies — there are just as many who argue that devolution would be the 'slippery slope' to independence as who contend that it would reform and strengthen the Union — nor in relation to individual policies, where in a changing Europe and an interdependent world concepts of 'total sovereignty' over areas of policy are less and less applicable.

It is certainly true, however, in terms of fundamental philosophical outlook. Devolution, by its very definition, means recognising the ultimate authority of the Westminster Parliament, or at the very least that its consent is required to implement any change. For it entails maintenance of a bilateral political relationship with England, and as with any such relationship any alteration in the terms must be agreed by both partners.

Independence, by contrast, involves an explicit rejection of the authority of Westminster; the basis of its claim is that the Scottish people are sovereign, not the English Parliament. If the English state is not prepared to accede to the demands of the Scots for a change in their relationship, then Scotland simply leaves the relationship.

It is, in political theory at least, a straightforward unilateral act. Mrs Thatcher may be able to 'veto' any demand for devolution, and she has reminded the Scots that she would not hesitate to do so. But she has no ability to apply a veto, on any grounds of legal, or political or moral authority, when it comes to a people exercising their sovereign right to self-determination, which is one of the cardinal and universally-recognised features of international law.

This is not some wishful thinking by a nationalist who does not recognise that Mrs Thatcher will attempt to place difficulties in the way of Scotland achieving independence. Overcoming such attempts will be a question of the respective political wills of the Scottish people and the English Government, just as it has been with every other nation which has won its freedom from London. It is not a matter of freedom being given to slaves, but of a free people deciding to exercise what is rightfully theirs.

This essential distinction between independence and devolution has been repeatedly and, indeed, most forcefully emphasised by the very opponents of any form of self-government for Scotland. When he was Secretary of State for Scotland, George Younger confirmed that the Government would have no choice but to recognise the Scots' decision if they voted for independence. Ex-Cabinet minister Leon Brittan said the same at the end of 1988, before departing for the European Commission in Brussels, And it has been one of the pet themes of our latest and self-styled Governor-General, Malcolm Rifkind. In one recent television interview, he stated quite emphatically:

> If you want to break up the United Kingdom, then if it's the people of Scotland who want to do that, or the people of England, or of Wales, then that can be decided by each individual country. If you want to leave a partnership, you leave it — full stop.
>
> If your objective, however, is different: if what you are wanting to do is to reform that partnership, to create a different kind of partnership, then no partner can dictate to the other two, or the other three, the new partnership that is to be created. That is something which has to be discussed by all those who are involved.
>
> (*Left, Right and Centre*, BBC Scotland, 10 February 1989)

The hard choice which has to be faced up to by devolutionists is not, therefore, a matter of the precise areas of policy over which any Scottish Parliament or Assembly should exercise control; it is not even whether they are unionists like Donald Dewar who see devolution as a way of improving and buttressing the UK, or quasi-nationalists like many Labour and Democrat supporters who do not regard the Union as sacrosanct and would be quite happy to see devolution leading on to greater things. The real dilemma is presented by the 1980s version of Archie Birt's question from the 1970s: what happens when Thatcher says no?

That question poses no problems for nationalists: we assert, supported by every single international treaty on the question of self-determination, that Thatcher has no legal or moral authority to say no to independence, and the issue becomes one of political

will and practical preparations for taking her on and defeating her
if she attempts to do so. The reaction of the quasi-nationalists,
however — those trying to sit on the fence between independence
and devolution — becomes at this point totally schizophrenic.

Symptomatic of this malaise is the body of thought emerging in the
nationalist wing of the Labour Party — in particular, the Scottish
Labour Action pressure group — on the fantasy of a 'dual mandate'.
Their wish is for Labour to fight the next General Election on such
a dual mandate, with the primary aim of electing a British Labour
Government which will deliver Scottish devolution, but that if — or
rather, when — that does not occur they will invoke a separate Scottish mandate for unilateral change of some hitherto unspecified kind.

On any logical analysis, this is sheer nonsense. The fundamental
issue is of sovereignty. Either you are a nationalist and accept the
sovereignty of the Scottish people, or you are a unionist and accept
the sovereignty of the British Parliament. You cannot have it both
ways — both cannot be sovereign.

You either seek a mandate for Government and constitutional
change at United Kingdom level and accept that you are or are
not given that mandate, or you assert all along that the Scottish
people possess ultimate authority, not Westminster. You cannot
retrospectively change the question depending on the answer.

This confusion of thinking is not confined to the quasi-nationalists
in the Labour Party, however. The very same dilemma crops up
again and again both in the *Claim of Right* document itself and in the
subsequent cross-party arguments over the nature of the proposed
Convention. Wherever there is an attempt to muddy the waters
between independence and devolution, the unbridgeable difference
which arises is less over policy than over sovereignty

The very language of the *Claim of Right* consists of a superb
collection of irreconcilable assertions. On the one hand, it has
drawn criticism from the Labour leadership for the repeated use
of such phraseology as 'the English Parliament' (1.3) 'the English
Constitution' (4.1) and the no-nonsense assertions that 'the Union
has always been, and remains, a threat to the survival of a distinctive
culture in Scotland' (2.2) and that 'the United Kingdom is a political
artefact put together at English insistence' (5.3.3). All of these imply
an external, even alien control of Scottish political life which our
people are no longer under any obligation to accept.

On the other hand, the *Claim of Right* has drawn equally as much
fire from the nationalist camp for talking about 'the constitutional
rights Scotland expects within the United Kingdom' (Prologue)
and for arguing that 'rectifying these defects [of the government

of Scotland] would improve the government of the whole of the United Kingdom' (1.2). An entire section of the report — Chapter 5 on the 'Fundamentals of an Assembly'—is furthermore devoted to defending the merits of a devolved Assembly within the United Kingdom: to arguing that such an Assembly would not be a 'slippery slope' to independence, to addressing the West Lothian Question, to refuting suggestions of an 'extra tier' of government or 'extra taxes' and concluding that 'for Scotland within the framework of the United Kingdom, strong regional economic policies are essential'(5.6.6).

For those of us who were involved in the Yes forces during the 1979 referendum campaign, the arguments have a depressingly familiar ring. While there has been a fever of intellectual activity over the past decade in nationalist circles, culminating in an explicitly left of centre SNP able to take on Labour and in the intellectual high ground of Scottish politics now being dominated by the concept of Independence in Europe, it seems that life among devolutionists has largely stood still. The last thing the *Claim of Right* should be about is a rehash of the tired old devolution arguments from the 'seventies. What it should have concentrated on was asserting the sovereign rights of the Scottish people — yet this was precisely what it seemed most anxious to avoid.

It is certainly true that the title *A Claim of Right for Scotland* conjures up visions of nationalist and even revolutionary demands which are anathema to all good unionists; and true to form, Donald Dewar made a point at the first cross-party meeting on 27 January 1989 of specifically objecting to the further use of the title in any part of the Convention's deliberations. Despite the historical analogies of the previous Scottish Claims of Right of 1689 and 1842 cited in the report, however, the title of the document is about as far as the comparison goes.

The *Claim of Right* proposes that a Convention would have three specific tasks, defined as follows: '(1) to draw up a scheme for a Scottish Assembly; (2) to mobilise Scottish opinion behind that scheme; and (3) to deal with the Government in securing approval of that scheme, or an acceptable modification of it' (12.1).

This remit sounds more like the aims of a pressure group, such as the Campaign for a Scottish Assembly itself, than the constitution of a body asserting the sovereign rights of the Scottish people, an impression given further credence by the *Claim of Right*'s throwaway line that 'the Convention will have more of the attributes of a campaign than a legislature' (16.11). Certainly, a Convention would not be a legislature in terms of determining laws of specific policy areas;

but to suggest that a Constitutional Convention, or a Constituent Assembly as it has often been known in other parts of the world, is nothing more than a campaigning body hoping to apply pressure to an intransigent British Government almost defies belief.

The *Claim of Right* does a reasonable job of analysing Scotland's problems within the current centralised state of the United Kingdom; it argues for remedies which sound suspiciously like a predilection for yet another set of devolutionary proposals, rather than a serious examination of all the options available for Scotland's future. What it wholly fails to do, however, is suggest how Scotland gets from (a) to (b) in the face of sustained opposition from a hostile English majority in the House of Commons.

The terms of reference were, to be fair, amended somewhat at the cross-party meeting on 27 January 1989. Item 1 was altered to read 'to draw up a scheme for an Assembly or Parliament for Scotland'; item 2 became 'to mobilise Scottish opinion and ensure the approval of the Scottish people for that scheme'; and item 3, at the insistence of the SNP delegates, now read 'to assert the right of the Scottish people to secure the implementation of that scheme'.

Some mention of asserting the rights of the Scottish people was thereby included in the terms of reference for a Convention; something which, almost unbelievably, had not been included in the original terms framed in the *Claim of Right*. While the report recognises that a Convention would represent 'a challenge to the authority of Government' (14.1) and that 'powerful indications of Scottish support for the Convention and resistance to the Government may be needed before the latter acknowledges the facts of Scottish opinion and the need to take account of them' (15.2); it adds that 'we cannot predict what this might involve' (15.3), other than the possibility of organising a referendum.

The next section of the report sums up, however, the dilemma over sovereignty facing the authors of the *Claim of Right*. It states that 'a wide range of other action is possible. Either to force a referendum or to force the Government to recognise the results of one. Whatever forms this action takes, it will achieve its object only if the Convention has effectively mobolised opinion on its side'. (15.3)

Precisely. Sovereignty, and success for any Convention, depends on the legitimacy which can come from the will of the people. The fundamental difficulty the Scottish National Party — which ranks the right of the Scottish people to determine their own future above all other considerations — faces with the non-elected, self-appointed type of Convention which has been proposed by the *Claim of Right* and subsequently by the Campaign for a Scottish

Assembly is that at no stage in the process will the Scottish people have their say.

They will have no say in the formation and composition of the Convention, either through direct elections or the compromise the SNP put forward of linking membership and mandate for the Convention to the European Elections in June 1989. They will have no chance to express their preference between the options available for Scotland's future — independence in Europe, devolution or the *status quo* — through a multiple choice referendum at the end. Instead, they will yet again be told what the politicians think is good for them — a single option of devolution, perhaps put to them in a referendum, perhaps not, which in any case will be subject to veto by Mrs Thatcher.

At this stage, a little of recent Scottish political history should be borne in mind. The SNP's opponents are trying to perpetrate a myth the Party never intended to participate in a Constitutional Convention no matter what its composition or remit. Nothing could be further from the truth.

It was with great regret that Gordon Wilson, Jim Sillars and Margaret Ewing—the Party's delegates to the cross-party meeting held 27 January 1989 — agreed that they had no other option but to recommend that the SNP should not participate in a 'rigged' Convention. Gordon Wilson, after all, had been the first politician to propose a Constitutional Convention as a way forward for Scotland after the 1979 referendum debacle. As MP for Dundee East, he introduced a Government of Scotland (Scottish Convention) Bill, proposing an elected Convention, in the House of Commons in March 1980 to mark the first anniversary of the devolution referendum.

Equally, it had been Jim Sillars who moved the resolution at the SNP Conference in September 1984 in Inverness committing the Party to supporting an elected Convention. That commitment was included in the SNP's manifesto for the 1987 General Election, at which Margaret Ewing was elected MP for Moray, at a time when no other political party was in favour of a Convention scheme.

There is a world of difference, however, between a directly-elected Convention and a self-appointed one. The latter offers the Scottish people no opportunity for them to express their view on the single issue of how Scotland should be governed; no party other than the SNP has ever asked them hitherto for a mandate for any form of Convention; it therefore lacks the legitimacy of popular consent which will be essential for taking on and defeating a hostile English Tory Government. The *Claim of Right* talks about the need for a 'significant level of support' to be 'indicated' for a Convention to get off the ground (11.6.2); it gives, however, no clue as to how any level of support is to be indicated at any stage prior to the Convention reaching its conclusions.

Quite simply, the Convention as proposed would be sewn up by the Labour Party unionist establishment, not as a means of articulating and developing Scottish demands, but of keeping them in check and watering them down. They know as well as anyone else that Labour's 1970s-style brand of devolution no longer matches the mood and needs of Scotland as we enter the 1990s, and that a series of polls have shown majority support for the SNP's policy of independent Scottish membership of the European Community. Donald Dewar's late conversion to the Convention cause near the end of 1988 was motivated by nothing other than a desire to try to take independence in Europe off the agenda and put devolution back on it. With the Convention as proposed — giving Labour a huge absolute majority of the membership and limited to the production of just a single option — he would be able to do precisely that.

Indeed, Mr Dewar gave the game away when, following the SNP's announcement of its intention not to take part in the Convention, he stated:

> The important thing is that a very broad range of Scottish opinion — political and non-political, but I think informed and representative — is going to meet and is going to look at how we hammer out the sensible changes within the structure of the United Kingdom that will allow Scots to control in a very direct way the areas of domestic policy which matter to us.

(*Scottish Questions*, Scottish Television, 2 February 1989)

Regrettably, such an attitude was not confined to the Labour leadership. Canon Kenyon Wright of the Scottish Churches Council, and one of the *Claim of Right*, expressed similar views the following night:

> The Convention represents the point of view that there is another way. We do not have to choose between total separation and unitary state as at present. There are other possibilities.

(*Scottish Question Time* BBC Scotland 3 February 1989)

It is certainly true that the SNP — the only organisation likely to argue a non-devolutionary case in the Convention — would have received a derisory 8 per cent share of the total membership under the scheme adopted by the other parties on 27 January 1989, at a time when a Party was standing at 32 per cent in the opinion polls. It is also the case that the *Claim of Right* itself, while not favouring direct elections, did insist that 'the Convention itself must . . . reflect reasonably closely the recent voting patterns of the Scottish electorate, otherwise its decisions will be open to serious question' (16.3). But that was not the central issue of concern to the SNP delegates.

The question of fair representation of the SNP, the Labour Party or anyone else was secondary to the fundamental issue of fair representation of the views of the Scottish people. At no stage did the SNP representatives suggest that they should receive 'x' per cent of the Convention membership; what they did argue was that the Scottish people should decide, through direct elections or the European Elections, the level of representation accorded to each of the viewpoints articulated by the various parties.

Going further than that, the SNP argued that even the question of the composition of the Convention was less important if the Scottish people were offered a choice between all the options available to them — from independence in Europe through to the status quo — in a multiple option referendum at the end of the process. Labour would have none of this, however, insisting on a single option over which they knew they would have total control. Their opposition to a free choice for the Scottish people — either through elections or a referendum — is all the more bitterly ironic when one considers the *Claim of Right*'s attack on the Tory Government's notions of 'freedom' and 'choice':

> The crucial question is: who edits the choices which are to be offered? The ordinary citizen's power to edit the choices that are to be offered can be exercised better through elective institutions than in any other way (7.2).

We come back to the question of sovereignty — a sovereignty which can only come from the expressed consent of the Scottish people. Apart from the SNP, no-one has ever sought a mandate from them for any sort of Convention; yet without that mandate any Convention will have one or both of its hands tied behind its back in taking on an intransigent Thatcher Government. That is recognised time and again in the *Claim of Right*:

> The essential is that a Convention, whether its origins are *de facto* or *de jure*... must achieve acceptance by those on whose behalf it presumes to speak and act (10.4).

The *Claim of Right* acknowledges the problem of sovereignty; it does not propose the answer because it cannot do so. That, not policies or strategies, is the irreconcilable gulf between a nationalist position and a devolutionist one.

The Scottish National Party may have received a lot of bad press for taking a hard stance by insisting that it would only take part in a Convention which genuinely reflects the wishes of the Scottish people and even more importantly, is able to implement them. Certainly there are many Scots not unsympathetic to the SNP who hoped the Convention would be the easy option to constitutional change, providing a focus for the overwhelming demand for some form of Scottish Parliament.

The truth however unpalatable, is that there is no soft option. The Convention, like the Scottish people as a whole, will have to face up to the hard choice on the issue of sovereignty. Either you accept that Mrs Thatcher and the English Parliament have a veto over Scottish aspirations, or you do not. There is no middle way.

The implications of that are that devolution, in whatever form, is not and will not be on offer as long as Westminster says no — which means the foreseeable future. There is no such thing as a unilateral declaration of devolution; but independence, as even Malcolm Rifkind has admitted, lies within the unfettered grasp of the Scottish people themselves.

It is time for a genuine *Claim of Right* — for the Scots to assert and take our internationally recognised right of self-determination, as a free, equal and independent European nation — rather than wasting any more time going cap in hand to London, begging for devolution.

# 9

## Scotland's Claim of Right

STEPHEN MAXWELL

The publication of *A Claim of Right for Scotland* in July 1988 shot a beam of republican optimism through the mirk of Scottish politics. It held out the promise of an escape from the long tunnel of depression in which Scotland had been trapped since the referendum of 1979. It suggested, even before the decade had been concluded, that the view of the 1980s as a cruel mould misshaping Scotland's foreseeable future might one day be replaced by the memory of a dishonourable interregnum between two complementary periods of national revival.

The 1970s had been years of hope borne up by rising expectations. By and large political debate had been infused with the spirit of reason. *Pace* Neil Kinnock, for all the excitement of those turning times, more thinking was done with the head than with the blood. Books like *Red Paper on Scotland* (ed. G.Brown, 1975), *Scotland and Nationalism* (C. Harvie, 1977), *The Radical Approach* (ed. G. Kennedy, 1976) and *The Break-Up of Britain* (T. Nairn, 1977), and journals such as *Scottish International Review* and *Question* applied some progressive thinking of the 1960s to a critical analysis of Scotland's political paralysis, its cultural dilemmas and its psychological preoccupations. As befits a nation of economists the political options were exhaustively assessed against their economic effects. As an active member of the Scottish National Party the optimistic rationalism of those years is symbolised for me by SNP's extended series of policy documents remaking Scotland in the image of Scandinavian social democracy.

In retrospect the defects in the intellectual foundations of this optimism appear obvious. The contradiction between the rhetoric of decentralisation and community control and the urge for a more powerful interventionist state — POWERHOUSE SCOTLAND in the headline slogan of Labour's Scottish manifesto for the Election of

October 1984 — was identified but never resolved. The powerful
impetus to individualism built into the consumer revolution was
barely acknowledged, its political ramifications not even guessed
at. English politics was assumed to be irredeemably pragmatic and
conservative. Feminism had to scramble for a place at the bottom of
the agenda. The dilemmas posed for a Nationalist movement by the
growth of international interdependence and integration were left as
vague question-marks. But if the intellect was often weak the will for
rational public debate was manifest.

By the mid-1980s the optimism had soured into despair. Here was
a nation which appeared to have lost its faith in the public role of reason, turned its back on a dazzling opportunity for economic revival
and resigned itself to chronic unemployment, spreading poverty and
political impotence. From the vantage point of the previous decade it
must have seemed that only the grim and graphic irony of Jonathan
Swift's *A Modest Proposal for Preventing the Children of Ireland from
being a Burden to their Parents or Country* was adequate to express the
depth of Scotland's humiliation.

If a *Claim of Right* for Scotland has a more modest claim to literary
fame than *A Modest Proposal* it is surely a more hopeful augury for
Scotland's future than Swift's satire was for Ireland's future.

In their Prologue the authors of the *Claim* place themselves in a
line of descent from the Scottish Claims of Right of 1689 and 1842.
Far more important is the *Claim*'s role in the modern revival of
republican thinking in Scotland. The first evidence of this revival
was the Scottish National Party's Constitution for an independent
Scotland published in the mid-1970s. It asserted the sovereign right
of the Scottish people to self-determination, laid down the principles
of a Written Constitution guaranteeing fundamental rights and liberties and provided, *inter alia*, for proportional representation, intiative
and referendum.

Notable developments of this modern tradition include Neal
Ascherson's *Ancient Britons and the Republican Dream* (1986) and
Tom Nairn's *The Enchanted Glass* (1988), each exposing the myths
and cultural stratagems by which the British, and more particularly
the English, conceal from themselves the gravity of their political
and cultural crisis.

*A Claim of Right for Scotland* makes a distinctive and very practical contribution to this modern revival of Scottish republicanism.
The first is the demolition of the presumption of Westminster's
democratic legitimacy in Scotland. It exposes the flaw in a constitution which permits — indeed through its electoral system positively encourages — the assumption, in the name of parliamentary

sovereignty, of absolute power by a party representing a minority of the voters in a General election.

In Scotland this perversion of democracy is measured by the powerlessness of parties which between them won 57% of the United Kingdom vote and 76% of the Scottish vote to redeem in Parliament their Election pledges to set up a Scottish Assembly.

The *Claim*'s second distinctive contribution to the development of republican thinking is the proposals it makes for a Constitutional Convention as a mechanism to allow the Scottish people to pursue their right of self-determination. If the *Claim* is revolutionary in its logic it is notably cautious and evolutionary in its conclusions. This caution is no doubt a by-product of the practical purpose which inspired its instigators. It was conceived by the Campaign for a Scottish Assembly not as an academic treatise on the defects of the British Constitution or relative democratic merits of popular and parliamentary sovereignty but as the intellectual underpinning of a campaign for a Scottish Assembly which would be representative of majority Scottish opinion. The fact that the Constitutional Convention has been launched — even though the composition of its crew and its course are as yet uncertain — may be considered sufficient vindication of the original project.

But the practical political purpose behind the *Claim* does appear to have blunted the subversive edge of its argument. The *Claim* is firm in its conclusion that the British Constitution offers the Scots no consistent opportunity for self-determination and that they are therefore entitled to act outwith the constitution. It is less confident in identifying the implications of the unrepresentative character of Westminster government for the individual citizen's obligation to obey the law of the land.

The moral legitimacy of democratic government derives from its observance of two principles — the inviolability of a core of individual rights and the right of the majority to determine issues of public interest consistent with those individual rights. Where either of these principles is consistently breached democracy falls. A political system in which *more often than not* a minority of voters assumes the power to govern, fails to satisfy the most basic requirement of democracy. When the elected representatives of that minority having assumed power deliberately use it to attack and undermine the values of the majority the very idea of democracy is mocked. Minority rule of this sort sacrifices the moral credit which democratic theory assigns to majority decisions.

Of course the fact that a law represents the preference of a minority does not of itself free the citizen from his obligation to obey the law.

A law passed by representatives of a minority of voters may still be a good law deserving of obedience. But it does mean that where a law passed by a minority administration offends the deeply held beliefs of individuals or groups it cannot deploy in its support the moral credit which is due in a democracy to the majority preference.

The dilemma of the individual citizen under the unrepresentative British system of government has a practical bearing on the political purpose which inspired the *Claim*. Many Scots find the policies imposed upon them by the present minority government offensive to basic moral beliefs. The more individual citizens are emboldened publicly to defy the unjust laws of an unrepresentative and in crucial ways an anti-democratic government the more likely it is the Constitutional Convention will command public sympathy when it is forced to act outwith the constitution in execution of Scotland's right of self-determination.

Perhaps the caution which the *Claim* demonstrates in extending its republican logic to the right of individual resistance is a tribute to the bourgeois character of the Committee which drafted the *Claim*. That is not intended in a dismissive sense. In the 1970s the middle classes in Scotland remained largely indifferent to, if not actively hostile to, the cause of constitutional change. The Nationalist movement suffered from the paradox that it was a bourgeois nationalism which lacked the support of any significant section of the bourgeoise. Today the capital owning and capital managing elements of the Scottish bourgeoisie remain hostile: indeed as a result of the polarisation of opinion secured by Mrs Thatcher and Michael Forsyth they are more purposefully hostile today than they were a decade ago. But under the pressure of the Thatcherite attack on Scottish institutions, particularly public sector institutions, other sections of the middle classes have been forced to reassess their political attitudes. Even so middle class support for a significant measure of constitutional change is a tender plant whose growth and flowering cannot be taken for granted. If sustained for long enough the Government's efforts to create by force of state a social and economic base for Thatcherism in Scotland may succeed.

One can imagine the passionate ambivalence with which Hugh MacDiarmid would have contemplated a radical *Claim* of Scottish Right drafted *inter alia* by a former Chief Planner at the Scottish Office, a former Permanent Under-Secretary at the Scottish Office, an Methodist clergyman, an Edinburgh Professor of Public Law, a former Foreign Office diplomat and a former chairman of the Scottish Postal Board. But such authorship reinforces the hope that the Convention can help to crystallise the sense of dislocation felt by many middle class groups in Scotland into a firm will for political change. It is this prospect which among other reasons makes a SNP withdrawal from the Convention a grave strategic error.

The launch in London of the Charter '88 with its call for constitutional reform within the United Kingdom prompted claims from some Right wing commentators that the Left had turned to constitutional tinkering, despairing of success on the ideological battle front. As we have seen the purpose of the *Claim* was to provide intellectual underpinning for a broadly based Scottish initiative for constitutional reform, not to provide a new image of democracy to challenge the ideology of 'freedom through the market'. But the political context in which the *Claim* was conceived, particularly the ideological dominance of market theories, makes it pertinent to inquire whether the *Claim* contains elements of a republican ideology capable of carrying the battle to champions of the market.

The immediate target of the *Claim*'s criticisms of Britain's system of government are the constitutional arrangements which make the Crown-in-Parliament the sole source of political legitimacy. Although alternative bases of legitimacy are not explored the *Claim* identifies the rights of the citizen as the chief victims of this monopoly:

> Every feature of the English constitution, every right the citizen has, can be changed by a simple majority of this subordinated Parliament.
>
> (*A Claim of Right for Scotland*, 4.3).

The belief that every citizen is a member of a political community of shared rights embracing individual liberties and the right to an equal share in the determination of issues in the public domain lies at the heart of the republican idea. The concept of political community as the basis of democratic rights may help to combat some of the New Right's cruder essays in market individualism. For example it helps to expose the undemocratic character of the Government's proposals to give a single generation of parents, by virtue of their role as proxy consumers, the power to remove a school from democratic control of their fellow citizens whose interest in education as a public good is no less than theirs, who have contributed through generations to build up assets of the school and who will continue to provide the funds for the school.

The Right's deployment of the individual's presumed right to choose through the market against the democratic presumption in favour of a collective determination of public issues can be countered only if the attractions of the market definition of freedom are first properly appreciated. The brief references to issues of individual

freedom contained in the *Claim* suggest that its authors may under-
estimate the appeal of market freedoms. The *Claim* asserts that there
are two kinds of choice — 'choice from what is offered and choice
of what is to be offered' (*Claim* 7.2) and asserts that stripping away
the power of politicians restores power 'not to the people but to the
powerful'.

It is doubtful whether in Britain, or in Scotland, in 1989 that
is how the majority of people actually experience the effect of
Mrs Thatcher's reforms. At least some of those reforms — the
privatisation of publicly owned industries (public utilities are a
distinct case), the sale of council houses, the Parents' Charter,
School Boards and opting-out, are as likely to be experienced as a
liberation from the bureaucratic power of public authorities than as
a subjection to powerful private interests. And if, in some areas at
least, freedom is felt to lie in choosing between the 'given' options
of the market rather than edited options of public authorities, the
issue of where the options are edited, in London or Edinburgh or
Brussels, and by whom, becomes superfluous.

The republican idea need not to be helpless before this public
perception. It can give a greater presence to the concept of political
community by reforming the electoral system to secure majority
government, by entrenching core liberties in a Bill of Rights, by
correcting some of the shortcomings of representative government,
by providing opportunities for direct democracy in form of initiative referenda or directly elected boards to supervise local services,
including School Boards elected not by the spurious community
of consumers but by the political community of citizens: and by
consolidating such changes in a Written Constitution asserting the
will of the people as the source of political legitimacy.

Secondly, republicanism's insistence that the only safeguard of
individual liberties is the community's will to defend them puts it in
a strong position to contest Mrs Thatcher's assertion that there is no
such thing as society only individuals and families. In almost every
aspect of life in a modern society the opportunities for the enjoyment
even of those goods which are indisputably private depend critically
on public policy, as the householders of Kent struggling to defend
the peace of their homes — in some cases the very existence of their
homes — from the British generation of TGV's will attest.

Thirdly, the republican idea is well equipped to contest the
colonisation of public good by private rights. The principle of
the community of citizens identifies the deliberative process of
democratic government as a public good in itself. In the same
perspective education, general culture including the arts and the

media appear as much as public good as they are private goods, while other goods such health and material prosperity contain at the least significant elements of public good.

The republican concept can be extended to issues of distributive justice. Gross inequalities of income and wealth conflict with the requirement that all members of the political community should have at least a rough equality of opportunity to participate in the determination of public issues. And the essential interdependence of the individual and the community is held by some to endow the citizen with social rights to accompany his or her political and civic rights.

However this extension of republican claims is not only theoretically problematic. From an egalitarian point of view it has the disadvantage of being open to 'minimalist' interpretations which would leave the materially less fortunate members of the community with no more than 'threshold' provision in an increasingly unequal society.

Egalitarianism needs to be supported within the republican framework by a more robust principle of distributive justice capable of responding to the dynamic of change in modern society. That 'principle' may be found to be nothing more, and nothing less, than an ethic of human solidarity creating duties to complement the citizen's political rights. In this 'social' republic each citizen will be assumed to have a core of common needs which it will be the prime purpose of the political community to meet, consistent with the principle that no citizen can accept for his fellows a level of provision lower than he judges necessary for his own welfare.

These republican speculations take us some way from the practical political concerns of the *Claim*. But Scottish self-government will be a poor thing if it is not informed by a vision of radical democracy beyond the ken of the market.

# 10

## Scotland's English Problem

CHRISTOPHER HARVIE

The summoning of a Scottish Constitutional Convention — the centre-piece of the proposals of *A Claim of Right for Scotland* — occurs in 1989, a year heavy with revolutionary auspices. We are being put on the spot, and the political consensus which has got the autonomy process so far will be put under maximum stress both by its traditional foes, the Conservatives, but also by the gathering pace of political change in Scotland, and the likely impact of world and European economic events. It is a notable irony that while the *Claim of Right* has gone on to inform the tone and purposes of the Charter '88 movement in England, the Scottish political situation which it was drafted to address has itself been changed by the revival of the Scottish National Party and its 'Independence in Europe' programme. While the Govan election and its aftermath has given the autonomy campaign an enormous boost, it has also presented the possibility of a breakdown in relations between its advocates.

The 'Independence in Europe' camp — with whom I would broadly align myself — envisage Scotland's relations with the rest of the UK, where not subsumed under the European Community, being subject to various confederal arrangements. Traditional devolutionists seem now to be moving in a federalist direction, envisaging a Britain organised on the lines of the German Federal Republic. Both of these positions can be reconciled, at least as far as the negotiation process is concerned, by the notion that the Convention puts the ball in the court of the Scottish people, not in Westminster, under the umbrella of 'renegotiation of the Union.' But the threat of a break-up is still considerable. The capacity of Constitutional Conventions to mystify and ultimately bore the voters is considerable; history is littered with their skeletons. The one that we, as Scots, contemplate, can only succeed if it is part of a political, as well as a constitutional strategy.

Recently, writing an article on Gladstone, I was struck by the fact that Gladstonian Britain, after the 'home rule' election of 1886, bore an uncanny resemblance to 'anti-Thatcher' Britain after the election of 1987. Scotland, Wales, the North East were still voting on the left. Lancashire was more radical than it had been in Gladstone's day; the West Country less so (although Alliance candidates lay close behind many Tory MPs). But the Conservatism of London and its suburbs had merged with the green fields of rustic Toryism, and swamped the rural radicalism once found among the farm labourers of East Anglia. The heart of international finance, as once the heart of empire pulsed with blue blood; the difference was that a century of demographic tilt meant that the London commuting region, which contained 25% of UK population in 1886, now contains 35%.

In 1886 the United Kingdom contained Ireland, in 1988 only Northern Ireland. The 'success', or at least the survival, of the unwritten UK Constitution was gained by thrusting out the greater part of a component nation which in 1911 would have settled for a generous measure of devolution. Many of the Conservative ineptitudes of inter-war government were due, more than is realised, to the absence of fifty-odd anti-Tory Irish MPs, and to the absence of the experience of a devolved legislature which enjoyed a fair field for political and social experiment.

The unbalanced nature of English politics is something we're going to have to come to terms with. As the *Claim of Right* eloquently pointed out, we are not seeing a constitution in malfunction but a structure of party dominance with a considerable potential for coercion. Likewise, if we observe the UK Conservative party's reactions, when its backers consider their interests threatened, we do not see a 'pillar of the constitution' in Ivor Jennings/Harold Laski terms — a great institution-of-state acceding to 'moderate', consensual leadership — but a feral creature capable of doing a lot of damage to such concepts and persons as get in its way, the 'rule of law' included. In July 1913 Bonar Law declared to the Ulster rebels:

> Whatever steps you may feel compelled to take, whether they are constitutional, or whether they are in the long run unconstitutional, you have the whole Unionist party under my leadership behind you.

A Scottish Conservative cornered has never been a pretty sight. Behind the programme of the *Claim of Right*, and the operations of the Constitutional Convention, we still have to cope with the problem of the 'predominant partner' — and we have to remember that we are only, now, at the point the Irish had, roughly, reached in 1884, before Parnell's Nationalists swept the 'English' parties away.

There are several reasons why the metropolitan English won't let Scotland go without a struggle. They would lose the transfusion of oil revenues (although so catastrophic has Nigel Lawson's trade deficit become that this isn't the argument it once was); nuclear bases and dumps would have to be relocated at appalling expense and great embarrassment to the UK's pretensions within NATO; and — not least — a Scots government would monkey around with absolute property rights in ways which would scare the City of London rigid. Any one of these could provoke Bonar Law-style reactions, and twenty years 'policing' in Northern Ireland plus nine years of unchecked elective dictatorship give the premier the means to make her presence felt. The 'I'll go away and then you'll be sorry' scenario brandished by Allan Stewart as one means of solving the Union's problems just isn't on, not with Thatcher around.

So among the essential tasks of any Constitutional Convention must be one of softening up the opposition. Nationalists don't like the sound of this very much, as it tends in the direction of 'Vote Labour and all will be well' (Neil will take a deep breath, swallow devolution, and shut up about it while it's expeditiously enacted at the head of his legislative programme). They will be right to have their suspicions, particularly about the present Labour leadership, but it will be easier to horse-trade with anyone other than Thatcher, particularly after the heels have been ca'd from under the traditional Tory verities of the constitution.

This ought to give to the Convention several specific tactical goals, i.e. goals beyond those of spelling out to the Scots electorate what the general options are:

(1) Settling on a single anti-Tory candidate in each of the remaining Tory-held Scottish seats.

(2) Giving full backing to a hard-and-fast alliance between the anti-Thatcher parties to win majorities in 60 key seats in England and Wales.

(3) Enabling publicity, sympathy and funds for the Scottish cause to be pursued in a much wider context than that of the British Isles.

To be more specific as to (1): The election in 1991 must be anticipated as a 'revolutionary' event, in which Conservative representation in Scotland is extinguished. Labour stands next to the Tories in Ayr, Stirling, Edinburgh Pentlands, and Dumfries. The Democrats are second in North Angus, West Edinburgh and Eastwood.

The SNP are second in Galloway, West Perth and North Tayside. There are, of course, problems here, as such a pact virtually implies a standstill elsewhere; a particular problem for the SNP who, after Govan, could put the finger on pratically any Labour seat, and must be raring to evict Brian Wilson or Martin O'Neill. Patience, brothers! This election is a one-off event which must set up the machinery for a definitive constitutional settlement — and if possible so put the fear of extinction into Rifkind and Co., to make the Conservatives anticipate their fate by conceding in advance. Such an electoral pact could also be used as a means of recruiting competent constitutional authorities by the main devolutionist parties 'for the duration' of the negotiations which must follow. Jim Ross, for example, could stand for Labour, Neil McCormick for the SNP. But it depends further on (2) and (3):

Disraeli always used to argue that big majorities were bad things, as more MPs got worried about losing their seats, and thus became more difficult to lead, Thus it figures that if a lot of ex-estate agents and merchant bankers face the prospect of being decanted by a centre-left pact back into now less-than-promising careers they are going to put Thatcher under increasing restraint and may even force her to go. Sans Thatcher — and her rigid discipline — the Conservative party could be very pliable indeed on this issue. Even the 'archetypal Scotch crawler' (Tom Nairn's words, alas, not mine) Andrew Neil in the *Sunday Times* has been allowing his underlings to suggest that Scots autonomy, nay independence may not be a bad thing.

This is an optimistic view, in that it suggests that Neil Kinnock (or his successor) can be persuaded to drop his veneration or 'Our Glorious Constitution' and that Paddy Ashdown will have to give up his hope of supplanting the Labour Party. But not perhaps entirely absurd: conversions to proportional representation seem to be accelerating in the Labour Party and the federal scheme reportedly developed by Alistair Darling offers a good basis for negotiations with the Democrats. Ashdown must realise that even a few good by-election results won't put him upsides with Labour in its heartlands, and Labour must feel further rigidity could lose it much of the support of the 'thinking' left — the sort of people involved in Charter '88.

Which brings us to a topic not usually discussed: home rule in England. Generally speaking, interest in English provincial federalism has been zilch. (I produced a Fabian pamphlet on this subject in 1982, which awoke zero resonance outside Scotland — which the Fabians had thoughtfully removed from the map on the cover). The

North's awakening interest in devolution can be cited as a counter-argument, yet if we plot the areas of Britain in which Labour withdrawal could hand seats to the Alliance, we find that practically half of those 'possibilities' outcrop in the West Country, an area whose radicalism has deep historical roots. Arguably, the region's tendency to vote for the non-socialist left has been strengthened by the low profile of the Labour Party over the last eighteen years (since seats like Exeter and Falmouth and Camborne were lost), and by a high seasonal unemployment rate and declining industries, things which naturally promote discontent. Even an elderly population, if anti-socialist in principle, has also got an interest in defending the welfare state, subsided public transport, etc. England west of Bristol thus seems to be shifting in rather the same direction which the Highlands took twenty-odd years ago. A Scottish Constitutional Convention would profit by inviting, and cultivating, members of English provincial local authorities, not as rivals but as potential allies. Even London, we must remember, is the seat of the former GLC and the ILEA and the cadres they once galvanised, as well as of the fat cats of the City.

This leaves the solidly Tory areas and their voters. And potentially worrying they are, in very deed. A decade of making loadsamoney or at least being in work, having the government behind you, and reading the London tabloids is not going to replicate the situation of the 1930s, where the strongly-unionised London working class was in the vanguard of British socialism. The 'enterprise culture' of the London yuppies is too firmly plugged into an international structure of exploitation to have much conscience left. If either group suffer an economic downturn through the ineptitude of their own government, they are unlikely to grasp for Keynesian remedies. The alliance of private monopolies, banks and an authoritarian political party exercising untrammelled power is too attractive to be thrown away.

Hence (3) the importance of nonparliamentary agitation, and the appeal to Europe. Our deep-rooted loyalism — and, frankly, our unwillingness to spend sensible amounts of money on politics — has held us back in this critical area. One function of the Convention, if only an informal one, must be to set up a publicity and finance organisation, with an adequate income and access to a large-scale participative membership. Our goal should be to influence Europe, an area in which Thatcherism is peculiarly vulnerable. Firstly, manufacturers seeking to integrate into the single European market will have less and less patience with the 'Little England' reactions cultivated by the Prime Minister. Secondly, if the UK economy continues its comparative decline, European institutions will be under pressure to sort it out on behalf of European businesses which have invested in British companies. Thirdly, it's already the case that insistence on a Scots identity acts as a certain indemnifier against being identified with Thatcher.

All of these resources for propaganda have to be developed, at the commercial, diplomatic and cultural level. The extent to which distinctive Scottish business views will be reflected by autonomous representation in Brussels partly explains the Government's lack of enthusiasm for the idea. This may also be explained by the absence of reliable Conservative chaps to man such a legation, and consequent reliance on bodies like the Scottish Council: Development and Industry. While it isn't beyond Rifkind to pack such bodies with his own creatures, even he must be made to acknowledge that dim reliability has its limitations in the representation game.

Furthermore, we can exploit the links already built up with communities in Europe, such as town-twinnings, university and regional exchanges. Glasgow's transfiguration into European cultural capital in 1990 will mean that in 1989-1990 Scotland will anyway have a much higher European profile, and a much higher capacity to embarrass the UK government. Saatchi and Saatchi should not have the last word.

Finally, we can usefully study historical examples in order to alert the international community to the Scottish issue. In the nineteenth century the cause of Italian nationality thrived because it was directly represented by articulate propagandists in the major European capitals, London and Paris; the Irish struggle for independence was similarly assisted by the mobilisation of the exile community, especially in Britain, the United States and Australia. In 1905, when Finland was threatened with 'Russification', Finnish intellectuals organised an effective mobilisation of academics throughout the world to protest against this. In the period during which preparations are made for the Constitutional Convention, it is essential that such a 'menu' of possibilities be drafted, and, if we are to think in terms of strategy and tactics, it is no bad idea to make the menu as broad as possible, to keep the enemy guessing, uncertain as to where the main thrust of our attack will come!

# 11

## A Glimpse of the Promised Land

TOM GALLAGHER

*A Claim of Right for Scotland* is a splendidly evocative title for a document which not only spells out how the inhabitants of Scotland have become disempowered in their own land — the easy bit — but offers a persuasive strategy for halting and reversing this perilous situation.

Paradoxically, one of its strengths is that it is not *clamorous* nor *self-righteous*. Thus it is difficult to imagine it being less like the revealing 1988 'Sermon at Bruges' delivered by the embattled leader of a shrinking power determined that Britain should stand once more against the rest of Europe.

Scots driven by a national purpose have not always avoided resembling their chief external antagonist in choice of symbols and basic posture. This sane and tightly argued document runs no such risk and succeeds in bringing Scottish emotion and reason into healthy alignment. It is a tremendous inducement for the emergence of an enabling patriotism that becomes a political as well as an emotional expression.

Not the least of its qualities is its refusal to advance the claim of the Scots at the expense of other political communities, nor does it diminish the worth of others, by which I mean our nearest land-based neighbours. Snide or superior comments about 'the poor brainwashed English' are absent. The present critical impasse is seen as political in origin rather than racial: a parliamentary system upon which hinges every right a citizen possesses has consistently allowed basic liberties in many areas of life to be whittled away or terminated: this is because it is subordinate to a government which has no higher view of parliament than as a conveyor belt for policies now undoing the paternalistic settlement that allowed the British state to get along for so long without a written constitution.

It is no coincidence that Scotland has displayed the greatest resistance to the infringement or removal of economic, social, or political
rights that millions of citizens once took for granted. After all,the
testing ground for many government policies which, when stripped
of their radical or emancipatory gloss, are designed to 'restore power
to the powerful' has been there. The replacement of the enabling
state with the coercive state rests particularly ill on the Scots since,
long before the emergence of Keir Hardie and the Labour Party, the
state played a vital role in knitting together the Scots and helping
to form a national community. Memories of statehood have been
persistent and enduring helped by the fact that 'the boundaries of
Scotland have been fixed for centuries and within Scotland there
are laws and policies which apply nowhere else' (7.4). Perhaps it
might be added that the cool Scottish climate, the unyeilding soil,
and the absence of natural resources that were easily exploitable,
also obliged the inhabitants of a poor nation to draw upon values
other than material ones. Of course, the Scottish past is not easily
summarised and it has provided enough consolation for the occu-
pant of the seat of power to proclaim that 'the Scots were the first
Thatcherites'; however, the electoral performance of the governing
party in Scottish seats where people are likely to have 'stood on their
own two feet' does not say much for the vitality of this tradition.

Neither does the document minimise the difficulties in restoring
a self-governing forum to Scotland. In this respect, the framers have
more respect than some politicians have for the judgment of the Scottish people who are instinctively aware of how determined and even
ruthless the regime which exercises its writ over them is prepared to
be when the occasion warrants it. Invaluable work has been done by
the former to counteract doubts which have been sewn in the minds
of the people when confronted by the mighty apparatus of London
power. The myths, potent in their day, that self-government in any
meaningful form would be a slippery slope to 'separatism' or else
would result in wasteful over-government, or else lead to the constitutional anomaly known as 'the West Lothian Question' are dealt
with here more convincingly than anywhere else I know of. A Claim
of Right *ensures that it will be far less easy to foster them in the future*.

Because it is the view of the signatories that Scotland 'faces a crisis
of identity and survival', flabby thinking or judgments coloured by
emotion do not intrude very far. By the time I reached 8.4 the
precision of the assessment even made me take seriously a view
which has not impressed me when voiced by others:

> we fully understand the pressure for refusal to comply with
> the requirements of the poll tax legislation. . .But we do not

believe that random rejection of the law on particular issues is
the answer to the problems facing Scotland. . .

Resistance to one mischief [8.5] will not prevent other mischiefs and may well fail because it does not address the real
weakness of the Government's case.

I needed less persuading when they mentioned the obstacles in
the way of restructuring the state in a democratic manner presented
by a voting system that places enormous power in the hands of a
Prime Minister whom a large majority of the electorate may have
voted against. My own party has benefited even more resoundingly
from this electoral lottery (69% of the Scottish seats on 43% of the
vote, due allowance being made for tactical voting) than the English
Conservatives and there is plenty of evidence to show how this warps
judgment and narrows the range of MPs in terms of background and
ability.

Having described in sober terms how a defective political system
(pre-dating the present incumbent of Downing St. but whose failings have been magnified by her actions) threatens the economic
future and political liberties of Scotland, the document argues that
a just remedy lies in restoring to Scotland a meaningful degree of
self-determination. *How to go about fulfilling this goal is the key part
of the text.*

No other approach is likely to prove as effective as setting up
a Constitutional Convention with the task of creating a Scottish
Assembly. In a situation where such an assembly is denied to them
even when Scots vote for it overwhelmingly and the majority of the
United Kingdom electorate backs parties that endorse it, we are left
with no alternative but to create our own constitutional machinery.
Its work of persuading the government is viewed as the most important part of the convention's remit. It must also achieve acceptance
by those for whom it proposes to speak and act. Civil disobedience
is not to be ruled out but only as part of an orderly programme to
work towards an Assembly. These are first principles that are likely
to produce strenuous debate but it is yet another sign of the clarity
of thinking underlying the document that they have been set out so
comprehensively.

What is a constitutional convention, how can it be set up, and what
are its specific tasks each are central questions tackled in depth; the
record of such bodies as they have emerged to fill the democratic gap
when the government of an existing state has partly or wholly failed
is traced from the US prototype in the 1770s down to the Northern
Ireland Convention of 1975 which was set up by a British government even though the local demand for it was miniscule compared

with the backing that it enjoys in Scotland. It says a lot for the British government's respect for popular opinion that a campaign of violence by an unrepresentative minority helped shape a response which has been stubbornly unforthcoming in Scotland despite the overwhelming verdict of the ballot box in favour of a parliament for Scotland.

Different precedents show that the creation of a constitutional convention is *a normal response* to the failure of democratic government, one far less drastic than the insurrectionary means whereby the present British state was created in 1688. But there is no standard pattern or formula, local traditions and circumstances largely determining this. The strength of a tradition of peaceful civil disobedience in recent Scottish history (ranging from Highland land raids, Glasgow rent strikes to the work-in at the UCS Govan shipyard), leads me to think that this initiative of 1989 can set down enduring roots in Scottish clay.

The architects of *A Claim of Right* come from many different walks of life. Presumably, in a self-governing context, they would not be ranged together on all issues. Perhaps in drafting this manifesto they had to resolve differences over outlook and strategy. If so, it is a tribute to their constructive endeavours that they have produced a guide so appropriate to Scotland's requirements at this crucial juncture.

I would even venture to say that if the politicians, whose role is now likely to be *the* critical one, display the same co-operative spirit, then the momentum for a self-governing forum could well become unstoppable. *Self-government is surely there for the asking if Scotland's political representatives want it hard enough that they manage to act in concert and shelve normal disagreements.* Of course our adversary is a powerful one but unaccountable regumes with tyrannical pretensions have been forced to relinquish control to democratic resistance movements with far less going for them than is the case in Scotland.

The strength of our cause will be augmented if it is recognised that allies are to be found, often in unexpected places. Already *A Claim of Right* has been hailed by radical democratic elements in England as a tremendous boost for their growing campaign to reconstitute the state on a more democratic and participatory basis. The evidence that strong antipathy to Scottish aspirations is harboured by the English remains very inconclusive. The decisive opposition that scuppered devolution at the end of the 1970s came from Scottish politicians based in the south or from those who viewed attempting to tamper with the Westminster system as bordering on the sacreligious. I do not think that Margaret Thatcher would find it easy to stir up resentment against the Scots — 'the enemy within that wants to get away' — unless it is made easy for her.

Scottish objectives are likely to be accomplished with more despatch if England becomes the scene of organised pressure to decentralise and re-democratise and, not least, to redefine what constitutes English patriotism and the 'national interest'. I agree that 'it is a mistake to suppose [epilogue]. . .that the route to reform must lie through simultaneous reorganisation of the government of all parts of the United Kingdom. . .', but tactical alliances with English confederates are worth pursuing. If they prove of good account, the message might at last be relayed to the rest of Europe that Mrs Thatcher's narrow chauvinism is a minority English view — albeit a vigorous one — a message which is surely overdue in order to reduce the distinct possibility — in my view — that European politicians of similar undemocratic temper will seek to emulate her by piling up votes on a tide of right-wing populist nationalism.

The need for external partnerships such as these becomes more pressing if the pulse of the Scots is taken to determine the collective temperature of the nation. A growing sense of outrage at what is being done to them is paralleled by a numbing feeling of despair about whether anything can be truly done to redeem the situation. Trends in western capitalist society since the 1950s from the decline of neighbourhood-orientated housing to the growth of a mass culture centred around private forms of consumption, have weakened the bases of solidarity among ordinary citizens. The experience of the blacks in the USA of the 1980s — far worse under Reagan than that of the Scots under Thatcher — perhaps bears this out. Who would have thought that the community which fought for, and won, political emancipation in the 1960s would put up with policies that now condemn them to being an economic underclass? Yet a process of economic depoliticisation has been at work as drugs, gang warfare, and rampant materialism smother radical impulses; it was exemplified for me by a recent small incident when Jesse Jackson's daughter, on arriving at college, met two blacks of her own age who were under the impression that Martin Luther King has been an old-time black singer.

The Anglo-American hold over mass culture — enormously important for shaping the context of politics — has increased even as an undeniable revival has occurred in Scottish popular and high culture that has been able to respond to the latest mediums of cultural expression. National consciousness still needs to be politicised, the Scottish cringe banished to the cellar. Among many desperate for better times, there is often the despairing feeling that the British state is the norm, even if it does not offer elementary justice or hold out the prospect for a decent life. There is little realisation that small nations blessed with less resources than Scotland can and do stand on their own two feet perhaps because mobile Scots tend to gravitate towards the large states making up the Anglo-American world. Even though the ancestors of not a few Scots hailed from Scandinavia, its potent experience is still beyond their comprehension — a terrible loss.

Much scope remains for deepening national solidarity which remains a *sine qua non* if Scotland is to be completely independent some day. A pervasive sense of Britishness is still reproduced in Scotland by the monarchy, the army, the presence of as many as a million Scots in the rest of Britain and, the oft neglected fact that the Scottish public sector is recruited from the British labour market; not surprisingly, there are workers in the public sector, increasingly aware, from their own everyday experiences, that Scotland is treated not much differently from a colony, and who are reluctant to speak in outright nationalist terms out of a desire not to alienate colleagues who hail from England.

Nationalists are imprudent if they fail to realise just how Scottish consciousness is impaired by its powerful neighbour and if they choose to remain deaf to the possibilities that the whole convention initiative holds out for placing Scottish awareness on a much higher plane. Understandably, many of them are straining at the leash after the past ten miserable years and are keen to press their maximalist demands now that the pendulum seems to be swinging their way. But if (by the time this is published), the convention initiative is discounted as an irrelevancy or has been exploited for short-term electoral purposes, I fear that a blunder of historic magnitude will have been committed. *A Claim of Right* does not rule out independence or dismiss it as an aspiration unworthy of the Scots, but it makes a convincing case for the view that a gradualist strategy should first be attempted, one that stands an excellent change of uniting a formidable array of Scots and attracting the participation of those whose voices are rarely heard.

If the debate is polarised between independence or union, then the advocates of the status quo will be occupying their own ground which they know well how to defend. *A Claim of Right* comprehensively rejects the numbing — and very British — formula that there can only be two sides to the great public questions of the day rather than a range of options and possibilities dependent on forces that are often in a state of flux. The care and deliberation with which the report has been draughted makes me think that its authors have sized up their opponents well. Beyond the veneer of reasonableness, it is easy to forget that the Whitehall state has a veritable arsenal of devices to wear down, confuse, or intimidate those who wish to remove its clammy hand from their affairs. At least until recent times Scotland has only glimpsed a small quantity of the black arts that the most feline and cunning of states has developed during centuries of imperial adventure and conquest.

*Inducements* as well as threats might be used with devastating effect. It may be too early to say whether elements of divide-and- rule are contained in the promotion of Glasgow for a mainly southern audience. The partial and incomplete revival of the city has gratified this native son, especially where its hard-pressed citizens have gained some benefit, but it is a very open question whether Glasgow's place in Scottish life will be strengthened by current trends. Not enough people are aware that the manipulation of cultural life is a major concern of the guardians of the state. The Highland threat was defused by subverting its traditions and turning them into a badge of submission; time will quickly show if Glasgow, the Celtic city *par excellence* is on the receiving end of similar treatment.

It goes without saying that hard thinking needs to be carried out to anticipate British skullduggery. This is perhaps the job of the politicians and analysts who know the Westminster–Whitehall jungle and are surprised by little that moves in it. It would be a fitting way to complement and extend the work of those who initiated *A Claim of Right*.

If the great possibilities contained in this document are vitiated by internal discord among those empowered to breathe life into its proposals, it will not be the end for Scotland. It is in the nature of a situation whereby much of Scotland is treated as an economic and cultural colony that other opportunities for effective resistance are likely to emerge. But, in the meantime, another brick will have been shoved into the powerful psychological construct that we Scots do not have what it takes to shape our own political future, that so many of us are born to encounter disappointment or defeat unless we forsake our native land.

Hopefully, the vision and sense of service which animates this document will be conveyed to the political parties: when I see Scots of all ages marooned on the streets of London as far from salvation as shipwrecked sailors on a desert island, I reserve part of the blame for domestic politicians *whose lack of vision* prevents them from seeing the awful damage their bickering over inessentials has done to the Scottish will to resist, while recognising that the major fault lies with an economic system that buys and sells people only to discard them when their labour ceases to be of value.

Perhaps it is not too much to hope that a few more people will be encouraged to enter the political process for whom this route has previously meant opportunism and dishonour. Among the young especially, the need to become active citizens has probably never been greater given the strong cultural conditioning towards leading me-centred lives. Alienation from the political process is a real danger, leading not necessarily to violence but to numbing apathy and a sense of despair. If this document draws more people into politics, the quality of political discussion is likely to be improved along with its representative character.

Too often the only road to freedom in this politically pathless land has been the one conveying *departing* Scots who despair of fulfilling their potential in their own land. By clearing a path through the thickets of Scottish politics, the architects of *A Claim of Right* have revealed a glimpse of an alternative future which could become an attainable prospect if public representatives show the wisdom and solidarity that helped to make this document possible.

# 12

## Educating the English

JOHN OSMOND

'Within the United Kingdom the Scots are a minority which can never feel secure...'[1]

This assertion, near the centre of the tightly worded argument in *A Claim of Right for Scotland*, is particulary striking when viewed from Wales. If it is true of Scotland, a country with such a relatively coherent framework for its identity, then how much more true is it for the Welsh?

Seen from Wales the Scots appear to possess an enviable clarity concerning who they are. Internally, Scotland may be riven by differences — Highland and Lowland East coast and West coast, islands and borders, Lallans and Gaelic — but outside their country they are just Scots and operate, most effectively, on that basis. In contrast the Welsh seem to have a prior loyalty to their local community, their 'bro', even when viewing Wales from the outside. The Welsh, in fact, have great difficulty in imagining their country as a whole, let alone in acting on the principle.

It is often said, for instance, that a person is 'very Welsh', as defined by linguistic fluency but more often by accent, and these attributes are generally linked to an idea of 'Welsh' Wales being towards the west and north of the country.

Geography, history and institutions account for the contrast. Wales is part of southern Britain. For the Romans it was a frontier zone, but nevertheless occupied by them: the Welsh language is the product of a mix between the old Brythonic and Latin. Wales was conquered by the Normans and later there was no Act of Union, but one of Incorporation of Wales into England, in 1536. The Welsh border, especially in the north, is close to major centres of English population. Cardiff, the capital city, is but two hours on a train to London.

Even in medieval history Wales only fleetingly possessed

institutions that covered the country as a whole. We celebrate Princes of the regions of Wales rather than Kings. The old Welsh laws of inheritance distributed property equally amongst all a man's sons rather than just the eldest, which promoted the dispersal of power in the community. The main fact, however, is that the separate system of Welsh law did not survive beyond 1536: Wales is ruled by English law and has no distinctive legal institutions. The Welsh education system is also indistinguishable from the English, apart from that conducted through the medium of the Welsh language.

Welsh identity has been carried mainly by a separate language and nonconformity in religion, rather than a distinctive network of institutions. The consequence is that the Welsh have virtually no sense of Welsh citizenship, even of the kind that may only be vestigial in Scotland. And in the 20th Century the two vehicles of inheritance have faltered in their tracks: the language has declined from being spoken by a majority of the population to around 20 per cent, and Wales like the rest of Britain, has become a secular rather than religious society.

It has been argued, not least by the author[2], 'that there has been compensation in the creation of an astonishing range of institutions since World War II that do assume an all-Wales territory and sensibility. Most importantly has been the Welsh Office. Created in 1964 this now controls an annual budget in excess of £3,500 million, a figure representing some 80 per cent of public expenditure in Wales, and administered by 2,300 civil servants. Moreover, most of the money is not spent by the Welsh Office by itself, but in conjunction with local government (eight counties and 37 districts) and a panoply of quangos ranging from eight health authorities to the Welsh Development Agency, the Welsh Water Authority, the Wales Tourist Board and the Welsh Arts Council, to name only twelve.

It might be thought that, as a consequence of the 1979 referendum — in which the Welsh voted four-to-one against an Assembly — the process of establishing new national institutions and extending the role of the Welsh Office might have drawn to a close. In fact, the reverse has occurred. Not only have both processes gained a fresh dynamic, but an entirely new dimension has been added as post-1979 Secretaries of State for Wales have demonstrated a new commitment to promote industrial regeneration in Wales. Post 1979 Wales has been marked by three related developments entailing the establishment of new national institutions, extending the responsibilities of the Welsh Office, and the formation of distinct strategies by Welsh Office Ministers aimed at securing economic regeneration.

In terms of the creation of new national institutions, 1979

inaugurated a phase of accentuated development, involving initially the establishment of S4C — the Welsh Fourth Channel — followed by a national body to oversee Welsh medium education and latterly the Welsh Language Board to promote the Welsh language more generally. Within the media Radio Wales and Radio Cymru, created as comprehensive channels in the mid-1970s have gained audiences in the 1980s, and efforts are being made to increase the proportion of English language programming on BBC Wales and HTV Wales. Wales does not have an integrated home newspaper network, as in Scotland, but during 1989 a new national Sunday paper is being launched, adding to Welsh-based daily newspapers in north and south Wales.

Earlier in the 1980s all-Wales bodies to promote health education and sites of historical interest were established. And as the 1980s were drawing to a close a National Curriculum Council, a Welsh Committee of the UK University Funding Council, and an all-Wales Housing body, Tai Cymru (Housing for Wales) were being created.

Within the Welsh Office and its related institutions there was a similar process of development. The most important occurred in the immediate wake of the referendum with the Welsh Office securing responsibility of a block grant for its expenditure responsibilities which it negotiates each year directly with the Treasury. Previously, the Welsh Office had been locked into the expenditure priorities of the Whitehall departments in the key areas of its responsibility such as education, health, housing roads, agriculture and economic development.

At the same time the Welsh Development Agency has been elaborated through the establishment of WINvest (to attract inward investment into Wales) and WINtech (to promote technological development within Welsh industry). Two further ventures, involving public sector initiative and participation, have been established in the financial arena. Hafren Investment Finance was created as a subsidiary to the WDA in 1982, whilst the Welsh Development Capital (Management) was made a joint venture between the WDA and the Development Capital Group in 1985 — both initiatives being attempts to cater for the financial need of Welsh industry. Alongside such developments were the creation in the late 1980s, by private sector and media interests, of the independent Institute of Welsh Affairs and the St David's Forum, both aimed at promoting research, debate and communication among Welsh policy makers.

With this economic and administrative infrastructure in place the key development in post-1979 Wales has been the promotion of strategies aimed at achieving autonomous Welsh economic regeneration.

For Nicholas Edwards, Secretary of State between 1979 and 1987, this entailed a commitment to use the Welsh Office to establish links between industry, the venture capital market and the University of Wales, with the WDA maintaining a supportive role. Peter Walker, who succeeded Edwards in the wake of the 1987 general election, has maintained this approach: it is clear, for example, that his insistence that a separate Welsh Committee of the New University Funding Council be established was part of this strategy to secure economic regeneration. The main thrust, however, is being carried by the targeting of resources: on the completion of the A55 dual carriageway across North Wales: the Cardiff Bay Development Project, comprising a £1,700 million investment in the 1990s and the construction of a barrage across the mouth of the Taff; and the Valleys Initiative, involving another estimated £1,500 million in the 1990s.

In the light of the above, the increasing reliance of Welsh identity upon a growing institutional infrastructure, it is sobering to read the dismissal of the same process in relation to Scotland in the *Claim of Right*.

> The apparent strengthening of Scottish institutions of government since 1885; the creation of a Secretary of State, the enlargement of the functions of the Scottish Office, the extension of Scottish Parliamentary Committees; has been accompanied by an increasing centralisation and standardisation of British government practice which has more than offset any decentralisation of administrative units.[3]

Earlier the document declared that the Secretary of State 'may be either Scotland's man in the Cabinet or the Cabinet's man in Scotland, but in the last resort he is invariably the latter'.[4] Perceptions in Wales are different and the reason is plainly because here we are nowhere near 'the last resort' of threatening the stability of the State as is the case in Scotland. On the contrary, the senior British unionist party, the Conservatives, recognise special advantages and opportunities in identifying themselves more strongly with the politics of Wales. This must be the main underlying explanation for the striking contrast in the profile adopted by the Conservatives in Wales compared with Scotland. It is not just a question of the contrasting stye and personalities of two Secretaries of State as admittedly different as Peter Walker and Malcolm Rifkind.

The interventionist approach to the Welsh economy, outlined above, is being built on the basis of annual increases in the Welsh budget. In the Autumn of 1988 Peter Walker boasted that he was pushing spending in Wales during 1989-90 to an 'all-time record' of £3.79 billion — 9.8 per cent higher than the figure estimated for 1988-89. It is clear that Peter Walker, who actually believes in 'the creative use of political power to improve the standard of living of the masses'[5], is playing a Welsh card in the Cabinet.

There is concern within Mrs Thatcher's Conservative Party of being seen as overwhelmingly an English party within the United Kingdom, and more than that a southern English party. The concern is highlighted by the poor showing of the Conservatives in Scotland, where there is little prospect of improvement at the next general election.

In Wales, however, it is a different matter. Here there is a possibility of increasing the present Welsh Conservative contingent of eight seats — Labour currently have 24, Plaid Cymru and Democrats three each. The Conservatives could win Brecon and Radnor, a Democrat seat, on a swing of just 0.05 per cent. Clwyd South (Labour) needs a 1.1 per cent swing for a Conservative win; Newport West (Labour) needs a three per cent swing; Carmarthen (Labour) four per cent; Montgomery (Democrat) 4.05 per cent; and Wrexham (Labour) 4.1. per cent.

If the Conservatives were to make gains of this order at the next general election, it would be a powerful boost for the party to claim it was reversing the trend of recent years of its strength and identity being concentrated in just southern England. This potential has created an opening to enable Peter Walker to create an entirely different interventionist image for the Conservatives in Wales from the one that Malcolm Rifkind has pursued in Scotland. It is a strategy that has left Labour, the major political force in Wales, uncertain how to respond and lacking a clear focus for its opposition to the Government.

*A Claim for Right for Scotland* acknowledges that economic disparities within the United Kingdom, and argument over how best they might be reduced, are at the heart of the debate concerning a Scottish Assembly. In this area, however, the document does not press the point far enough. It could have argued more strongly that politics and the political/constitutional structure are central to understanding the reasons why there is so much concentration of wealth, power and the resources of the whole United Kingdom in just the south-eastern corner of England — to the detriment of the rest of England, let alone Scotland and Wales.

*A Claim of Right* notes:

> Since before the Second World War, British Governments have acknowledged the need for regional policies. Doubts are beginning to arise as to whether the present British Government

acknowledges that need, yet the need is as great as ever and may intensify when the Single European Act comes into force.[6]

Yet it is not just a question of the efficacy of regional economic policies to ameliorate the problems of the outlying parts of the UK economy. Rather it is the existence of active investment policies being pursued as a form of positive discrimination in favour of south-eastern England. This is quite simply the budget wielded by the Ministry of Defence whose size outstrips by massive proportions what has been spent on traditional regional economic policy. For instance, the equipment budget alone of the Ministry of Defence amounted to some £8.3 billion in 1985-6 (spending on regional economic policy in the UK was halved between 1979 and 1986, cut by £1 billion, and being halved again by 1990)[7]. The defence equipment budget accounts for about half the output of the aerospace and some 20 per cent of the electronics industries in Britain, and an enormous number of jobs, especially in research and development establishments.

It is, of course, the geographical spread of the defence spending that is the most sobering reality so far as Scotland, Wales and northern England are concerned. England, south of a line drawn from the Severn to the Wash accounted for 68 per cent of it in 1985-6 — the South-West 11 per cent, East Anglia 3 per cent and the South-East a staggering 54 per cent. In contrast northern England received 15 per cent; the Midlands 9 per cent; Scotland 6 per cent; and Northern Ireland and Wales came bottom of the pile with just 1 per cent each.[8] The Ministry of Defence budget is, in practice, an unofficial regional economic policy, working to the advantage of the South-East of England.

Partly in response to such underlying inequities in the distribution of resources within the United Kingdom, but more clearly in reaction to a decade of Conservative rule from London, devolution began to creep back on to the Welsh political agenda in the late 1980s. The first signs came from within the higher reaches of Welsh local government when a number of senior figures publicly declared a change of mind on a Welsh Assembly in the wake of the 1987 general election. In 1979 Welsh local government had been very largely opposed to an Assembly, seeing it as a first step to a merging of the eight Welsh counties and 37 Welsh districts into a single tier. However, the effect of years of Conservative centralisation of local authority power and finance into Whitehall changed perceptions. The Labour leader of Gwent county council, Lloyd Turnbull, for instance, declared: 'I chaired and spoke at most of Neil Kinnock's anti-devolution meetings in this country in 1979. But I've changed

my mind and would now campaign the other way.' Another oppo-
nent of an Assembly in 1979, John Alison, Labour leader of West
Glamorgan county council, said 'I'm not a Welsh nationalist and I am
not talking about our separate history and culture. Now, though, our
democracy is being assailed. Because of government policies, areas
are being deprived of services they want and are prepared to pay for,
and which are available in the south-east of England.'9

Another indication of a change of heart on the question came
in the House of Commons when an Early Day motion tabled
by Social and Liberal Democrat MP for Ceredigion and North
Pembrokeshire, Geraint Howells, in July 1988 soon attracted a
majority of the signatures of Welsh MPs. The motion urges the
Government 'to bring forward proposals to devolve power to the
people of Wales, so that they will have their own parliament before
the century is out.' Among those who signed were some who had
campaigned actively against an Assembly in 1979. The Labour MP
for Caerphilly, Ron Davies, was one. He quoted a slogan painted on
a railway bridge in his constituency — 'We voted Labour. We got
Thatcher.' He conceded that no Assembly could offer full protection
against the onslaughts of a Tory government, but in conjunction with
pressure from Assemblies in Scotland and also the North of England
it could offer some defence. Another who switched sides was the
Labour MP for Wrexham, John Marek. 'The climate was wrong
last time,' he said. 'But now we've had nine years of Mrs Thatcher
centralising power to London. We must have real decentralisation of
economic power to a Welsh Assembly with revenue raising powers
as well. Both were missing in the 1979 proposals'.10

Opinion poll evidence on support for a Welsh Assembly is sketchy.
However in November 1988 BBC Wales's *Public Account* current
affairs programme announced the results of a second poll on the
issue, following one it had held just prior to the June 1987 general
election. To the question, 'Would you vote for or against an elected
Assembly for Wales with substantial powers over public spending?'
the replies, in percentages, were (with those for June, 1987 in brack-
ets):11

| | | |
|---|---|---|
| Yes | 48% | (41%) |
| No | 10% | (10%) |
| Undecided | 22% | (27%) |
| Would not vote | 20% | (22%). |

At the same time as this poll was being undertaken a Campaign for
a Welsh Assembly, modelled closely on the Cmpaign for a Scottish
Assembly, was being launched. A grassroots affair, it had sprung
up in the wake of the 1987 general election as a response to much

the same sentiments articulated above by local government and parliamentary figures. Before coming together to formally launch the Campaign at a public meeting in Merthyr in November 1988, its leader had created some 20 small informal groups in all parts of Wales. At the Merthyr meeting the Campaign, which has in membership people from all parties other than the Conservatives, adopted an objective precisely similar to that of the Scottish campaign: 'to secure the broadest understanding and support for the creation of a directly elected legislative Assembly or Parliament for Wales, with such powers as may be desired by the people of Wales.'[12]

In early 1989 the Campaign circulated a letter to all Welsh local authorities canvassing support and outlining four reasons why Welsh devolution was once more on the agenda:

— Increasing concern that the powers of local government are being eroded, especially in the fields of housing, education and economic development, and being handed over to Welsh Office-appointed quangos. Imposition of the poll-tax will substantially undermine what little financial discretion local authorities have left.

— While the powers of local authorities decline, those of the Welsh Office and its appointed quangos increase ... Here is, in practice, a tier of bureaucratic government already operating at the all-Wales level and largely unaccountable to democratically expressed opinion.

— Greater understanding that a fully integrated economic strategy, to ensure the balanced development of a Welsh economy as a whole, is unlikely to materialise without the political force mobilised by a democratically elected Welsh Assembly.

— A growing appreciation that as integration between the nation-states within the European Community develops apace, beyond 1992 the case for a democratic Welsh voice in Brussels and Strasbourg will become unanswerable. Britain is now the only large EC member-state not to have an evolving Regional Structure of Government between its central and more local levels...

This last reference to the European Community dimension is an indication that the politics of devolution are ultimately a matter of identity. One of the striking contrasts between Wales and Scotland is that the Welsh feel more strongly British alongside feeling Welsh. There are signs that, as in Scotland, the British dimension of their identity is being replaced, perhaps blended, with a wider European sensibility. In turn, and just as in Scotland, this is allowing a more imaginative approach to the potential for creating a democratic political community based upon Wales as an entity within the European Community.

The virtue and the challenge of a *A Claim of Right for Scotland* is that it offers a sharply defined constitutional route for addressing both the economic inequities and the politics of identity that characterise the governance of the United Kingdom. The Scots, it says 'must create their own constitutional machinery'[13] and 'create for themselves a focus of resistance and political negotiation'[14]. In so doing the Scots will lever open an opportunity for the other peoples and communities of the United Kingdom, not least the Welsh. For, as the *Claim of Right* concludes:[15]

> The crucial questions are power and consent: making power accountable and setting limits to what can be done without general consent. These questions will not be adequately answered in the United Kingdom until the concentration of power that masquerades as 'the Crown in Parliament' has been broken up.

In its proposals for a Constitutional Convention *A Claim of Right* offers a political route for the constitutional leverage that is so desperately required.

The report also rightly points out it can happen in Scotland first. There is no need, as it puts it, for simultaneous reorganisation of the government of all parts of the United Kingdom. However, the claims of Scotland will be most effectively met if it is recognised that they entail important and progressive changes for the rest of the peoples of the United Kingdom as well: for the Welsh; for the communities of the northern part of Ireland; and, not least, for the English. As usual the English will be the last to become aware of the realities that face them. The Scots and the Welsh have a common interest in their education.

Notes

1. *A Claim of Right for Scotland*, paragraph 4.8.
2. See 'The Dynamic of Institutions' in John Osmond (ed) *The National Question Again — Welsh Political Identity in the 1980s*, Gomer Press, 1985. A more contemporary analysis is Emyr W.Williams' 'The State without The People — On the challenge confronting the Campaign for a Welsh Assembly', *Planet* 69, June/July 1988, available from P.O.Box 44, Aberystwyth.
3. *A Claim of Right for Scotland*, paragraph 2.8.
4. Ibid, paragraph 2.7.

5. The words are those of Joseph Chamberlain, quoted favourably by Peter Walker in his book *Trust the People*.

6. *A Claim of Right for Scotland* paragraph 5.6.3.

7. See John Osmond, *The Divided Kingdom*, Constable, 1988, pages 51-4.

8. Ibid.

9. John Osmond, 'Dreaded Devoultion. . .Back on the Agenda' in *Planet* no 65, October/November 1987

10. John Osmond, 'Wind of Change Blowing in Favour of Devolution'. *Western Mail*, Cardiff, 18 July 1988

11. Results reported in the *Western Mail* 17 December 1988.

12. Details of the Campaign for a Welsh Assembly can be obtained from its secretary Maldwyn Pate, 53 Alfred Street, Roath, Cardiff.

13. *A Claim of Right for Scotland*, paragraph 6.10.

14. Ibid., paragraph 8.5.

15. Ibid., Epilogue.

# 13

## For My Fellow English

BERNARD CRICK

For myself, I am a deliberate immigrant to Scotland because I came to love the country. I gave up a job to live in Scotland not to take a job. But so different is the culture, and so strong my Englishness, that however Scottish my political and constitutional views have become (for good reasons, as I'll seek to convince you), I am now, to be honest, too old to believe that I'll ever think of myself or be thought of as Scottish, as my young college friends in the late 1940s, whose Jewish patents had sent them from Germany as young children, were already English. (If, of course, it ever came to that, I'd take up citizenship at once in an independent Scotland, though I'd probably have voted against it.) At the heart of the matter there is, what Mrs Thatcher cannot grasp, or only grasp in an English context, national feeling, indeed nationalism. But nationalism does not necessarily imply separation. Most Scots, like most Welsh, have an intense sense of dual identity, and for most purposes live with it comfortably, indeed find an enhanced quality of life in being able to live in two worlds, enjoy two cultures and their hybrids. But they perceive this, of course, as being Scottish and British, not Scottish and English. The real difficulty is that this sense of dual identities is not shared by most of the English.

The English immigrant in Scotland should be very sensitive to the 'English-for-British' linguistic and cultural well. My tongue often betrays me. But there is such a thing as being so sensitive that reality is obscured. The heart warms to the honest clarity of mind of the third paragraph of *A Claim of Right for Scotland* (an exemplary piece of political thinking, even if almost totally ignored by the London media — they don't yet take the issue seriously and they don't read much):

> In this report we frequently use the word 'English' where the word 'British' is conventionally used. We believe this clarifies

many issues which the customary language of British government obscures. Although the Government of the United Kingdom rests nominally with a 'British' Parliament, it is impossible
to trace in the history or procedures of that Parliament any constitutional influence other than an English one. Scots are apt to
bridle when 'Britain' is referred to as 'England'. But there is a
fundamental truth in this nomenclature which Scots ought to
recognise — and from which they ought to draw appropriate
conclusions.

I now want to draw the appropriate conclusions for my fellow
English, or more formally to consider the consequences of *A Claim of
Right* for the constitution of the United Kingdom as a whole. It does,
indeed, call into question the whole character of the constitutional
settlement that followed 1688 and 1707. And this is precisely why
many English Conservatives so vehemently oppose any Devolution
or Home Rule, as well as why most Scots and a growing minority of English (I mean a probable majority of those who think
about constitutional issues at all) now favour it. The traditional
response of English politicians was to make conciliatory gestures
and to search for compromise or compensatory positions, either
Burke's great virtue of 'prudence' or Macmillan's or Wilson's soft
fudge. But Margaret Thatcher practices a melodramatic either-or
confrontationalism, the Union (God bless it) or Separation (shudder, shudder!). She dismissed any middle ground whatever in her
Glasgow speech of 4 February, 1989: 'This Government believes
in devolution to the individual citizen, a devolution now being
practiced in the United Kingdom. . .This Government remains
committed to the Union, as committed as ever'.

\*\*\*

Let us go back to the beginning, to the Act or Treaty of Union
of 1707: part of the living memory of Scotland and just one part
of the dead past in England. The very name and nature of it is
still in dispute. The canny Scottish Lords of Appeal have never
been drawn in judgement in any case meant to test whether alleged
breaches of the Treaty of Union by Act of Parliament could be
illegal. The response of English judges would be more robust and
less equivocal: that Parliament has absolute power to legislate on
anything it chooses, therefore no Parliament can be bound by Acts
of its predecessors, however solemn; so the Act or Treaty of Union
is simply an ordinary enactment, and even if it was a treaty, treaty
obligations can be overridden by future enactments (presumably
even the Treaty of Rome).

The 16th, edition of Sir Erskine May's *Treatise on the Law . . . of Parliament* intones:

> The constitution has assigned no limits to the authority of Parliament over all matters and persons within its jurisdiction. A law may be unjust and contrary to the sound principles of government; but Parliament is not controlled in its discretion, and when it errs, its errors can only be corrected by itself.

Practical men of both kingdoms in 1688 and 1707 saw the new abstract doctrine of parliamentary sovereignty as a gigantic bluff (a *Leviathan* indeed) to maintain order, or in specific terms to ensure the Protestant succession and the end of religious and dynastic civil war, to ensure the predominancy of Parliament over the Crown, and to maintain the unity of the United Kingdom. Power was to be checked and balanced within Parliament, but if divided among the kingdoms, even under one crown, was to risk anarchy. And men felt that they had come close to 'anarchy' or perpetual civil war in all three kingdoms. Yet every man of affairs in Scotland and England knew that the claim to absolute power was a legal fiction tempered by political reality and mediated by skilled statecraft, sometimes by good or ill fortune.

Did prudence or corruption predominate in the last debates of the old Scottish Parliament? The *Claim of Right* is still coloured by an old romantic nationalist view of history, in a specific 19th century form: that a Parliament must embody the life of a nation. 'The nation was not conquered', they say, 'but it did not freely agree to the Union of Parliaments in 1707' (Para 2.5). Certainly there was bribery and corruption in Edinburgh, just as there was in Westminster to get the Bill through the English House of Lords with the Bishops in uproar. Yet modern historians suggest that most Scots believed that a hard bargain had been driven. 'The matters on which the Treaty guaranteed the Scots their own institutions and policies represented the bulk of civil life and government at the time; the Church, the Law and Education' (Para 2.6), indeed. And add to that commercial union and military security against the Highlands, vastly important and urgent matters. And Parliament itself was not as respected at the time as it became in legend. True, 'the nation' was not consulted, but nations never were until modern democratic times, and only then most rarely. Much public opinion of the day saw Parliament not as the national institution and the nation's pride but as a corrupt entity mainly serving the interests of the landowning class. But there was a national institution in which the middle classes and the people took pride, the Church of Scotland itself, the Kirk. And by the standards of the time it was a remarkably representative institution, at least the elect proceeded by elections. The elected Church Assembly had at least as strong a claim to be seen as the national institution as the parliament. That is why its establishment was so bitterly fought in the English Upper Chamber.

It was not the case that Scotland suddenly became directly governed by England, but that what government there was (leaving aside trade and foreign affairs) became secured in the hands of the of the Kirk, local government and the legal profession. And with the growth of the modern Scottish Office, Scotland still exhibits an astonishing spectacle of almost complete administrative devolution, and one, moreover, mainly in Scottish hands. And that is, of course, *the minimum case for a representative institution in Scotland: that all this existing machinery should be subject to democratic control.* What happened was less that Scotland has suffered from having, in an aberrant epochal and regrettable moment, 'lost' its Parliament, but that the established church it gained gradually lost its dominance over the nation's life and its role as the national institution.

Scotland is full of what the eighteenth century called 'peculiar institutions' but it now lacks an elected national institution. Therefore the common sense argument is for some form of subsidiary Parliament. But it is not a wholly rational or a common sense matter. On the one hand, there is nationalism — Scotland is a unique culture and has its own history, it is not a meccano set of institutional arrangements that can be adjusted into the 'greatest happiness' equilibrium position; and on the other hand there is what I call the English ideology of parliamentary sovereignty. It may have outlived its usefulness, but it has left behind deep fears that the creation of any national representative institution in Scotland will lead to the breakup of the United Kingdom.

The English ideology of parliamentary sovereignty arose because from the end of the seventeenth century right up until the Government of Ireland Act, 1920, the major business of British politics was holding the United Kingdom together. Churchill's generation, even after the formation of the Irish Free State, had the history and mythology of this at their finger tips. They did not always succeed, as the Irish rebellion showed, but they knew they had to try, and it was part of 'the Great Game'. Irish historians once painted a lurid canvas of continuous coercion, but their modern successors paint a more complex picture in somewhat softer colours: firstly, they see the culture, commerce and politics of Britain and Ireland as inextricably intermingled, quite apart from claims of right and justice; and, secondly, they see British policy in the nineteenth century reactive more than settled, as alternating spasms of coercion and conciliation. And these spasms did not always follow change of office between Whig or Tory, Liberal or Conservative.

Scotland was once almost as worrying to the English as Ireland. Memories of 'the 45' lived long. A barbarian army had got as far south as Derby. The depth of the scare, among Scottish unionists not least, is reflected in the savagery of the reprisals. When in 1780, in desperate need of recruits in the unpopular American War, the Government lifted some proscriptions on Catholics partly to increase the recruitment of Highlanders (the Gurkhas of the First British Empire), it provoked the Gordon Riots in London, anti-Catholic and xenophobic. And the fear of these, as shown in two novels of Dickens, echoed into the next century. The harsh treatment of Scottish radicals in the Napoleonic Wars was not just an aberration of Lord Braxfield. The maintenance of law and order and the preservation of the Union were inseparable concepts to both the English and Scottish political classes of that time. After the wars, the old memories and fears were still strong enough for the Government to feel the need to play cards from the other hand: conciliation. There was the ludicrous state charade of George IV's visit to Edinburgh produced by Sir Walter Scott and commissioned by the Cabinet. Only for political necessity did the dropsical Prinny wear the kilt that immortal once. And in the next reign but one, the young Queen was persuaded by Melbourne, at first reluctantly, of the desirability of spending 'an appreciable part of the year in Scotland'. Luckily she and Albert liked it. And at that time there was virtually a state cult of Celtic song, poetry and dance. Victoria's children wore tartan plaid and the children of a Viceroy of Ireland wore the green. It was later called 'cultural politics' in other contexts, but it was not then an insensitive and centralising imposition of southern English culture and values.

By the last quarter of the nineteenth century any residual English fears that Scotland might become Ireland had vanished. Yet this very time saw the creation of the office of Secretary for Scotland in 1885 and the beginning of the gradual process which led to the modern Scottish Office in Edinburgh. This was part of, once again, an instinctive, almost routine, English conciliatory politics, triggered more by dubious analogies with Ireland than by actual threats or immediate pressures in Scotland. There was a Scottish Home Rule Association from the 1880s. Its ideas were prescient but its influence was minimal. And, to complete this stumbling gallop, when Liberal leaders in 1910 and 1911 began to talk of 'Home Rule All Round', and Asquith discussed in cabinet whether to bring in one Bill, or to take the difficult or the easy one first, again the impetus was analogy with Ireland, a pre-emptive or reflex action rather than something dictated by the political power of the Scottish Home Rule movement. Also many ministers of the day, not just thinkers, were coming round to the federalist position of Gladstone's *The Irish Question* pamphlet of 1886. They were beginning to see the drawbacks in 'sovereignty of Parliament' and the constitutionless constitution it entailed. They were influenced by Canadian and Australian experience, American of course, and more immediately by the federal settlement in South Africa after the Boer War. Even a few Tories played with ideas of an Imperial federation. The Great War brought an end to such speculations, and to much else. But the old English political class could exercise sovereign power with more flexibility, restraint and conciliation than they are usually given credit for. The inner paradox of the theory of sovereign power is the need for good judgement in when not to use it. Holding the United Kingdom together called for all kinds of restraints.

When the going is hard they can change their rigid ways. Since 1974 I've seen some very unlikely Northern Ireland Office ministers (seemingly sent there for punishment or to destroy themselves) mug the subject up, talk to the right people, get quite a feel for the ground, and do, for such circumstances, reasonably well. And things inherently inimical and contrary to the British Constitution suddenly become possible, indeed necessary: statutory referenda, power-sharing, proportional representation and 'conditional sovereignty', even.

The Anglo-Irish Agreement of 1985 stated: 'The two Governments. . .declare that if in the future a majority of the people of Northern Ireland clearly wish for and formally consent to the establishment of a United Ireland, they will introduce and support in their respective Parliaments legislation to give effect to that wish.' And provision for such a poll or referendum was already in the Northern Ireland Constitution Act of 1973. It should give heart to the SNP. Why cannot this flexible attitude to the union be extended to Scotland and Wales, though a majority of Scots might wish to vote for something different? Must political imagination only arise from the unhappy stimulant of violence?

\*\*\*

The concept of sovereignty itself is the great obstacle to empathy and imagination in the English political mind. 'Our direct concern is with Scotland only', began *A Claim of Right*, 'but the failure to provide good government for Scotland is a product not merely of faulty British policy in relation to Scotland, but of fundamental flaws in the British constitution' (Para 1.2).

As I have said, the wide acceptance of the sovereignty of Parliament only took place in the eighteenth century. Blackstone set down the classic statement of the doctrine in his *Commentaries on the Laws of England* (1765-69).

> Parliament has sovereign and uncontrollable authority in the making, confirming, enlarging, restraining, abrogating, repealing, reviving and expounding of laws concerning matters of all possible denominations. . .: this being the place where that absolute despotic power, which must in all governments reside somewhere, is entrusted by the constitution of these kingdoms. . .

His sweeping assertion that all government needed 'absolute despotic power' did not go unchallenged. The parliamentary debates over the repeat of the Stamp Act in 1766 show that some still took the old-fashioned view that there were limits, other than practical limits, on parliamentary sovereignty. Taxation, then and now, roused deep passions. Could the Americans be taxed if they were not represented in Parliament, except by their own provincial Assemblies? The great director of the Seven Years War, William Pitt, had no doubts, and dragged himself in his last illness to protest in Parliament:

> . . .that this kingdom has no right to lay a tax upon the colonies, to be sovereign and supreme in every circumstance of government whatsoever. They are the subjects of this kingdom, equally entitled with yourselves to all the natural rights of mankind and the peculiar privileges of Englishmen. . .the Americans are the sons not the bastards of England. Taxation is no part of the governing or legislative power. The taxes are a voluntary gift and grant of the Commons alone . . .Here I would draw the line.

He was, however, in the minority.

Edmund Burke in his great speeches on 'Conciliation with America' and on 'American Taxation' was to rail at Lord North's claim that the American refusal to pay taxes threatened the sovereignty of Parliament. Do not ask, he said, 'whether you have a right to make them miserable, have you not rather an interest to make them happy?'

> Leave America, if she has taxable matter in her, to tax herself. I am not going into the distinctions of rights, nor attempting to mark their boundaries. I do not enter into these metaphysical distinctions; I hate the very sound of them. Leave the Americans as they anciently stood. . .They and we, and their and our

ancestors, have been happy under that system. . .Be content to bind Americans by laws of trade; you have always done that. Do not burden them by taxes, you were not used to do that from the beginning. Let this be your reason for not taxing. These are the arguments of states and kingdoms. Leave the rest to schools; for there they may be discussed with safety. But if [not]. . . you will teach them by these means to call that sovereignty itself into question.

*And that is precisely what has happened, then and now.* By opposing all concessions and slamming the door on any discussions of change (even within her own party in Scotland), Margaret Thatcher, very like Lord North, has raised the stakes dramatically and foolishly. Some will think that she has, indeed, strengthened the hands and hearts of separatist nationalists in Scotland. Perhaps. But I think it more likely that her intransigence has swept mere devolution off the agenda and is turning, almost overnight, devolutionists into federalists in the Scottish Labour Party (however slow our leaders are to catch up with their followers). The whole constitution of the United Kingdom is called into question, and there is no secure way forward for Scotland unless it is.

Unhappily while Mrs Thatcher has turned her back on Burke, Labour's leaders still echo him. They plead for *and rely upon* a prudence which is not there. They seek vigorously, like Mr Hattersley, to fudge the sovereignty issue. They can sound equally magnificent, perhaps, but the impact is equally futile. Like Burke, they are hedging the fundamental issue. For Burke clearly in the above passage, was not attacking sovereignty as such, but its abuse in bad policies. Labour's present leaders also believe in 'unlimited and supreme. . .sovereignty' but want it in their hands, and would, indeed, if it ever fell into them, exercise it more prudently and benignly, truly chockful of radiant and sincere concern. But by the time Burke spoke it was too late. The Americans did not just want better treatment, they wanted constitutional guarantees for a defined area of self-government. They were not prepared to wait for a more friendly government, and to trust for restraint, like good English politicians, to friendship alone.

★★★

It used to be argued, in private by the main draughtsman of the Scotland Act of 1978 before he retired from the Scottish Office, and in public by John Mackintosh, MP, who had he lived might have given the campaign that lift it needed, that the details of the devolution Bill were of secondary importance. Not to worry, get

an Assembly of some kind off the ground and as its authority
grew so its powers could be amended. Such a process would be
politically irreversible. But Jim Ross has recently seen the catch
in the Burkean argument for prudence. His 'A Fond Farewell
to Devolution' (*Radical Scotland*, Dec/Jan 1989) is a remarkable
and important document. He was, of course, the secretary of the
committee who produced *A Claim of Right*.

Ross simply argues that in 1978 'we were innocent enough to
suppose that future Ministers would not dare withdraw powers once
granted. We now know better. We used to think that Governments
under the British constitution were fussy and interfering but not
fundamentally undemocratic. We now know that the British constitution is inherently authoritarian and is quite capable of spawning a
Government to match.' So he concludes that the objective must be,
however politically difficult, a constitutionally protected Scottish
Parliament, such that only by some special and difficult procedure,
involving that body too, could Parliament wind it up, change its
powers or cut its funding (as has been done to local government).

In 1981, with the events of 1979 very much in mind, I remember
trying to set this question for an English school examination board:
'Devolution was a concept invented by Harold Wilson to obscure the
hitherto clear distinction between local government and federalism'.
*Explain and discuss*. The teacher assessors understandably threw it
out as too difficult. There was plenty of choice in the paper. I just
wanted to see if *any* English sixth-formers would go for it. But it
would have been fully comprehensible, then and now, to any Scottish sixth-former. Assessment might have raised some difficulties.

The *Claim of Right* sees the English constitution as a barrier to
Scottish rights to a national representative institution. But it is now
widely canvassed, as never before (except within the old Liberal
Party for most of this century!) that the constitution is an obstacle to
all our British civil liberties. The lack of restraint upon government
has reached epic proportions.

*The Political Quarterly*, a journal not famous for sensational-
ism, had a recent issue on 'Is Britain Becoming Authoritarian?'
(Jan. 1989). Wyn Grant wrote comprehensively of 'The Erosion
of Intermediary Institutions'. There is no need to labour the point
that many political thinkers have seen intermediary institutions as
essential conditions for liberty. But Wyn Grant sombrely pointed
out that the erosion is not simply a product of Thatcher's deliberate policies but follows from another strong tradition, rooted in
the classical economists, which sees any intermediaries between
individuals and the state as threats to true competitive, atomistic

individualism. And Mark Stallworthy wrote in the same place of 'Central Government and Local Government: the Uses and Abuses of Constitutional Hegemony.' It is an almost definitive listing of the extent to which powers and discretion of local government have been radically diminished (contrary to Tory tradition quite as much as to Labour's — in some respects more so). He sees it as a new, imposed constitutional settlement, and concludes: 'A constitutional settlement which is resistant to dialogue and which confers an unconditional legitimacy on imposed central solutions is antithetical to reasonable expectations within a purported liberal democracy.'

There has been a centralist tradition in the Labour Party (as Wyn Roberts reminds). Old Fabianism had one thing in common with Leninism: that the party should act for the good through control of the central state, and a belief that most intermediary institutions were irrational, reactionary or obstructive. But there was also a pluralist tradition, more concerned to do good through people, in ordinary social groups and communities, than to do good to them from however heavenly a height. This centralist tradition was unhappily apparent in the half-hearted support, if not open opposition, given both by Government Ministers and by many Scottish Labour MPs to the Devolution Bills of 1978. Things done by a Government simply for political survival carry little conviction among ordinary people,

Yet the fear was real among Labour activists, in Scotland as well as in England and Wales, that the welfare state would suffer if central power declined. But that was before Thatcher's massive demonstration of how much of welfare, nor merely in the personal social services and housing, depended on the strength of local government. So in the last ten years there has been an extraordinary conversion among Labour intellectuals and thinkers to constitutional reform. It is hard to think of any prominent figure on the Left who now makes the old Footite defence of parliamentary sovereignty. Some of the motives for this change are obvious, a process for constitutional traditionalists, of Left and Right, not unlike aversion therapy. But there has also been a movement away from mere pragmatism in the Labour centre and right, a recovery of thought by the thoughtless, a reanimation of values. Among those values are a positive sense of community. And at the same time, for quite different reasons, former hard or obscure Marxists, in searching for a basis for an humanistic and liberal approach, have been rediscovering pluralism. Philosophically, they now say with Harold Laski that 'all power is federal': and empirically they say that while class divisions are still important, other social groupings are too; therefore the old 'class analysis' is too simple to describe modern or post-industrial society.

These two groups have, together with Liberals and Social Democrats, swelled the adherents of Charter '88's call for constitutional and electoral reform. Charter '88 arose in London, with no direct reference to Scottish conditions, but a remarkable cross-section of people have come together convinced that, because of a breakdown of traditional restraints on which civil liberties depended, a formal constitution is now needed.

The actual Charter '88 statement only says of Scotland that 'Scotland is governed like a province from Whitehall' (well-meant but not wholly accurate). Among Charter's eleven demands there is 'Guarantee an equitable distribution of power between local, regional and national government.' So do even they see Scotland as just a 'regional government'? This is far less than the *Claim of Right*. But some of the original sponsors read that demand more radically than the bare words suggest. Antony Barnett called his inaugural article on Charter '88 in *New Statesman and Society* (2 Dec. 1988), *A Claim of Right for Britain*. He said that 'along with the sustained and detailed *A Claim of Right for Scotland* Charter '88 points towards a new kind of politics in Britain.' And he quoted from Neal Ascherson's Mackintosh Memorial Lecture:

> It is not possible to build democratic socialism by using the institutions of the Ancient British State. Under that include the present doctrine of sovereignty, Parliament, the electoral system, the civil service — the whole gaudy heritage. It is not possible, in the way that it is not possible to induce a vulture to give milk.

This is not merely true for democratic socialists, though the admission is long overdue from many of us; even to build a more liberal, decent regime needs formal constitutional law. The kind of reasoning behind the Charter is found in *1688-1988 Time For A New Constitution* (edited by Richard Holme and Michael Elliott), in which I was not the only Labour contributor to a kind of Liberal Democratic popular front. So the climate of reformist opinion in England for *Claim of Right* ideas could be favourable, if they are argued. The English dimension must not be forgotten or neglected by Scottish publicists, or simply made a target of abuse. Potential allies need to be convinced in terms relevant to themselves.

National movements can spend, like political parties, too much time arguing among themselves. English Charter supporters, let alone Mr Hattersley, need to be convinced that Scotland's rights go beyond being graciously given the powers of a hypothetical

English region. The case for English and Welsh regional government may be good. It rests on democratic and on administrative theory (there are few signs of any popular support). But in Scotland there is massive popular support for Home Rule, substantial support for independence (though some of that may be tactical), because Scotland's case rests on nationalism and a long national history. How can any of my fellow English be so obtuse as not to recognise that Scotland, for all the interconnections and friendliness, is a nation? Or so condescending as to think that what Texans, Bavarians, Quebecquois, Gujaratis and white Tasmanians do, cannot be done by Scots — that is operate a federal system? And why should a federal solution be deemed impossible because of the numbers of English? It depends what constitutional guarantees are given and how and by whom they are guaranteed. The Scottish Convention will have some proposals to make.

As all of us write, the Convention faces great difficulties. Will the SNP return to it? Both parties have their internal difficulties, not unknown to the other. But may I just say this to fellow Labour Party members, always remembering what Pericles said in Athens so long ago, that 'the secret of liberty is courage'? We must have the courage of our democratic convictions, let alone of our electoral numbers, to make things as easy as possible for those separatist nationalists who would want to come into a devolved Assembly or a federal Parliament and leave to the future the 'final decision'.

Can we not say, as even Mrs Thatcher has said over Northern Ireland, that if at some future date the people of Scotland should vote in a referendum for separation, 'independence in Europe' or whatever, then so be it. As I've said, I'd take up citizenship happily, not trek South to Yorkshire or Surrey again. And a referendum should offer the Scottish people the three realistic alternatives which everyone knows there are: the status quo, a federal parliament or independence. The Campaign for a Scottish Assembly might have been wiser to picture the Convention as producing, initially, three such packages (one needs little work) and to put these to the Scottish electorate. Let them decide. Then would come the time for an elected Convention, officially or unofficially, to provide a fully drafted constitution. And can anyone seriously doubt the practical sense and justice of conducting those elections on any other but some form of proportional representation? Again consider Northern Ireland, which has set, in that respect, no precedent for the mainland, even by having PR for its European seats. Should we be less flexible and inventive than Thatcher's ministers?

What if the Government refuses (as is overwhelmingly likely) to hold such a referendum, nor to facilitate an official election for a Constitutional Convention, nor to respond to the proposals of a Convention however constituted? And what if, as is at least possible under the present electoral system, the Conservatives are still in office after the next election (the heart will not let the head say, 'if Labour loses again overall')? What will happen then? There is no knowing. Opinions might grow stronger but still not translate into appropriate, understandable, historically precedented behaviour. Or there could be real trouble. But my vision of civil disobedience is neither of riots, nor of Jim Sillars and Donald Dewar politely disputing who shall cast the first symbolic stone at the windows of the Secretary of State for Scotland, but of respectable, worried, conventional local government officers all over Scotland beginning to ignore injunctions and to organise an election for a Scottish Parliament.

The heroic version of Irish independence centres on fighting, bloodshed, atrocities and 'the lads of the column'; and the realistic version on the resulting stalemate and war-weariness on both sides. But there is a civilian version also: that at some stage law-abiding and home-abiding family men in three-piece suits and watch chains began to post their official returns on this and that to Dublin's Mansion House. Pray God Scotland's right can be obtained peaceably and without 'troubles'. Much will depend on the character of the response when propositions are made. It will be a test for the English political mind at a bad time. It is dangerous to affront the rights and pride of a nation for whom the present English Government has lost politically all right to speak.

# 14

## The Timeless Girn

TOM NAIRN

The SNP's dramatic desertion of the Scottish Constitutional Convention at its crucial opening meeting has already won its place in tradition; a theatrical coup in all respects worthy of 1979, 1843, and before. It superbly evokes all the aberrant, self-destructive grandeur of our nation's history: everything (in short) which has over the centuries made the Scots a people of gallant losers and political imbeciles.

I well recall a personal rediscovery of this Scotch-pessimist philosophy of history, one freezing January morning back in 1975. It came back to me in the hardy shape of William Thompson, the Liddesdale postman. He made his way among the hundreds of mole-hills to the door of a cottage with some re-directed mail, noticing as he left again the piles of political and history books standing inside the front door.

'Ach, politics. . .' he said as the most natural of conversation-opener '. . .the trouble wi' us is we've never been able tae agree amang wirselves'. I had only returned to Scotland the night before, after some years abroad, and it was the first thing anyone had said to me, apart from road directions. Still in the grip of returnee fever, I didn't know what to reply; but no doubt thought something along the lines of 'Have they been left a bit behind, in God-forsaken places like this?'

The conversation turned to getting rid of moles. He gave me a long and useful account of the local methods of mowdie-trapping and disposal.

That moment has often come back to mind over the years. Especially, since our great *Claim of Right* appeared and all those serious moves took place to turn it into the political reality of a Constitutional Convention. At last, I thought, Willie is being proved wrong. Yet in the same breath (having reacquired much of

the equipment of 'Scottishness' in the intervening years) I couldn't
help simultaneously feeling 'How will it go wrong?' And as all other
sufferers know, in the God-forsaken sub-conscious 'It's bound to go
wrong!' sits in sour-breathed proximity to another timeless, girning
old drunk: '*Who* will ruin things this time?'

Well, we ken noo.

### Problems of Identity

In the 'Prologue' the *Claim of Right* presents itself as an 'ar-
ticulation' of Scotland's need for political institutions: the voice
of a common identity as yet unrepresented by instituitons of its
own. The task of the Constitutional Convention proposed by the
*Claim* will be to design and legitimate these bodies before — 'in
due course' (p.20) — presenting the plan to a British government
and negotiating with it.This of course assumes the Convention's
right — its effective if *de facto* embodiment of the Scottish national
sovereignty. It will be asserting only those 'rights of the people'
inscribed in all contemporary constitutional systems: all (that is)
except the one which Convention spokespeople will be confronting
in such a situation.

Now this is sure one day to raise many genuine problems of the
'What happens when Mrs Thatcher says "no"?', kind. The SNP's
Convention delegation made flamboyant use of that question, and
has been brandishing it remorselessly ever since. The great walk-out
was done on the pretext that (unlike the SNP) the other bodies
represented there had no answer to it now. Mrs Thatcher's 'No' and
the party's new magic charm, 'Independence-in-Europe', have been
the main part of the Nationalist argument against the Constitutional
Convention process.

But it was Jim Ross, secretary of the committee which produced
the *Claim of Right*, who outlined the problem of a British 'No'
better than anyone else in his comments on the Govan by-election.
Independence may indeed, eventually, prove 'the least of the evils
available to Scotland'; but, he pointed out quietly, this is unlikely
to happen 'without fighting in the most literal sense of the word':

> The nature of power in Britain breeds a thicker skin than
> most. Even if the SNP won a majority of Scottish seats in
> a general election, a Tory Government wouldn't hesitate to
> profess that such a vote had nothing to do with independ-
> ence. . . The attitude of any United Kingdom Government
> will be conditioned by the interests of England and at present
> these demand the continued attachment of Scotland. . .The

day when Scottish independence will be a friendly process is
not in sight, nor is there any sign that Scots are yet ready to
tough out a thoroughly unfriendly process.

*(Scotsman* Nov 14 1988)

For the unfriendly process, however, what counts is widespread
support going far beyond voting: the participation of different classes
and social bodies in their own way and to varying extents, the transformation of the social and cultural climate, a massive rather than
an elite consciousness. The Convention process is part of this. Only
a part, true: but — given Scotland's peculiar fragmentation on the
relevant plane of consciousness — probably a vital one.

It can't do it on its own; but it may be a precondition of serious
advance beyond the shallow mobilization of the 'seventies.

Beyond (that is) the kind of mobilization historically associated
with the electoralism of the Scottish National Party.

### *'They're Stealing ma Scones!'*

Although verbally similar, it must be stressed that Ross's sombre
problematic is not really that put forward by the SNP delegates to
the Convention, and reiterated ever since by its leadership. He is
envisaging the transformation of Scotland's new, emergent political
identity into a movement of national resistance or liberation; the
disappearance of the 'Scottish cringe' in a political rather than a
metaphorical or psychological sense. This process is still at an early
stage, and its later development (if it happens at all) is inevitably
hard to imagine. What the SNP is playing with, by contrast, is best
understood as a kind of strip-cartoon version of the independence
scenario; 'national liberation' for British idiots to be attained by
the simple short-cut of voting SNP at Her Majesty's next General
Election.

Ross and C.S.A.'s Convention wonder (and have earned the right
to wonder) what a rediscovered Scots political identity might do to
us and to Britain. The SNP's comic-book edition wonders nothing
of the kind. Why should it, since it owns the monopoly on national
political identity? The latter's terms and conditions are set out in
a policy-booklet and purchasable along with the party card. 'Scots'
prove themselves such by voting SNP. Other Salvation is there none.
And all true party-folk are naturally suspicious of any competition
undermining the Godly simplicity of this assumption.

For a time it may have suited SNP-ers to be nice to the assorted
small-'n' nationalists arising in other movements. They were lost,
poor things, and deserved a little time to find the light. A little, but

not too much; for there can be no real need for the 'rediscovery' or development of something long ago awarded the Royal Patent for exclusive sale to the Scottish electorate. Still less (therefore) for a tedious Convention aiming to debate for a year or so and set out alternative wares; so many devolutionary distractions from the only significant flag in the wind, the tattered one with the 'VOTE SNP' on it. We already have as much political identity as is good for us. 'Conversion' is really the game not persuasion or strategic compromise. Anyone thinking differently just can't have seen the old flag (held up higher than ever after Govan). If they have, and yet still draw back from the light, they may well be hireling knaves.

In the same article Ross underlines how disenchanted the Scots generally have grown with 'the total sovereignty of Westminster' and the special kind of dry-rot destroying the United Kingdom's political system. But such despair was premature, back in November. Only three months later we can see the dry rot is in good hands; British 'Parliamentary cretinism' (to use Lenin's old phrase) has found its last abiding refuge within the SNP, where sectarian infantilism seems likely to keep the old thing warm until a true Doomsday comes. The strange SNP version of *Sinn Féin* ('ourselves alone') we can now see means not the Scottish people alone, but the Scottish National Party alone: sole and Providentially-nominated guardians of the national ballot-box. Their first duty has come to be protecting the imaginary Grail from the Constitutional Convention — a new parcel of rogues, assembled together to pinch it from them.

Once more the primal scream of offended British Scotia rings out: 'They're stealing ma scones!' This soul-cry came from Labour in the 1970s, when it first saw serious competition arising in the SNP. Now we hear it the other way round as in the 1980s a broader nationalism has arisen to challenge that party's mortgage upon the national heart. The insult could be tolerated, even wanly smiled on, while the SNP was still hard up for votes. But since Govan the prospect of redeeming the mortgage by traditional means has suddenly reappeared. So, protection of both SNP property-rights and (for the time being) of Her Majesty's Constitution have become a first priority; fundamentalism under the Crown, a rapid rush to Westminster, and then triumphant exit (without too much of all that 'unfriendly' business, thanks to Europe).

### The Tough and the Toothless

In Ross's perspective, the point of the Covention is to forge a wider and more popular Scots political identity — that separate democratic identity and self-confidence which contemporary Scotland so evidently lacks. It was this lack (not flaws in 'devolution' as such, or economic slump) which brought the ruin of the later 1970s. The main tide of events since 1707, whatever it has preserved, inevitably brought near-obliteration at the political level — an annihilation derived from submergence in one of the greatest State-polities of modern times. And re-emergence from this is naturally slow, and halting. In a country where (Praise be) religious, linguistic and ethnic factors don't automatically underwrite political identity, the latter has inevitably to be constructed 'in its own terms': just what the Scots (overshadowed by Anglo-British political grandeur, and moulded by their own collusion in it) find most difficult. Even with Thatcher to help them, decades may be needed to reverse these centuries of responsible paralysis.

Ross's point is, surely, that without the formulation of such an identity — the popular sense of 'Scotland' as a distinct *political community*, erected on a far broader basis than one electoral party — there can be no chance of our 'toughing out' any of the less friendly aspects of nationalism. A kind of bubble-nationalism — a longing for identity rather than the actual building of it — may blow up now and then in favourable conjunctures: we saw it in the 'seventies. and it may be happening again now. But such balloons are always likely to deflate again under real challenge. This is because they are filled by windy but fugitive enthusiasm, rather than the steadier mixture of accumulated collective resentment and offended interest which fuels enduring nationalism.When such mixtures discover a valid contemporary myth of mobilization, national-political identity is born. But contemporary Scotland is still in search of such a myth; while the SNP's surrogate wobbles back and forth between Bannockburn (1314) and the ballot-box ('next time').

'Toughness' here is not to be confused with the vulgar and toothless rhetoric of SNP fundamentalism. All this spluttering creed of 'Independence, nothing less!' actually means is 'Send us to Westminster!' (to pull independence from the constitutional hat). In reality 'toughness' can only refer to mobilizable identity, not rhetorical posturing; to a more resistant and many-sided communal consciousness which, if its to amount to anything historically, must eventually be determined upon its rights *at all costs*. These costs may (and customarily do) include action outside the law, forms of civil war, the risk of economic upset, and eventually a willingness to rock (or sink) every boat in sight, starting with the Westminster Ark.

The Constitutional Convention is of course (and must remain) a peaceable body: but what it is actually doing is far more revolutionary than anything which can be undertaken by any British-system party like the SNP. That most of those doing it are so un-revolutionary is merely a comment on the times. We are living through a successful counter-revolution, and the Campaign for a Scottish Assembly is trying to make the Scots opt out before it's too late. Mild-mannered, over-respectable folk have been drawn into this effort, as into all similar political upheavals of the past. Elements of our corporate, canny Establishment have entered the fray at last; and 'devolution' and Utopian federalist schemes do indeed often figure among their motives. But these motives and ideas are no true measure, either of the process itself or of its consequences.

Here, the hammer-effect of Thatcherism seems to have brought about a curious reversal in the Scottish arena. While the histrionic radicalism of 'Independence, nothing less!' has turned into a form of dowtit conservatism, along the Convention's route a certain pragmatism which once underwrote the Union has become, for the time being, a profoundly unsettling and formative force.

The Convention, after all, is trying to set out a principled political alternative — a Scottish constitutional way — incompatible with the very nature of the United Kingdom State. This is plainly spelt out in the *Claim of Right*'s argument, with its sober denunciation of Westminster's 'illusion of democracy' and the *de facto* tyranny concealed behind it. In his reflections on Govan. Ross put the same point in another way. 'Pay no attention to comparisons with Norway and Sweden in 1905'. He advised:

> The economic and social interactions of Norway and Sweden then were far different from those between Scotland and England now. Also, Norway's big brother was Sweden, ours is England, a very different and much more brutal polity.

### 'Nationalism' versus nationalism

However, the Convention's prelude to effective presentation of this alternative has now been threatened (and possibly aborted) by the sectarian posturings of the SNP leadership. The principal immediate barrier to the development of nationalism has, paradoxically, become Nationalism itself. In other words the current expansion of democratic consciousness in Scotland has now collided with the older narrower version of nationalism pioneered by the SNP. Beyond a certain point the new, more realistic and resistant form of national awareness hammered out under 'Thatcherism' has turned out to be profoundly unwelcome to this old philosophy. SNPism remains what it always was: the conviction that one body is *the* irreplaceable, Historically-patented stand-in for political Scottishness — party, Movement and embryonic State all in one, complete with foreign and economic policy, doormen's uniforms, 'Flooer o' Scotland' and an Independence Scroll up for the Queen to initial. What need is there to plan a new State, when we can already boast an Independent Scotland-in-Waiting, chafing for its solemn procession from No.6 North Charlotte Street up to Parliament Hall?

In a recent TV debate about 'Independence in Europe'. Mrs Ewing replied to a cheeky jibe about a possible Socialist Republic of Alba in these words:

> This is an easy question to answer. Ever since 1926 the SNP's policy has always been Commonwealth Status, Loyal to the Crown. This position is so invincible that we've never even debated it, it's never been called in question once. . .
>
> (*Left Right & Centre* Dec. 1988)

Anybody recalling a relatively recent SNP conference debate about a referendum on Republican status might have questioned this Presidential verity (the motion got substantial support, but did not end up defeated). However, the secure tone and refulgence of *Madame Écosse* were making a much more important point (before proceeding to her inevitable encomium on Norway and Sweden). She was underlining SNPism's impregnable home base in the identity of the 1920s, when George V was National Dad and Councillor Alfred Roberts had just been blessed with a daughter.

Some optimists thought that this addled identity–surrogate had died off years ago. Though occasionally taken down and lovingly dusted at moments like the one just mentioned, the presumption was that it might really have gone the way of the Labour Party's 'Clause 4', and would cause little more trouble. That happy notion was apparently confirmed after Jim Sillars' election triumph last November when the victor of Govan made a remarkable series of measured statements seeking out new common ground with Labour and the other likely Convention participants. These were important in preparing the atmosphere for the Convention's preliminary moves, and suggested that progressive nationalism had indeed consigned political Lauderism to the wings, if not to the back exit and the dustbin.

Now the truth is clearer. We have seen the old mummy leap malignantly out of its specimen-jar and take over the SNP's National Executive again. Its cheeks appear suffused with rosy new life, as if the rest had done it good. The rows of sober-suited young politicos have melted away from the centre-stage limelight, and confine themselves for the time being to embarrassed choruses of the old fundamentalist ditties. 'A rush of blood to the head' is how one or two of them have been overheard describing the shame, with the implication that such tides have — however reluctantly — to be swum with rather than resisted then and there. Poll-intoxicated atavism might be another description.

People are supposed to remember what they were doing when President Kennedy was assassinated. I will certainly always recall the moment of realization that the Convention had been crippled (whether mortally or not remains to be seen). It was during the suspenseful day following the initial January 28th meeting; there was still some lingering hope in the air, as the SNP delegation debated its final stance. Then a radio announcer brought the grim news; SNP President Mrs Winifred Ewing had pronounced herself 'largely satisfied' with the decision reached (and due to be formally divulged next day).

Hope dropped dead on the spot, and a darkly inebriated *fin-de-siècle* swam suddenly into focus, where loyal 'Scots' might still be sending *Madame Écosse* up to Strasbourg and the 1997 batch of Lauderite fundamentalists down to Westminster — all still crystal-balling helplessly about what to do if England keeps on saying 'No!' to Commonwealth Status and Independence-in-Europe-under-the-Crown into the next Millenium.

### Tartan Sectarianism

'Atavism' entails harking back. But just what is SNPism reverting to in such moments of crisis and decision? It's hardly the first time that the syndrome has been observed. In fact it is the third time since the last general election in June 1987 that this unmistakable style has been seen in operation.

'SNP-ism' was forcefully displayed (for instance) in September 1987, when the STUC sponsored a march and 'Rally for Scottish Democracy' at Glasgow Green. Then too the Nationalists refused to take part. Hence what had been conceived as a new popular-front response to the tightening grip of Thatcherism declined (inevitably) into an old-fashioned Labourite event — a culturally adorned celebration of their one-legged 'victory' in Scotland. And the following year, after prolonged arguments, the SNP withdrew from the united anti-poll-tax campaign (again STUC-led) in order to set up its own ordained version, Say No to Poll-tax.

As with the later Convention walk-out, these gestures were carried out amid a fuliginous reek of embittered accusations about Labourite treachery and conspiracy; no movement in which that detested party is involved can, it seems, be other than poisoned from the outset — a 'front' for continued English domination rather than Scottish common interests.

What does this common pattern express? The Scottish National Party's general outlook and credo — its reflexes, rather than its policies — were formed in that other era so dear to Mrs Ewing I already mentioned. It is chronologically quite recent yet already spiritually and developmentally remote. They belong integrally to a pre-Thatcher Britain of Imperial decline, 'consensus', evolution and Labourism, where 'class' (in the quaint old Queen's-English sense) was all, and British Constitutional problems (finally solved in 1832) did not exist. The first half-century of the SNP's existence was passed under those conditions — that is, in a Scotland still predominantly (sometimes overwhelmingly) loyal to Empire, Throne and Labour's turn.

In such circumstances, political nationalism could only exist as an embattled, more or less hopeless, minority sect. To say that a movement is a 'sect' does not imply triviality or worthlessness; this case alone would prove that point. From the 1920s until well after the Second World War the SNP and its predecessors sought to revive the idea of Scottish independence and they should be honoured for that. However, they did so under such cripplingly adverse conditions that both the idea itself and the politics which grew up around it suffered badly. Suffered such deformation, in fact, that a 'Scottish Nationalism' arose not only very different from other nationalist movements but — in the end — at odds with the wider nationalist movement which would later develop in Scotland itself.

SNPism anticipated the more normal situation of the 1980s; the aggressive assimilationism of 'the Englishing of Scotland' and the Poll-tax, and signs of real mass disillusionment with the political Raj and its more markedly colonial effects. But — precisely — it *anticipated* them from a pre-natal position, rather than expressing a democratic-popular nationalism already in existence. It was the voice of a land as yet without mass political identity, and looked forward (instead) to a curious, stage-managed resumption of Scotland's pre-democratic Statehood. The party was bearing the gift of modern political identity to the nation, rather than vice-versa. That gift being (of course) itself: an ideological stance even more favourable to egomania than the normal theatre of Westminster politics.

Now, it can be argued that in the circumstances this was better than nothing — a lot better (e.g.) than the national nullity of Scottish political consciousness once Labour had forgotten about

Home Rule after 1918. Equally one could maintain that only such a blinkered and narrowly arrogant creed could have accomplished the break-through of the early 1970s: a broader, less philistine movement would have been too caught up in (or 'contaminated' by) all the compromises of British culture. However the price for such limited success had to be a confirmation of the traits in question — the formation of that contemporary SNP 'fundamentalism' predicated wholly upon the need *not* to 'change with the times', not to compromise and accommodate for fear that any inflexion may sabotage the Gift. Fifteen years after its historic 'high' of 1974 this legacy is not only alive but quite capable at crucial moments of reasserting its command over the movement. However, since reality has changed — for the good as well as for the bad — this capacity has now become destructive as well as preservative. It is holding back progressive nationalism as well as — in effect *rather than* — combating the Auld Enemy.

In the United Kingdom politics most sects have based themselves upon purist doctrine of 'class', a Marxist concept filtered (inevitably) through the weird prisms of a primarily English hierarchy and backwardness. On the extreme right there are also sects like the National Front using the concept of white or Anglo-Saxon 'race'. SNP sectarianism owes nothing to either of these. Its rigidly idealized picture is of a pure 'Scotland' embodying certain mythic social and psychological virtues regardless of class, race or creed — the nation of undefiled 'Scots' who, once awakened to their virtuous inheritance, will cast aside the false garb of Englishness and vote pure Nationalist. Although SNP discourse blames 'the English' for everything (exposing itself to accusations of ethnic narrowness) this rhetoric is in function most akin to Trotskyite denunciations of 'capitalism'; something which ideology renders inevitable but is very rarely meant literally or personally.

In these ideological terms, what anti-Englishness so conveniently obscures is *Britain*. But politically speaking, the SNP's 'Scotland' is also a function of Britishness: the obedient, constitutional path of Her Majesty's electoral system, restoring full partnership in Crown, Commonwealth and (nowadays) 'Europe' too. It has always been hard to explain to southern observers that all those anti-English tirades were only studio-Tibers, foaming with much ketchup. The 'England' in them is an ideal construction made necessary by the other one, 'Scotland'; and both belong within a wider structure of signs and silences which takes 'Britain' for granted. Inside that, over-emphasis upon 'England' consistently distracts attention from many profoundly British aspects of the actual Scots (including their

Nationalists). After all, the Scots and Welsh invented 'Britain' and retain a (sometimes unwittingly) large stake in the notion, while the English rarely view it as more than a tiresome if necessary overcoat.

The reason 'Britain' *has* to be all an English plot in Nationalist rhetoric is in order to legitimate a 'Scotland' whose claims were *not* — or not yet sufficiently — justified by persecution and minority status. Yet at the same time, the factor of pretence in such pretend-nationalism could be sustained in practice solely by tacit, grudging allegiance to a British Crown and Parliamentary system which couldn't (therefore) all be just an English plot. Were that so, Nationalists would hardly be pinning all their hopes upon the Constitutional path, and electoral success at Westminster: they would probably have been in jail.

Thus, nationalist sectarianism and Crown-and-Commonwealth Britishism have in fact propped one another up, in an increasingly contradictory and odious symbiosis. The SNP's sect-mentality derives from the need rigidly to adhere to this idealized pretence-factor — the principal ideological bond of the movement: that's why it has always been so suspicious of intellectual culture, in the way so memorably described by H.J. Hanham:

> The SNP was to be a party fighting for the small man to whom culture was something that he had already. . .
>
> Hanham, *Scottish Nationalism* (1969), pp. 175-6

Culture one doesn't have already contains a display of theoretical doubts and alternatives, constantly menacing the explosion of the contradiction and the sabotage of party-spirit by egg-heads. Hence, consciousness-raising is best avoided. The special philistinism which sets the SNP apart from every other variety of modern national movement derives from this underlying dilemma. And now, in the 1980s, it is under threat from an evolving political culture too — the nascent, more concrete sense of national identity generated by the mounting oppression and political brutalism of the Thatcher years.

## The Fossillization of SNPism

The tenacious after-life of SNPism (in honour of the charismatic spirit one might also call it 'Ewingism') can probably be explained in a number of ways. The sheer conservatism of political movements — notably those with revolutionary goals — should never be underestimated. Also, until the shocks of the Thatcher era, the profoundly apolitical nature of Scottish society offered little intellectual stimulus or opposition to the Nationalist belief–system.

It let the philosophy of the *Scots Independent* be embalmed in a strange time-warp.

But the main explanation must surely be that already referred to: the success of the early 1970s. After the decisive failure of British social-democracy in the mid-1960s (when it became evident that British modernization could never assume a left-wing form), political restlessness began to mount in both Wales and Scotland. Along with the English North, these were the principal fiefdoms of a Labour corporatism now doomed to stagnation and decline. But unlike the North, both had a long-stifled national dimension capable of mobilizing some of the resultant resentment and uncertainty. In Scotland this happened quite quickly and (as everyone said at the time, and ever after) 'sensationally'; Winifred Ewing's by-election victory at Hamilton in 1967 led on to a fitful electoral advance culminating in the 30% and 11 seats of the October 1974 parliament.

What this rapid fluctuation of voting patterns did was to carry forward an essentially sectarian movement into a position of party-political power. Carry forward, but not transform; the very speed of the changes, as well as the nature of the support behind them, meant that there was a big change in 'support' (defined mainly in voting and opinion-poll terms) but very little in other ways. That was why sectarianism emerged confirmed by the experience, not discredited. After all, an astonishingly large proportion of Scots had apparently responded to the call — had nodded assent to SNP 'Scottishness' at least in the polling booths.

It was soon realized how shallow and unreliable this gesture towards political identity still was, as support dropped away again in 1977. 'Sensation' was succeeded by relapse into normal shoulder-shrugging apathy. Yet its effect upon the political plane were to be lasting. Here — where 'Scottish' consciousness is at its feeblest and most ambiguous — the consequence could only be the ratification of the party's world-view: the 'fundamentalist' certainty that 'we can do it again', on essentially the same grounds and by the same means — do it again but (obviously) with more votes next time round, correspondingly bigger leverage over the Crown, and an even quicker Constitutional exit to Commonwealth and European status.

Among the faithful, the intensification of such certainty occluded the alternative perspective on the 1967-77 decade. This other explanation was that SNPism's heady surge forward of the early 1970s was due to one particular conjecture of events, unlikely ever to be repeated. It was a shallow-level mobilization made possible by the impact of 'Scotland's Oil' in what were to be closing years of that 'decent' old British regime to which Mrs Ewing's 1920 philosophy integrally belonged.

During these years, after Edward Heath's brief experiment with pre-Thatcherism in 1970-72, it was Labourism which found itself struggling to sustain consensus and compromise on (inevitably) too many fronts at the same time. One of them was the partially reborn 'national question' in Wales and Scotland. Its operations in that direction were (like most of its policies) futile. But they did prolong the crucial fantasy SNPism depends on — that of a Crown-State reluctantly making way for the Scots to resume their rightful 1707 place. The brutal and thick-skinned polity behind 'Parliamentary Sovereignty' continued to be hidden or made light of.

Hence the abortion of 1979. Post-euphoria did produce a shift to the Left among Nationalists, associated with the 79 Group which (after expulsion and readmission) went on to produce so many new leaders and spokesmen in the 1980s. However, movements within this Left-Right policy spectrum occur on an axis quite distinct from that of Realism versus Sectarianism — and it is the latter, unfortunately, which remains most fundamental to the SNP's self-image and ideology. It used to be a rather right-wing sect with as many members as voters. It has now turned into a rather left-wing sect which a large number of people vote for.

It has always been erroneous to identify SNPism primarily in terms of this Left-Right polarization; popular distrust of the movement has rested as much upon perception of its inherent crankiness and unreliability, as upon its right-wing or 'Tory' character. Recent history has shown all too well how parts of the working class can be won over to the political Right. But it is far less likely to move over and stay with a palpably sectarian movement — with the politicos who still put up with *Scots Independent* in the age of satellite broadcasting and desktop publishing. In the sense, the real connotation of the old 'Tartan Tory' jibe may lie as much with the adjective as on the noun. Tartanic purism is not necessarily right-wing, but remains an inescapably friable and indeterminate quantity — somehow more likely to turn the key in the door to open it up. I need scarcely add that the often ultra-conservative antics of many SNP leaders and spokespersons — including, notably, the current President of the Party — have done nothing to allay the distrust.

### Modernizing Scottish Politics

I suppose it all means a lot more disagreement amang wirselves before we can fight back effectively. In both the Labour Party and the SNP, new generations will have to kill off the old before the promise of the *Claim of Right* can be fully realized. And the rest of us? 'We belong to that big movement without a name or a leader, which loves none of the political parties and judges them by how they go about getting Scotland a democracy' wrote Neal Ascherson in *Observer Scotland* on February 5th 1989. In this perspective, what we need is the national movement prefigured by the *Claim* and the Convention, and not (as he concludes) 'an Independence League of Purity in the desert'.

His diagnosis of the last Independence League gesture is that it reveals 'just that miserable, contemptible weakness for which the SNP have with justice mocked Labour: the fear of power'. However, fear of power in this sense is the same as sectarian desire *for* power: a moral might imaginable solely as patented property-right and justification by the Almighty. Sects fear power, in fact, *and* think of nothing but the awesome power which reality so unrighteously denies them — a thought so compulsive that it may (usually in the name of realism) wipe out all that threatens to contradict it. Marxist sects end up in this way with a fantasy proletariat unfairly prevented from following *the* recipe for Socialism; the SNP equivalent is its fantastic Nation of 'Scots' betrayed by most really existing Scottishness — the weirdly apolitical projections of an apolitical and anti-cultural nationalism unique in the world.

What the Ascherson-democratic Party sees in the Convention row is the likelihood of relapse into the climate of inveterate feud and denunciation which, until 1988, was Scotland's substitute for national political debate. After the great betrayals of the 1979 referendum, the 40% clause and the 'Labour Says "No"!' campaign, all serious strategic arguments about Scottish political identity had for well over a decade been locked into this vicious, seemingly inescapable circle of hatred and recrimination: Scotland's Corsican-style war between an undemocratic mass movement and a democratic sect. Journals like *Radical Scotland* have provided a valuable forum for the battle, and tried to move it as a whole into a more constructive direction: is this to be their reward too — defeat by the *Geist* of *Scots Independent*?

I won't try to deal here with the Labour side of it. However, having been in quite early on the business of denouncing Labourite backwardness and structural hopelessness (around 1965), I feel no great need to apologize for this. Most of the grim things said about Labourism in most situations of the kind we are dealing with here are likely to be true. In defence of SNP non-participation Jim Sillars has argued that taking part would have been liking 'putting the party's

head in a noose' held by the Labour Party (*Scotsman*, Feb. 1989)
How could he, of all folk, ever have imagined it would be anything
else? In a Scotland dominated by the electoral system which had
just returned him to Westminster and the SNP to the top of the
opinion polls?

The point, perhaps, was that all movement towards a Scottish
democracy must start from a situation of preposterous unfairness:
our historical part-interest in the collapsing legacy of Britishness. But
what the Convention process offers is a broader way of challenging
that legacy; a challenge which, had Labourism later betrayed it for
its own ends, Nationalists could then have effectively defended in
the name of (Scottish) democracy and popular sovereignty. The
withdrawal tactic might then have been a national success, rather
than a national disgrace.

By contrast, no amount of corruption and conniving mediocrity
can itself justify a response of hysterical purism. The fact that it
has returns us to the real dilemma; Labour's dreadfulness, however
unreformable and depressing, remains that of a political party; the
SNP's stridency and abstraction, its passionate substitution of rhetoric for reality, remain the attributes of an incorrigible sect. And no
embryo polity worthy of the *Claim of Right*'s new initiative can be
made from the collision of these elements alone.

About 'Europe' too I won't say much here. I supported European
political integration as a form of modernization when most of the
U.K. Left and the Scottish National Party were still denouncing it
as a fiendish conspiracy, and see no need to rehearse old arguments
again. But of course, SNPism's version of them can only be a sectarian one: a new achievment upon plane of electoral rhetoric for
Britain's most important electoral sect. Its use of 'Independence-
in-Europe' is as a deeply ambiguous slogan to take the sting out
of 'separatism'. It invites voters to a wider horizon, beyond insular
British parochialism; but simultaneously conjures up there a *Deus
ex machina* who will somehow smooth the forward path, history's
'Yes' to set against the English 'No'. In practice, this now means one
more reason to vote SNP — *rather than* organizing in the broader,
pragmatic spirit of the *Claim*. Thus, the new urge for autonomy in
Scotland is transposed on to the foggy plane of a post–1992 Europe
whose overall political configuration is unclear.

The new Europe is absolutely preferable to the United Kingdom
as a broader political arena; but the question of what new forms
of self-government that arena will favour (or disfavour) can only
be fought out well into the coming century, And Scotland's influence on that argument will (again) depend upon the nature of the

national-constitutional movement she evolves now, in her struggle
to get out from under Anglo-British hegemony. On her national
*movement*, not upon this or that electoral party pretending to be the
Nation.

'We've never been able tae agree amang wirselves' — and for a
time it looks like being harder than ever. Unity isn't an unqualified
marvel, or something to aim for at any price at all. However, there's
a difference between disagreeing or even fighting within a framework
of some agreement, and trying to wheedle or extort some scraps
of agreement out of a sub-politics of endless paranoid feud and
vendetta. The Constitutional Convention remains Scotland's best
chance to move from the latter to the former — to translate conflict
on to a higher level of achieved identity, as the necessary condition
for getting out of the U.K. and getting anywhere in the new Europe.

# 15

## Birth Without Beauty or Terror

OWEN DUDLEY EDWARDS

When in the course of human events it becomes necessary for one people to dissolve the political bands which have connected them with another, and to assume among the powers of the earth the separate and equal station to which the laws of nature and of nature's God entitles them, a decent respect to the opinions of mankind requires that they should declare the causes which impel them to the separation. And when in that course it becomes necessary for one people to dissolve some of the political bands, and alter others, which have connected them with another. the same decent respect also requires a declaration of the causes of the impulse. The essays in this book are the work of persons some of whom are convinced of the necessity for an absolute dissolution of all political bands that unite Scotland to England, while others demand some dissolution, some alteration, some retention.

In one respect our collection has a wider span than is covered by the attitudes of the authors of *A Claim of Right for Scotland*. Two of the most vehemently argued essays are from different standpoints hostile to *A Claim of Right*, those of Mr Michael Fry, and of Mr Chris McLean. It is not enough to see them as simple poles of Right and Left, seeming to invite, and seeking to repudiate, charges of 'impossibilism' from their more ecumenical colleagues in these pages. In other matters Mr Fry rejoices in his Rightness, while Mr McLean has well proved his Left-wing credentials. But for all of his hostility to the *Claim of Right* Mr Fry is implacable as a devolutionist in the teeth of his party's hostility while Mr McLean's position places him in SNP territory traditionally associated with the SNP's Right although now also inhabited, in many cases more uneasily than Mr McLean by prominent figures usually identified with the SNP Left.

Politics is but the tip of iceberg in the movement of Scotland away from England, and the fissures which may end by causing the Scottish iceberg to break totally from the United Kingdom (or Ukanian) icepack are largely invisible to the observer whether assessing polls, listening to taxi-drivers or taking his own temperature. Scotland's social and political lives are much more intermingled than are those in England, though other small countries, like Wales, or more federalised ones, like the U.S.A., will know something of its intricacy. Hence Mr Fry's courage and outspokenness make him encounter a colder social climate in his party than is found by more diplomatic colleagues who silently share his views and publicly deny them. Mr McLean is sundered in these pages from Mr Maxwell, with whom he was once expelled from the SNP, and from his former tutor, Professor MacCormick, whose efforts resulted in these expulsions being overturned on appeal, although it is impossible to imagine any lessening in his seniors' affection for Mr McLean. They may find it less easy to forgive prominent members of the SNP whom they have good reason to suspect share more of their views on this question than he does, but who have followed the fashionable thinking at present carrying so much before it in the party.

Nor could my affection for Mr McLean be lessened by his paper, although I, too, believe that the SNP should have remained within the Convention, and I want to see an independent Scotland. On the contrary, I owe Mr McLean an exceptional debt of gratitude for what he has done here. When this book was planned, editor and publisher assumed that it was the Labour party to which we must go for several statements, as we imagined that the challenge of the *Claim of Right* must prompt at least immediate divisions in Labour party sentiment. It seemed otiose to seek more than two SNP opinions. The SNP break with the Convention threw us into a wholly unlooked-for situation. Our two writers from within the party were selected for their long standing seminal contributions to the Scottish debate and their high repute in the party crossing ideological boundaries, but with one, Mr Maxwell, on the party Left and the other, Professor MacCormick, in the Centre. But both were whole-heartedly opposed to the S.N.P's break with the Convention. Mr Chris McLean would in any event have been a most worthy contributor to this or any other volume on the Scottish debate; but when at the eleventh hour we found that our volume would include nobody in agreement with the now official policy of the SNP, Mr McLean came to our rescue at a time when his official duties as press officer must have been at their most arduous, with every political journalist in the country battering at his door. The rest of us all disagree with him but we must be united in our gratitude to him. It must be stressed that his position as expressed here is one of absolute conviction, a spirit in which all our contributors have sought to write, but he declares himself loneliest of all of us, most implacable of all of us. Mr Fry shares a belief in some kind of devolution with his fellow-contributors; Mr McLean will have none of it.

The American Declaration of Independence, whence I plagiarised my first sentence, was an official document issued formally on 4 July 1776 by delegates acting in the name of the thirteen United Colonies and duly chosen by a representative process. Nevertheless its nature is that of a document which seeks to convince the majority of those in whose name it declares itself to act. Historians now seem to agree that the Declaration of Independence represented the views of roughly one-third of the adult white male colonists when it was issued, that a comparable number were opposed to its views, and that the largest third — to employ a logic inadmissible in mathematics, essential in history — were undecided or apathetic. At the present time it seems that at least one-third of the Scottish voters of both sexes favour independence, though it is unclear how many of these would like to see that independence obtained by a clean break and how many would prefer the growth of institutions preparing the country for independence. Many often vote Labour and some never vote SNP Support for the constitutional *status quo* is limited to much less than a third — possibly much less than the quarter who voted Tory in 1987 (Mr Fry may be much more representative in his devolutionary stance than his highly placed Tory opponents imagine, or perhaps many of them do secretly suspect as much but dare not say so). The greatest fraction of the three consists of Scots who want a lot of devolution but not independence.

The American antecedent is instructive in other respects. The Declaration of Independence polarised debate in ways that SNP policy today assumes to have already happened, and, like Thomas Jefferson and his associates, the SNP may be asserting conditions in order to create them. As Mr Tom Nairn argues in these pages, there is much in the SNP that is very old fashioned. Its thought, especially when expounded either by fundamentalists or by non-fundamentalists taking up a fundamentalist position, seems to have been shaped at a time when popular concepts of history were simpler, not to say cruder, than today. This continues to be so despite the SNP's having shown itself from time to time more modern than any other political party in Scotland: it was a pioneer in the politics of environmentalism, it is still ahead of all other parties in relating land ownership to land use, its structures were more democratic, it was conspicuous by the number of women in significant positions in its ranks. It thought much more deeply about constitutional questions than did others and formulated an impressive Constitution. In its youth the SNP was a much more deeply intellectual and cultural

than were other political parties (although here again what it gained
electorally it sometimes seemed to lose culturally) and when its time
of success dawned it showed sophistication in canvassing, use of
volunteer enthusiasm and skill in public relations which forced
its stronger opponents to adapt its techniques while vehemently
denouncing them. But it also wallowed in historical sentimentalism
of the bad-King-Edward variety, although it was impressive in its
assimilation both of the Schumacher small-is-beautiful thesis and of
the radical challenge to conventional Scottish historiography posed
by the 7:84 Theatre Company. Mr Nairn's anger remembers its
former receptivity to new ideas with a promise of breaking the
intellectual strait-jacket of British politics, and finds it superseded
by an SNP performance as Bourbons who had learned nothing and
forgotten nothing. It was hardly a way to celebrate 1789. Sherlock
Holmes in one of his less profound moments explained American
Independence as the fruit of the folly of a King and the blundering
of a Minister. The SNP now seems to assume the arrival of Scottish
independence on similar logic.

What gives the S.N.P position some credibility, however dubious, is that Mrs Margaret Thatcher seems hell-bent on acting out
the part of Bad King George and Blundering Lord North. It is
instructive that it is the caricatures of George and North that she
insists on performing; in reality King George had moral standards
in government, as for instance in the use of secret service, which she
would dismiss with the contempt of a Machiavelli or a Nietzsche,
while North was an intensely self-sacrificing person readily setting
aside his own glory in the cause of public service. Just as the cause
of American independence owed much to George and North, that
of Scottish independence has flourished as never before because
of her intransigence and insensitivity. In the 1970s polls showed
independence *less* popular than the SNP; in the 1980s it was *more*
popular.

The SNP is not going to state that it chooses to appear crass and
archaic because Mrs Thatcher is apparently incapable of appearing
anything else, but this is what its logic amounts to. Mrs Thatcher in
Scottish matters is, to be as polite as scientific analysis will permit,
politically illiterate. In their various ways the SNP's critics in this
volume accept this (it is hardly fair to insist that Mr Fry implicitly
agrees with them: we must not ask even more of him when he is
being very courageous indeed). But their answer is that, however
relevant to Mrs Thatcher, political illiteracy is a rotten way to eman-
cipate Scotland. A nationalism basing itself on anti-Thatcherism
will have the greatest of difficulty in immunising itself from the

infection of counter-Thatcherism. The SNP has a rich heritage of community-consciousness which could not be farther removed from a politician to whom the idea seems at once reprehensible and incomprehensible. But Ireland has recently shown in its support for Mr Charles Haughey against the bullying of Mrs Thatcher how much it is possible to identify with the nationalism all too reminiscent of its enemy. Mr Haughey's chauvinism, self-interest, materialism, enterprise-consciousness, favour for dubious associates of questionable means of self-enrichment, personality cult, ruthless control of party, and so forth, are the marks of gross Thatcherism, painted a shamrock green. Mrs Winifred Ewing's unilateral hi-jack of the SNP into alliance with Mr Haughey in the European Parliament is particularly ominous in this connection.

There are certainly short-term advantages in Scottish Haugheyism, although it should not be forgotten that advantages under Haugheyism are seldom evenly distributed. The SNP cry of 'Independence in Europe' has elicited Thatcherite replies, notably from the lady herself, that it would be unpopular with her European partners. The answer to this lies not in the constitutional cat's cradle which emerges when the matter is subjected to supposedly intellectual disputation. The SNP's case in plain fact is that Mrs Thatcher's European partners are sick of the sight and sound of her, and that they would be delighted at any development which made her look a fool. She has bullied them, bored them, blistered them, in language priding itself on endowing her severe intellectual limitations with Pecksniffian moralising. Mrs Thatcher's inability to understand European problems is consistently interpreted by herself in condescending tones obdurately proclaiming itself wisdom of an awesome and an ancient sanctity. The public proof of her self-admiring inability to understand Scotland would offer sweet revenge for her self-admiring inability to understand Europe. Perhaps the Tories may have a case in asserting that an acknowledgement of nationalism within E.C. existing frontiers could seem a Pandora's box to many powers, who may not wish to give flesh and blood to similar skeletons in their own cupboards. But just as Mrs Thatcher drives Scots towards independence not in spies but in battalions, she may drive her European partners towards enthusiasm for the claim of Scotland. Hence in imagining that Mrs Thatcher may provide an appropriately reversed image of the elder Pitt capturing Canada on the banks of the Elbe by losing Scotland on the carpets of Brussels, the SNP may have some justice in its pursuit of the lowest intellectual common denominator. The SNP is perfectly correct in pointing out that Mrs Thatcher claims to speak for Scotland in Europe and that

Europe will be deeply interested in any proofs Scotland can furnish to the effect that her claim is false. There is an unpleasant analogy here, of which Mr Haughey could, if he chose, remind Mrs. Ewing. European powers interested themselves from time to time in Irish aspirations for independence from Britain, Germany in the early twentieth century being a conspicuous example. The Germans were delighted to outflank Britain on the moral front, a propaganda victory they sorely needed, by fomenting insurrection in Ireland in Easter 1916 and then leaving the insurgents catastrophically in the lurch. It was an unlooked-for bonus that the severity of British punishment of the rebels played the Germans' game so thoroughly as to alienate an Irish population which had been massively hostile to the Easter Rising. Granted that Europe thirsts for the humiliation of Mrs Thatcher, the powers might find ways to accomplish that laudible enterprise while ultimately leaving Scotland in the lurch. In trusting to European hostility to Scottish independence the Tories are living in a fool's Paradise, on the fool's orders, but that gives no certainty that Scotland will ultimately dismember Ukania by imagining for itself knights in shining armour in Ruritania. In this connection important points are made by Mr Maxwell, and in a somewhat different way, by Mr Martin.

What ails the SNP, as I see it, is its self-consciousness as a political party. It was not ever thus. The movement for independence in Scotland in its first twenty years after the formation of the National Party of Scotland allowed for the independence-minded to join the Party while also being members of any other political party of their choice, and while the subsequent proscription of non-SNP party membership in Scotland was probably necessary to force the other parties towards Scottish nationalism by defeats which taught them lessons they would not learn from a soft infection, the spirit of the S.N.P's founders seem to have been forgotten by their party. It is, I think, time that the party began to ask itself questions about its means and ends. Politics, for the SNP as for everyone else, should be recognised as means. The infection of Haugheyism invites the thought that after independence a nationalist party should continue to exist, rewarding its friends and penalising its enemies. It would be far healthier for the party to tell itself firmly that it wants independence and that everything else, including its own political future, is secondary to that end. What is happening now is that the party political gains are being interpreted as the real ends. Such a lack of proportion is suited only to a party which believes itself to be in permanent opposition.

Mr Jim Sillars after Govan opened his arms to persons in other parties who would embrace independence and dazzled the many believers in independence who do not necessarily vote S,N.P. — and there are many such — by the vision of a 'coupon' election in which the SNP would not oppose any candidate pledged to independence. The Convention offered a perfect means to such an end. The whole basis of revolution, including the American revolution, lies in giving sufficient momentum to institutions which draw those involved more and more deeply within the development of a nationally conscious ideology. There is the risk that the convention might produce a halting place, as other political party representatives insist it would. But the SNP needs to put greater faith in its cause, and less in its party. We must stand with Milton in *Areopagitica*:

> Though all the winds of doctrine were let loose to play upon the earth, so Truth be in the field, we do ingloriously, by licensing and prohibiting, to misdoubt her strength. Let her and falsehood grapple: who ever knew Truth put to the worse in a free and open encounter?

Party Politics has done much; it has been Scotland's stimulus, and it is now in extreme danger of becoming another bolt for Scotland's prison. There is ample evidence that Scotland does not want Thatcherism, and while its anti-Thatcherite politicians war among themselves they perpetuate Thatcherism. *The Claim of Right*, even as it is discussed here, shows that Scottish national consciousness is not to be graded, as it once could be, by a chart showing various political persons and parties in fixed positions. We are into a moving scenario. What is startling about the Labour Party contributors as presented here, is that they show an entirely new willingness to learn. They exhibit a much more impressive capacity for self-criticism than has hitherto been associated with them. The Labour Party in Scotland was as famous for its reduction of its ranks to lobby-fodder in the interest of its ruling English hierarchy as were the old Tories for their identification of the true Scotland with servile ghillies and attractive grouse-moors. Our three Labour contributors from Westminster — perhaps not so much our Labour MEP — seem to affirm that no longer will Labour demand that Scottish national consciousness must be perpetually sacrificed to the Moloch of party. Or, if orthodox London-based Labour still demands it, the Labour in Scotland will insist for itself Scottish dynamics and recognise itself in its Scottish identity. Yet as it does, Party becomes an SNP Moloch in its turn. Macaulay once recognised a similar phenomenon:

> Dante tells us that he saw, in Malebolge, a strange encounter between a human and a serpent. The enemies, after cruel wounds inflicted, stood for a time glaring on each other. A

great cloud surrounded them, and then a wonderful metamorphosis began. Each creature was transfigured into the likeness of its antagonist. The serpent's tail divided into two legs; the man's legs intertwined themselves into a tail. The body of the serpent put forth arms; the arms of the man shrank into his body. At length the serpent stood up as a man, and spake; the man sank down a serpent, and glided hissing away. Something like this was the transformation which, during the reign of George the First, befell the two English parties. Each gradually took the shape and colour of his foe, till at length the Tory rose up erect the zealot of freedom, and the Whig crawled and licked the dust at the feet of power.

(Second Essay on Chatham, *Edinburgh Review*, October 1844)

Labour has still a long way to go before reaching High Noon of self-realisation. Our essayists may criticise their party's past; they are slower to criticise their own. There is only one person amongst all of us here who has shown the greatness of mind to censure himself for possible mistakes; and that is an SNP writer, Professor MacCormick, whose action reminds us how much there is for Labour yet to learn from the SNP.

The Democrats have perhaps less to unlearn than Labour, but they had fewer recent sweets of power from whose sticky memory to detach themselves; Mr Kennedy's contribution was written before he had occasion to contemplate the additional virtue for an independent Scotland that it would not only be free from Mrs Thatcher, but from Dr David Owen as well. That consideration should concentrate the minds of the Scottish Democrats wonderfully.

It might be argued that in its present mood the S .N.P. would be more likely to drive people away from the ideal of independence than to draw them in its direction, were it to return to the Convention. It will be interesting to see whether, on their own, the other parties have the wisdom to look closely on the case going by default in the absence of those who should be defending it. It is not much of a justification for the SNP but, such as it is, they have it.

The bloody-mindedness attending the SNP's insistence that the 'people of Scotland' demand this and forbid that, in ways that seem to project Mr Gordon Wilson — as the Delphic oracle's priestess — it is the classical method of Eamon de Valera but Mr Wilson (rather to his credit) is not of the stuff of which priestesses are made — has the danger of taking our eyes off a truth behind this promiscuous reiteration. Mr Neal Ascherson remarked that after the referendum defeat of 1979 he had supposed Scotland would now 'agitate, drink and learn' but that in 1989 he must add that in the ten years it had also grown up. He could have added something else. In the ten years it has refused to grow down. Thatcherism has done everything it can to bribe, bully and blackmail Scotland into bowing down before its gods of materialism and British chauvinism, self-enrichment and self-regard, community-destruction and beggar-your-neighbour, and Scotland in varying ways, some represented in our pages, has shown its refusal to crawl to the false and alien idols. I think it was I who spoke of the 'Scottish cringe' first, and as Mr Tom Nairn and others are now arguing, it is part of the old cringe that the SNP now clings to Westminster parameters while their former rivals, once self-abasing appendages to English parties, now try to straighten their backs. But behind them the Scottish people as a whole have made it clear that their past deference to the English connection will not now make them fall to their knees and bellies when the connection pulls them to do so. Whether the Americans were right or wrong in arguing that their revolt of 1776 was against a British revolution, there can be no question but that there has been a Thatcherite revolution. The Ukanian state has existed on the basis of certain agreed norms: these norms have now been shattered by a government which persists in invading and occupying what had largely been accepted as no-go territory. Broadcasting, the social theology of the state churches, universities, the monarchy, national health — all had been subjected in the past to mild pressure, nibbling, manipulating, complaining from successive governments, but none had been seen as potential targets for government control and remodelling to government ideological specifications. The relative independence of these had become part of the unwritten terms of Scottish participation in the United Kingdom, and the implied contract has now been unilaterally severed.

There was much voluntarism in the Scottish enlistment in British modernisation, and the Scots could tell themselves they had begun it, from the prophets of their Enlightenment down to Lord Reith. Their own eighteenth-century universities had begun a missionary process of civilising England, indeed even of inventing a sophisticated British sense of identity. Little by little the missionary-field overwhelmed the missionary nursery. William Turner arrived at Edinburgh University in the mid-19th century to find his English accent mocked for its uniquely alien character; as Sir William Turner in 1903-16 he was Edinburgh's first English Principal. In this he would have many successors and his fellow-nationals on the teaching staff would ultimately far out-number their hosts. Many of the English staffing Scottish institutions would do much for the advancement of Scottish national consciousness and in some instances far outstrip native colleagues in their love of Scottish culture. Many others would seek simply to establish intellectual dependence on England, with its corollary of a superiority of comparable English institutions which had not, alas, yet chosen to honour the efforts of their exiled sons by posts at home, that just reward of the virtuous and faithful coloniser. But however much Scots seemed to acquiesce in this, the terms of the bargain were clear. If Scotland sold its birthright for a mess of pottage, it is entitled to insist that the pottage remain pottage, not a reduction to thin gruel accompanied by offers of pheasant under glass at fancy prices. If the pottage be withdrawn the birthright is resumed.

There is much suspicion that hostility to Scottish moves towards some form of self-government will be countered by Thatcherite attempts to sow fear. The ten years in the wilderness for Scotland have helped strengthen the Scots against frighteners, but it is reasonable to acknowledge the potential of a judicious manipulation of fear especially in future elections where disproportional representation can maintain inequitable hold on marginal seats.

The major frighteners are said to be Taxation and Defence. It is believed that the 1979 referendum on a Scottish Assembly, although gaining a majority of those who voted in it, failed to produce a stronger mandate because of the use of fear by the Assembly's opponents, and that the most effective weapons were the threat of higher Taxation under an Assembly and the dangers to Defence implicit in the widening Devolution. The British Defence budget, and the Taxation involved in its realisation, may be likened to the judgment which said of the prisoner that one did not know whether to be more appalled by the folly of his wickedness, or the wickedness of his folly. For a country to make the keystone of its supply-raising the building of weapons of unspeakable human destruction, to glory in them, to parade them, and to steep its people in self-admiration at the capacity for using them, is to indict itself as an enemy of the human race. In theory at least it offers no choice between Thatcher and Tamberlaine. The whole costly and ludicrous exercise of weapon mongering, in the cause of which health, education and welfare have been pared perilously near the bone, is in itself the product of mental sickness: Britain is shrunk to a tiny fraction of her former world power. The only use of the spending spree on the arsenal of death is to feed delusions of grandeur. In plain language, on Defence, Thatcherism is in an extreme stage of alcoholism. For Scotland, to squander its taxes on sodden mirages of nuclear glory is catastrophic nonsense. A Scotland in control of its own taxation will give its citizens the benefits they need instead of infecting their starved and crimped existences, physical and mental, with the most despicable of all forms of chauvinistic *delirium tremens*.

It is true that Scotland seems to have considerable significance in the minds of Defence thinkers. That is to say, the geographical position of Scotland is said to be of importance to the supposed security of England and of the United States. If that is so, they may wish to make the Scots some satisfactory terms for their use of Scotland. Scotland does not need massive expenditure on these things any more than Ireland does: devolved or independent the Scottish People's wish should be to do what they can for humankind, not to see as their greatest basis for pride the possession of the means and will to annihilate it. In specifically material terms, it is utterly contrary to Scottish interests to have Scotland littered with nuclear dumps. nuclear targets, nuclear launching-pads. If the English and the Americans want these arrangements in Scotland, then they cannot do so by right or by any pretence that it is to Scotland's advantage. At best one (and certainly 'one' is not employed here in the modern snob usage of meaning 'I') would only grant them facilities if they were made to pay. So the answer to high taxation scares is that taxation will fall when the alcoholism of defence is cured; and the answer to inebriate mirages about Red attack or Blue Defence is to tell the frighteners to dry up and dry out. We have paid far too much for far too long and seen the household savings squandered on this poison. Whether we choose to accept the Convention as a marriage counsellor or insist on going to the SNP as a hard divorce lawyer, we can no longer accept slavery to nuclear intoxication.

The SNP insistence that their electoral opponents must go under the yoke of accepting the SNP's terms for participation in the Convention commends itself to its supporters by its justice in seeing the Convention's present basis as unrepresentative. It is unjust, but in the present situation the escape from imprisonment by the political forces which produce the elective dictatorship at Westminster is not going to be achieved by a short-term distribution of political justice. As Mr Fry's much-admired A.J. Balfour said in an aphorism which it is to be hoped is not one of Mr Fry's strongest bases for his admiration, 'Justice? There isn't enough to go round'. At present, if one set of horses reach the water, another set will not drink. The answer lies in making the most of what we have. Mr Donald Dewar and his associates are not where they are because of the natural wishes of many of them, although it is clear from our Labour contributors that they are enjoying the taste of Scottishness in a much more real form than hitherto.

Behind Labour, behind the Democrats, lie huge shoals of Labour voters who demand a large and powerful measure of Devolution, and many who shun the SNP but want independence. The Govan by-election was an indication that their loyalty to Labour and, still more, to the Democrats, can no longer be taken for granted, Professor Christopher Harvie and Dr Tom Gallagher are in this book because of their professional expertise, Professor Harvie as historian of modern Scotland and of its nationalism, Dr Gallagher as analyst of modern ethnic division in Scotland. But all of our contributions are here as products of dissectors and as material for dissection. Both of these writers, as it happens, are long standing members of the Labour Party. Both supported the SNP at the Govan by-election. The SNP need to ponder particularly carefully the implications of their stance then, and their stance now. The SNP has made its mistake in viewing its political rivals as ideological constants, where they are now ideological variables.

As for the Convention, Mr Ascherson has cut the Gordian knit by pointing out it cannot claim authenticity in advance. 'It must earn it.' And he argues that it is 'politically and morally wrong' to hold out for an evolution of Scotland to independence in one step. The people need the experience of developing structures leading to autonomy. The SNP may have been influenced by the thought of the Irish Convention of 1917, and Professor Bernard Crick has written here very perceptively of many lessons to be drawn from Ireland. But the Irish Convention, however much the SNP's friendship with Mr Haughey may prompt it as an analogy, differs drastically from the present case. It is undeniable that the two forces who boycotted its proceedings, *Sinn Féin* and the Ulster Unionists, were the two who ultimately profited by the constitutional solutions of 1920 and 1922. Firstly, the Irish Convention was set on foot by the U.K. Government; the Scottish Convention comes into existence in the teeth of opposition from the U.K. Government. This simply makes it an entirely different animal. Secondly, the Irish Convention was set on foot in the middle of a world war in which militarism was proclaimed by both Government and the insurgents of 1916 from whom *Sinn Féin* now accepted inheritance, as the higher solution to the problem of human existence. Pearse had preached the ideal of blood-sacrifice with all the fervour of British army recruiters and had indeed partly derived his faith in it from them. The Convention operated in an assumption that the finest representatives of the Irish and British peoples were those engaged in the shedding of blood.

*Sinn Féin* indeed at first sought to operate its own brand of civil disobedience in 1919 and steer clear of any active practice which might continue the holy cult of blood-sacrifice. But the legacy of 1916 and 1914-18 proved too strong, and the creed of passive resistance was quickly overwhelmed by irregular and unsanctioned acts of republican violence and bloodshed which the *Sinn Féin* politicians were left ingloriously to sanction in retrospect. The result was a poisoned chalice of freedom for Ireland, to convulse immediately after the Treaty of 1921 into civil war among the ranks of *Sinn Féin* and in the long term into the far longer civil war which now so cruelly scars Northern Ireland. Among the many causes of gratitude Scotland owes to the SNP is the party's hatred for and proscription of any flirtation with violence. The party's long history was dominated by persons who suffered imprisonment from their refusal to use violence, and later by supporters of the Campaign for Nuclear Disarmament. Its own history therefore cries against its adoption of a *Sinn Féin* stance, even *Sinn Féin* in its moments of non-violence: after 1916 *Sinn Féin* could never escape the condition of a movement owing its popular credentials to the martyrdom of persons who had resorted to militarism.

Moreover Ireland, unlike Scotland, was maintained in the Union by paramilitary police, and however hopeless the Irish insurrections of 1848 and 1916, they remained a pattern of high moral nationalism unsullied by political bargaining. It was in constitutional revolt that Irish nationalism really distinguished itself, but it did so while singing rallying-songs to the militaristic ideal. There is a flavour of this in SNP favourite songs, but it goes little farther than Bannockburn. Scotland has achieved its nationalist victories, including the SNP's own in a clear tradition of non-violence. The new Convention is in that tradition. It is part of the *Claim of Right* that Scottish democracy is being eroded by alien Thatcherism; it is essential, then, for nationalists to show their renewed faith in democracy by seeking what the strengthening of its tradition can achieve. Professor MacCormick has elsewhere pointed to Canada, Australia and New Zealand as examples of independence being acquired by non-violent means through a process of evolution or, as he says, gradualism. The importance of the Irish example is the terrible necessity of avoiding it. Nor is it possible to assume that it can be avoided simply by good intentions. The SNP abhors violence; Thatcherism worships it. Can simple anti-Thatcherism remains immune to it? Daniel O'Connell and Michael Davitt had preached and practised non-violence in their mature years with truly impressive effects; but in the end Ireland capitulated to the attractions of violence very suddenly. *Sinn Féin* was itself non-violent for almost a decade until it was overtaken by the Rising of 1916, and — in a single step — all was changed, changed utterly, the terrible beauty was born.

Belief in Scottish democracy admittedly carries with it the danger that the devolutionists who, unlike Professor MacCormick, do not want to culminate in independence, may produce a viable Assembly and that Scotland will decide it wants nothing more. But the SNP itself prides itself in that belief, and moreover has spent its life to date in the conviction that education and experience will ultimately convince the Scottish people of the need for independence. The other political parties, equally, require to put their faith in Scottish decisions as to their ultimate faith. Nor should Scottish Labour or Democratic party members, sympathetic if no longer subservient to their colleagues in England, think of devolution or even independence as an abandonment of them. As Mr Ascherson says, the prospects in all reality are for Thatcherite rule of Britain to the 21st century if the present electoral system and monolithic United Kingdom are maintained. He continues that what would make Labour, or Labour and the Democrats, a visibly alternative regime for England would be the sight of their success in Scotland for those increasingly unable to imagine any non-Thatcherite government. Mr Ascherson did not plagiarise the younger Pitt, but let us do so: Scotland can save herself by her exertions, and will then, we hope, save England — and Wales — by her example. Mr Osmond is our reminder that other parts of Ukania hungrily await that example.

It is one of the most appealing qualities of Scotland, and one of which Mr Kennedy's essay should remind us, that it is a phenomenally diverse country. That is all the more reason for its rejection of Thatcherite monolithic conformity. The Convention must certainly have as one of its priorities a sense of devolution within any devolved or independent Scotland. No part of Scotland — certainly not my own Edinburgh — must be permitted to subject the rest of the country to its dictation as the south-east of England now subjects the United Kingdom. Mr Ascherson's cheerful response to the West Lothian question — 'So what?' — does not answer the much more serious Lothian question and the Strathclyde question, nor does he intend it to. An independent or devolved Scotland must be protected from becoming a Lothian or Strathclyde appendage, and it will be the more resolute on this by its ugly experience as a London appendage. In this, as in so many other respects, SNP thinking has led the way. But the diversity should not be the cause of disunity, and while serious differences exist as to the Convention's means of proceeding, we should coalesce in the best unity as we can obtain. Without concerted action now we face dismemberment of Scottish institutions, legal, educational, social, in welfare, in communications, in sense of individual communities. And for all of the criticism showered on it, the *Claim of Right* in its dignity and resolution gives us our start. It gives us what Martin Luther King called a stride towards freedom.

# Some Potentially Relevant Dates

1320    Declaration of Arbroath by Scottish nobility and clergy pledging independence of Scotland irrespective of any Scotish ruler's submission to England.

1503    Marriage of James IV of Scotland to Margaret Tudor, elder daughter of Henry VII of England.

1513    James IV defeated and slain by English army at Flodden.

1603    James VI of Scotland, great-grandson of James IV, succeeds Elizabeth I of England, niece of Margaret Tudor, as James I

1689    Scottish Convention resolves James VII has forfeited the Crown, April 4 (English Convention had resolved he, as James II, had abdicated by leaving England) elaborating argument in the Claim of Right (accepted by Convention 11 April): Claim prohibits royal prerogative from overriding law, requires Parliament's consent for the raising of supply, declares for frequent meetings of Parliaments with freedom of debate.
'On 11 May William and Mary accepted the crown of Scotland, arguably, though not certainly, on the terms of the Claim of Right.' (William Ferguson, *Scotland 1689 to the Present* (1968), p. 6).

1707    Union of Parliaments of England and Scotland.

1714    George I, Elector of Hanover, great-grandson of James VI and I, succeeds to the Kingship of Great Britain by exclusion of all nearer heirs as Roman Catholics.

1842    Claim of Right drawn up by the General Assembly of the Church of Scotland insisting on the complete spiritual independence of the Church (arising from anger against lay patrons' 'intrusion' of ministers against the wishes of congregations). Claim rejected by Tory Prime Minister Sir Robert Peel.

1843    470 out of 1,200 establishment ministers (taking with them 40 per cent of Church of Scotland communicants) withdraw from the General Assembly and establish the Free Church of Scotland: the 'Disruption'.

1853-6 Association for the Vindication of Scottish Rights.

1872    National schools system established under Scotch Education Department.

1879    W.E. Gladstone's campaign in Midlothian, orchestrated by Rosebery, first mass agitation in British electoral politics.

1881    Rosebery leads campaign for Scottish governmental reforms in response to growing national sentiment, blunted by his appointment to abortive under-secretaryship for Home Affairs (Scotland).

1885   Scottish Secretary established below cabinet rank, Whitehall.

1886   Scottish Home Rule Association founded.

1882   Highl;and Land League formed under influence of Irish Land League.

1888   Scottish Liberals' central association adopts Home Rule policy.
Foundation of Scottish Labour Party led by Crofters' MP Gavin Clark, R.B. Cunninghame-Graham, MP, and James Keir Hardie.

1893   Scottish Labour Party assist in forming and then enter Independent Labour Party.

1897   Scottish Trades Union Congress formed.

1900   Scotish Workers' Parliamentary Election Committee formed.

1906   Scottish Committee styled Scottish Labour Party.
Scottish Federation of Women's Suffrage Societies formed by Elsie Inglis.

1909   Scottish Labour Party merges in Labour Representation Committee whence the Labour Party.

1915   Scottish Advisory Council of the Labour Party created.

1918   Scottish Home Rule Association, lapsed since 1914, refounded.

1923   Scottish Home Rule Association leads march of 30,000 in Glasgow.

1924   Scottish Home Rule Bill (federalist) introduced unsuccessfully at Westminster by George Buchanan, MP, supported by all Scottish Labour MPs.

1925   All parliamentary control finally removed from Church of Scotland.

1926   Tory Government under Baldwin upgrades Scottish Secretary to Secretary of State for Scotland.
Hugh MacDiarmid publishes *A Drunk Man Looks at the Thistle*.

1927   Government of Scotland Bill introduced by the Rev James Barr, MP, and 'talked out' in the House of Commons amid wild scenes.

1928   National Party of Scotland founded (fusing Scottish National Movement, Scots National Leagure, Glasgow University Scottish Nationalist Association and Scottish Home Rule Association) under the leadership of J.M. MacCormick, aided by Cunninghame-Graham and C.M. Grieve (Hugh MacDiarmid).

1929   Union of Church of Scotland and United Free Church.

1931   Compton Mackenzie elcted as Scottish Nationalist to Rectorship of Glasgow University.

1932   Scottish Party founded under Right-wing nationalist auspices.

1934   National Party of Scotland merges with Scottish Party in Scottish National Party whose first meeting resolves that if Mr. C.M. Grieve attempts to pay his shilling it was to be returned to him.

1935   SNP contents 8 seats in general election, with an average of 16%.

1936   Saltire Society founded.

1937   SNP pledges itself to oppose conscription save by Scottish government.

1939   John MacCormick of SNP plans all-party Scottish Convention to discuss Home Rule set for September 27 but destroyed by onset of

World War II.
Scottish government departments transferred from London to Edinburgh with opening of St. Andrew's House.
Labour Scottish Self-Government Campaign founded.

1940    Scottish Labour Conference sets up Committee on Post-War Policy in Scotland without seeking approval of NEC.

1941    Tom Johnston, Labour MP for West Stirlingshire, appointed Secretary of State for Scotland by Winston Churchill and establishes 'council of state' in Scotland.
*The Plan for Post-War Scotland* published by Labour Committee, pledging a self-governing Scotland with Parliament of Scottish (Westminster) MPs meeting in Edinburgh.

1942    Johnston establishes Scottish Council on Industry.

1945    Dr Robert McIntyre wins Motherwell for SNP at April by-election, losing it at subsequent general election.

1947    John MacCormick, having left SNP in 1942, calls together Scottish National Assembly embodying most sections of Scottish opinion including Unionist: it demands parliamentary devolution.

1948    Labour Government under Attlee rejects enquiry into devolution.

1949    MacCormick organises National Covenant movement pledging signatories 'within the framework of the United Kingdom to do everything in our power to secure for Scotland a Parliament with adequate legislative authority in Scottish affairs', winning nearly two million signatures.

1950    Scottish Coronation Stone (removed from Scotland during the Wars of Independence by Edward I of England 650 years earlier) removed from Westminster Abbey by Scottish nationalists.

1951    Stone supposedly recovered at Arbroath.

1952    Balfour Commission on Scottish Affairs told to ignore Home Rule issue.

1957    Compton Mackensie publishes *Rockets Galore*, an attack on British nuclear policy use of Scottish sites at the expense of Scottish communities: it prefigures subsequent strong Scottish nationalist growth in anti-nuclear agitation.

1960    Sydney Goodsir Smith's play *The Wallace* performed at Edinburgh Festival.

1966    Gwynfor Evans elected for Carmarthen as Plaid Cymru candidate at by-election.

1967    Mrs Winifred Ewing elected for Hamilton as SNP candidate at by-election, overturning a Labour majority of 16,000.

1968    (May) Tory Opposition Leader Edward Heath sets up Scottish Constitutional Committee under former Prime Minister Sir Alec Douglas-Home.
(December) Prime Minister Harold Wilson sets up Royal Commission on the Consitution under Lord Crowther.

1972    SNP lose Hamilton at General Election but carry Western Isles with Donald Stewart who holds it until his retirement in 1987.

1972   Death of Lord Crowther, replaced ultimately as head of Commission by Lord Kilbrandon.

1973   Kilbrandon Commission supports legislative devolution for the historic nationalities.

      SNP win by-election at Glasgow Govan with Margo McDonald.

1974   (February) General Election. SNP lose Govan, capture Dundee East (Gordon Wilson), also East Aberdeenshire, Banff, Moray & Nairn, Argyll, Clackmannan & East Stirlingshire (first and last from Labour, rest from Tories).

      (May) Tory Oppostion Leader Edward Heath promises indirectly-elected Scottish Assembly.

      (October) SNP hold existing 7 seats, capture Galloway, South Angus, Perth & East Perthshire and Dumbartonshire East from Tories, with 30% of Scottish votes (Tories 24.9%; Labour 36.4%).

1975   Gordon Brown edits and publishes *The Red Paper on Scotland*.

      British referendum on endorsement of previous entry into European Community, Scotland voting 60% (England 66%) in favour out of 62% poll; SNP opposed to entry (despite significant minority among major party figures); Labour divided.

      (November) Labour (Wilson) Government issues White Paper offering legislative Assembly with no real economic powers to Scotland.

      (December) Jim Sillars, Labour MP for South Ayrshire, announces intention to found 'parallel' party: the Scottish Labour Party.

1976   Scottish Labour Party supported by one other MP as well as Neal Ascherson, Tom Nairn and other intellectuals, but becomes target of envenomed Labour attack for apostasy, and Sillars loses credibility by ferocity of hostility to militant left-wing infiltration, with conference purge.

      Devolution Bill passes Second reading of Commons by majority of 45, with 55 of 71 Scottish MPs in favour, 6 of 7 contraries being Tories. Margaret Thatcher, new Opposition Leader, imposes a 3-line whip against Bill: leading shadow spokesmen on Scotland (Buchanan-Smith, Rifkind) resign and Heath opposes Tory policy.

      Michael Foot promises referendum.

1977   Devolution Bill destroyed in committee, new Bills introduced for Wales and Scotland separately.

1978   (January) George Cunningham (Labour, London Islington S.) forces requirement of 40% of Scottish voters to favour Scottish Assembly before referendum result implemented: Cunningham amendment supported by 5 Labour Scottish MPs (Cook, Dalyell, Doig, Hamilton, Hughes).

      (February) Scotland Bill passes third reading: 'Labour Vote "No"' campaign formed.

      (April) Labour unexpectedly successful in retaining Glasgow Garscadden at by-election (with former South Aberdeen MP Donald Dewar as candidate).

      Labour victories over SNP in by-elections at Hamilton, and then at

Berwick & East Lothian (latter following death of principal Labour proponent of Scottish devolution John P. Mackintosh).

1979    (1 March) Referendum narrowly votes 'Yes' for Scottish Assembly (Welsh substantially vote against more limited Welsh Assembly).

(March) Government refuses to make repeal order on Assemblies a matter of confidence, being unable to withstand pressure from Labour dissidents on devolution: SNP support 'no confidence' Tory motion and Labour (Callaghan) Government falls.

Thatcher Government elected: Labour takes 42% and 44 Scottish seats, Scottish Labour Party MPs both defeated, SNP overall vote falls to 17.2% and SNP retains only Western Isles and Dundee East. (June)Thatcher government repeals Scotland Act.

Mrs Winifred Ewing elected MEP for Highlands and Islands.

1982    SNP expels left-wing leaders of '79 Group' interim committee (Sillars now in SNP but while in 79 Group not expelled): expulsion overturned on appeal. Party membership falling.

1983    General Election. Second Thatcher victory. Labour still victorious in Scotland with slight losses. SNP hold 2 seats.

1984    SNP Conference declares for a Scottish Convention, strongly urged by Party Chairman Gordon Wilson, MP as well as by Jim Sillars. Winifred Ewing re-elected MEP.

1987    General Election. Third Thatcher victory. Tory vote falls in Scotland; party reduced to 10 seats; SNP lose 2 seats, gain 3; 'Alliance' (incorporating Liberals and Social Democrats) have 11 seats, Labour have 50. Result follows 'tactical voting' in which some party faithful crossed lines to favour anti-Thatcher candidates.

Attempted joint demonstrations by Liberals, SNP, Communists and Labour broken down by sectarian recrimination.

1988    (November 10) Landslide SNP (Sillars) defeat of Labour in Glasgow Govan.

1989    Thatcher and Tories celebrate ten years of non-implementation of Scottish vote for Assembly; Britain only major West European country without devolution.

# A Note on Contributors

*Dennis CANAVAN* Elected (Labour) MP for West Stirlingshire (now Falkirk West), February 1974 and consistently re-elected since. Previously Deputy Headmaster, Holy Cross School, Ferry Road, Edinburgh. Distinguished for his highly informed opposition to corporal punishment in schools, and hence a significant force in its abolition. Vociferous advanced activist on the need for recognition of Scottish demands, sometimes employing Parnell-style obstructionism.

*Bernard CRICK* Professor Emeritus of Politics at Birkbeck College, University of London. Honorary Fellow, Department of Politics, Edinburgh University. Also taught at London School of Economics, and at Sheffield University. Author of: *The American Science of Politics*; *In Defence of Politics*; *Crime, Rape and Gin*; *Political Theory and Practice*; *George Orwell: A Life*. Edited Orwell's *1984* (1984). Joint editor, *The Political Quarterly*, 1965-80. Is engaged on a major study of nationalism in Scotland, Wales and Ireland. Has lived in Scotland for the last ten years. Writes frequently for *Observer*, *New Statesman*, etc. Labour Party member.

*Owen Dudley EDWARDS* Reader in History, University of Edinburgh. Came to Scotland in 1966 to teach at Aberdeen University and in 1968 was appointed to Edinburgh. Contributor to *The Red Paper on Scotland*, *The Radical Approach*, *Scots Independent*, *Question* and *Scottish International Review*. Member, Edinburgh University Student Publications Board 1975-81. Also author of books on James Connolly, P.G. Wodehouse, Conan Doyle, de Valera, Macaulay, Burke and Hare, and co-author with Hugh MacDiarmid, Gwynfor Evans and Ioan Rhys of *Celtic Nationalism*. Working on a historical study of religion, romanticism and nationalism in Ireland, Scotland and Wales. Member SNP 1974-82; now member of Plaid Cymru.

*George FOULKES* Elected (Labour) MP for South Ayrshire in 1979, decisively defeating incumbent Jim Sillars (then Scottish Labour Party). Previously major figure in Edinburgh District Council, especially as vigorously egalitarian Convener of Education. Rector's Assessor to Kenneth Allsop on Court of Edinburgh University, 1968-71, during period of challenge to University establishment and thereby significant link with major area of Scottish student protest. Had been Edinburgh SRC president in mid-1960s. Advanced activist at Westminster in demands for recognition of Scottish needs. Magistrate.

*Michael FRY*    Prominent Right-wing English journalist who came to Scotland in late 1970s, swimming strongly against the Labour and Nationalist tides, initially on *Scotsman* staff, subsequently freelance. Co-author (with John Cooney) of *Scotland and the New Europe* and author of *Patronage and Principle: a Political History of Modern Scotland*. His *Tories in Trouble* will shortly be published in this 'Determinations' series. Is engaged on a major study of the younger Pitt's Scottish partner, Henry Dundas. Member of the Conservative Party.

*Tom GALLAGHER*    Reader in Peace Studies, University of Bradford. Glaswegian; member of Labour Party; author of *Portugal* (a study of its twentieth century politics and history); *Glasgow: The Uneasy Peace* (on ethnic relations, rivalry and conflict); *Edinburgh Divided* (on Protestant action movement of demagogic proportions in the 1930s). Writes regularly in *Scotsman, Glasgow Herald* etc. Working on a study of Edinburgh politics since 1945. Holds a Ph.D. from Manchester.

*Nigel GRIFFITHS*    MP (Labour) for Edinburgh south since 1987 (when he ousted incumbent from seat held by Tories since 1918). Previously Edinburgh District Councillor with special responsibility for Housing. Graduate in psychology. Social worker. Now a Scottish Whip. Has been mildly identified with activist Scottish policy including occasional disruptive tactics at Westminster. Consultant and worker on productions of Edinburgh University Student Publications Board, late 1970s.

*Christopher HARVIE*    Professor of British Studies, University of Tübingen, West Germany. Previously Lecturer in History, Open University. Member of Labour Party. Reported Scottish politics for *Tribune* in 1970s. Edinburgh Ph.D.; author of *The Lights of Liberalism: University Liberals and the Challenge of Democracy 1860-86*; *Scotland and Nationalism: Scottish Society and Politics 1707-1977*; *No Gods and Precious Few Heroes: Scotland 1914-1980*. Co-editor and contributor to *Forward! Labour Politics in Scotland 1888-1988* in 'Determinations' series.

*Charles KENNEDY*    Elected MP (Alliance: Social Democrat) for Ross, Cromarty and Skye, 1983, ousting Tory (seat had previous history as Liberal party stronghold). Re-elected 1987 with heavily increased majority. Now Democrat, having been prominently in favour of integration of Liberal and Social Democrat parties from 1987 election. Weekly Westminster columnist for *The Scotsman*. Before election prominent in Glasgow student politics and debates, being President of Glasgow University Union 1981-82, and foremost Debates Awards-winner of his time (Glasgow being the leading University in the British Isles for debate since 1953).

*D. Neil MacCORMICK*    Professor of Jurisprudence and Public Law at Edinburgh University and Director, Centre for Criminology and the Social and Philosophical Study of Law. Previously Fellow and Tutor in Jurisprudence, Balliol College, Oxford. Glaswegian. Member of eminent

Scottish Nationalist family (son of John MacCormick, National Party of Scotland and SNP leader until 1942; brother of Iain MacCormick, MP (SNP) for Argyllshire, 1974-79). Has been Dean of the Faculty of Law at Edinburgh University and has served many terms as Member of National Executive, SNP. Publications include *The Scottish Debate: Essays on Scottish Nationalism* (editor and contributor), which forcefully intellectualised public discussion of Scottish nationalism in 1970. Leading draughtsman of SNP Constitution for Scotland in 1970s. Has been SNP candidate for Edinburgh seats. Identified consistently in SNP with pro-devolution, pro-European Community forces. Signatory of *Claim of Right*, and prominent in its defence at SNP.

*Chris McLEAN* Press Officer, Scottish National Party since early 1980s. Previously SNP student leader at Edinburgh University. Founder-member, 79 Group in SNP, and expelled from party with other members of its transition committee after dissolution of Group by party order in 1982. Readmitted on appeal. Graduate in Law. Has continued tradition of previous SNP press officers in 'tutorial' briefings based more on scholarly political analysis than on propaganda. Co-operated actively with non-SNP devolution activists in 1979 and subsequently. Identified with advanced activist policy and support for carefully considered civil disobedience.

*David MARTIN* Member of European parliament (Labour) for the Lothians since 1984. Previously Edinburgh Regional Councillor. Graduate from Heriot-Watt University in Economics. Has been Labour delegation leader in European Parliament. Vigorous contributor to *Scotsman* on European Community questions. Identified with strong opposition to SNP 'Independence in Europe' policy before and since Glasgow Govan by-election of 1987.

*J. Stephen MAXWELL* Honorary Fellow in Politics, Edinburgh University. SNP Press Officer in 1970s. Edinburgh-born, raised and educated in England, including Cambridge and London School of Economics. Senior Policy Analyst, Scottish Council of Voluntary Organizations. Author of a study of impact of multi-national capitalist organizations with particular reference to Scotland. Contributor to *The Radical Approach*, *Question*, *Scotsman* etc. SNP candidate, Edinburgh Pentlands, 1979. Founder member, 79 Group in SNP, and expelled from party as leader of its transition committee after Group dissolution. Readmitted on appeal. Has been Member of National Executive, SNP on several occasions. Inaugurated system of 'tutorial' briefings of individual press persons when Press Officer and hence strongly intellectualised Scottish political debate, as acknowledged by Labour Party opponents. Formerly lecturer in Politics, Edinburgh University, and before that in Sussex. Director of SNP referendum campaign, 1978-79.

*Tom NAIRN* Born in Freuchie, Fifeshire. Studied at Universities of Edinburgh, Oxford and Dijon and the Scuola Normale in Pisa. Art student and teacher, especially at Hornsey College of Art, late 1960s.

Fellow of the Transnational Institute in Amsterdam. Editor and extensive contributor to *New Left Review*. Former Director, Scottish International Institute, Edinburgh. Author of *The Beginning of the End*; *The Left Against Europe?*; *The Break-Up of Britain: Crisis and Neo-Nationalism*; *The Enchanted Glass: Britain and Its Monarchy* (joint winner of Saltire Society Award with Neal Ascherson's *Games with Shadows*). Contributor to *The Red Paper on Scotland*, *Question*, the *New Statesman*, the *Scotsman* etc. Member of Scottish Labour Party in late 1970s. Engaged on a major study of Marxism's need to accept Nationalism.

*John OSMOND*   Journalist and intellectual identified with Welsh nationalism. Formerly political analyst of Welsh affairs, *Western Mail*, editor *Arcade*, Editor at Harlech TV. Currently Assistant Editor, *Wales on Sunday*. Author of *The Centralist Enemy*; *Creative Conflict: The Politics of Welsh Devolution*; *Police Conspiracy?*. Editor and contributor to *The National Question Again: Welsh Political Identity in the 1980s* and author of *The Divided Kingdom* (based on his Harlech TV series studying Northern Ireland, Scotland, Wales, England North and South etc.). Born in Gwent. Has reported frequently on Scottish political developments in relation to nationalism and devolution.